1993

Mercy or Murder?
Euthanasia, Morality and Public Policy

Edited by Kenneth R. Overberg, S.J.

Sheed & Ward

For acknowledgments, please see "Appendix C: Sources."

Sheed & Ward™ is a service of The National Catholic Reporter Publishing Company.

Library of Congress Cataloguing in Publication Data

Mercy or murder? : euthanasia, morality, and public policy / edited by
    Kenneth R. Overberg.
        p.   cm.
    Includes bibliographical references.
    ISBN 1-55612-609-3 (alk. paper)
    1. Euthanasia--Moral and ethical aspects. 2. Euthanasia--
Government policy. I. Overberg, Kenneth R.
R726.M48   1993
179'.7--dc20   92-43734
                                                      CIP

Published by: Sheed & Ward
                  115 E. Armour Blvd.
                  P.O. Box 419492
                  Kansas City, MO 64141-6492

To order, call: (800) 333-7373

Cover art and design by Tim Botts.

To Muddo:

may comfort, peace, and love
fill your final days

Contents

PART III: PATIENT SELF-DETERMINATION ACT (PSDA)

PART IV: NUTRITION AND HYDRATION

PART V: APPENDICES

Preface

EUTHANASIA IS A COMPLEX AND CONTROVERSIAL TOPIC. Both as a moral dilemma and as a public policy issue, euthanasia challenges our hearts and minds. Headlines describe dramatic cases of physician-assisted suicides. Citizens confront aid-in-dying legislation. Many of us face the severe suffering of dying patients, parents, or friends. We ask: What can be done? What ought to be done? Is euthanasia mercy or murder?

As the debate intensifies about the right thing to do, so does the need for careful reflection and discussion. Yet the emotions involved and publicity generated often make such reflection difficult. Fine-tuned campaigns, for and against euthanasia, evoke strong feelings—perhaps compassion for the dying, perhaps fear of widespread and involuntary euthanasia. Immediate reactions may be powerful, but they are not sufficient for sifting through a complex issue and coming to an informed decision. Our country already has widespread experience in the abortion debate of rhetoric playing on the emotions as a way to determine moral and legal issues. No, more than this is needed.

In his article in this book, Leon Kass emphasizes this need for appropriate argument, even while recognizing its limits. He writes, "Discursive arguments against, say, incest or cannibalism can never yield the degree of certitude intuitively and emotionally felt by those who know such practices to be

1

abominable . . ." Yet when prohibitions against such practices are breaking down, then there is "no other choice" than to argue for their soundness.

My hope is that this text will contribute to this difficult-but-necessary reasoning concerning euthanasia that is so important in our society today. While reading John Paris's article in *Theological Studies,* I found myself thinking what an excellent resource for the euthanasia discussion this could be—not just his article, but also many of those he cites. Put into people's hands articles of both views; allow them to wrestle with the complexities and implications of the issue. This anthology, then, offers the opportunity for reasoned discourse on this topic, which probably will challenge more and more persons, as moral decision-makers and as citizens. It can be used for private study and reflection, and many types of classes and discussions.

To facilitate this study, Paris's article is presented first, giving an overview of the current debate. Articles generally favoring euthanasia and/or physician-assisted suicide follow. Articles opposed to euthanasia are given next, including several that consider the 1991 referendum in the State of Washington. (It should be noted that as more states propose aid-in-dying legislation, some details will be refined, but the fundamental question remains the same.) Articles about two other issues, advance directives and withholding nutrition and hydration, are included because of their relationship to euthanasia. Finally, there are three appendices, the first presenting medical cases for discussion, the second giving definitions of terms used in the articles, and the third listing all the articles along with brief identifications of the authors.

I want to thank John Paris for his initial work and for his support of my project. I appreciate the cooperation of the authors and journals. Thanks to Forrest Calico, M.D., Christine McHenry, M.D., Frank Giese, M.D., and John Tew, M.D., for their assistance. Special thanks to Linda Loomis and Susan Ernsberger for their work in preparing the manuscript.

Kenneth R. Overberg, S.J.

Overview:

Active Euthanasia

John J. Paris, S.J.

TWO RECENT PROPOSALS ON MEDICAL DECISIONS TO END LIFE, one defeated and the other passed, dominate and define the ongoing debate over killing and letting die. In a November 5, 1991 referendum in the State of Washington, Initiative 119,[1] which would have legalized physician-assisted suicide as well as active euthanasia, was defeated in a surprisingly close vote of 54 to 46 percent. Barely a month later, on December 1, 1991, the federal Patient Self-Determination Act (PSDA)[2] went into effect. That Act, passed by Congress as part of the Omnibus Budget Reconciliation Act of 1990, mandates that every health-care facility receiving Medicare or Medicaid funding—hospitals, nursing homes, health-maintenance organizations (HMOs) and home-healthcare programs—must inform its patients or clients of their right to decline unwanted medical treatments, including those that potentially prolong life.

The PSDA is the culmination of nearly two decades of concern in the United States over the use of medical technology to maintain life when life itself has proven overly burdensome or painful to the patient. From the *Quinlan*[3] case in New Jersey in 1976 to the U.S. Supreme Court's ruling in *Cruzan*[4] American courts have been challenged to recognize the right of patients—competent and incompetent—to decline unwanted and

3

unwarranted medical interventions. That right is articulated in the Vatican's 1980 Declaration on Euthanasia, which states:

> [O]ne cannot impose on anyone the obligation to have recourse to a technique which is already in use but which carries a risk or is burdensome. Such a refusal is not the equivalent of suicide [or euthanasia]; on the contrary, it should be considered as an acceptance of the human condition, or a wish to avoid the application of a medical procedure disproportionate to the results that can be expected.[5]

The Vatican Declaration, summarizing some four hundred years of church teaching on the right to decline extraordinary or disproportionate means of preserving life, makes a sharp distinction between refusing measures that would serve "only [to sustain] a precarious and burdensome prolongation of life" and suicide or active euthanasia. The former is permitted; the latter is prohibited.

The word *euthanasia* ("a good death") is subject to widely differing understandings, and the distinction between active and passive euthanasia (killing and letting die) is frequently collapsed into the one term. James Rachels' now famous essay on "Active and Passive Euthanasia"[6] denies that there is any real difference between the two. For him, "if a doctor lets a patient die, for humane reasons, he is in the same moral position as if he had given the patient a lethal injection." In fact, Rachels argues that, since the latter action spares the patient from prolonged suffering, it is "actually preferable to passive euthanasia." Marcia Angell, Executive Editor of the New England Journal of Medicine, makes the same point in a recent editorial; after stating that "many of us believe that euthanasia is appropriate under certain circumstances and that, indeed, it should be legalized," she concludes that this should be done because "euthanasia is more humane than forcing a patient to continue a life of unmitigated suffering."[7]

To avoid confusion in the debate, it is imperative to distinguish euthanasia from termination of treatment. It is also imperative to have a clear definition of terms. For the purposes of this note, euthanasia is defined as the deliberate action by a physician to terminate the life of a patient. The clearest example is the act of lethal injection. Singer and Siegler's "Euthanasia—A Critique" provides the helpful distinction between such an action and such other acts as the decision to forego life-sustaining treatment (including the use of ventilations, cardio-pulmonary resuscitation, dialysis, or tube feedings—the issues raised in the *Cruzan* case); or the administration of analgesic agents to relieve pain; or "assisted suicide" in which the doctor prescribes but does not administer a lethal dose of medication; or "mercy killing" performed by a patient's family or friends.[8]

Church tradition, as the Vatican Declaration makes clear, opposes euthanasia or the direct intentional killing of innocent life, whether of "a fetus or an embryo, an infant or an adult, an old person, or one suffering from an incurable disease, or a person who is dying." Furthermore, the Church holds that "no one is permitted to ask for this act of killing for himself or herself," nor is it morally licit to consent to such an action for one entrusted to your care. The reason for these moral imperatives is clear: "Only the Creator of life has the right to take away the life of the innocent." To arrogate that right to ourselves, whether as patient, guardian, or caregiver would be a "violation of the divine law" and "an offense against the dignity of the human person."

Initiative 119 stood as a challenge to that tradition. In the State of Washington, for the first time anywhere in the world, voters were asked to approve what its proponents labeled "a new medical service": authorization for physicians actively to assist a terminally ill patient to die. Initiative 119, which was sponsored by the Hemlock Society, was circulated with the official ballot title, "Shall adult patients who are in a medically terminal condition be permitted to request and receive from a physician aid-in-dying?" Beneath that innocuously worded heading was the reality that "aid-in-dying" meant "aid in the form of a medical service, provided in person by a physician, that will end the life of a conscious and mentally qualified patient in a dignified, painless, and humane manner, when requested voluntarily by the patient through a written directive . . . at the time the medical service is to be provided."

Albert Jonsen, a medical ethicist at the University of Washington Medical School, noted that this was not just a simple amendment to earlier living-will legislation; it represented a radical change in medical practice.[9] For the first time since the Hippocratic tradition established prohibitions some 2,500 years ago against physicians directly taking the lives of their patients, physicians would be authorized to kill dying patients. Jonsen, who is no alarmist, wrote in *Commonweal* just prior to the vote: "The state of Washington is on the edge of a moral cataclysm." Public opinion polls suggested that he was right. A Louis Harris poll indicated that 67 percent of the voters in the state approved of the proposal. A more nuanced poll conducted by the Harvard School of Public Health[10] revealed that 64 percent of Americans favor physician-assisted suicide and euthanasia for terminally ill patients who request it. Of adults under thirty-five, 79 percent supported the idea. The most startling finding of that poll was that, of the religious groups surveyed, Catholics were the greatest supporters of the proposition. Seventy-one percent said they would vote for the initiative if it were on their ballot.

The debate over euthanasia is not new. Only the emphasis has shifted. In a thoughtful and thorough survey of the euthanasia movement, Humphry and Wickett[11] trace the issue from classical Athens, where magistrates kept a supply of poison for anyone who wished to die ("If your existence is hateful to you, die; if you are overwhelmed by fate, drink the hemlock"), through to the rise of Christianity, in which suicide was denounced as a violation of God's will.

In the United States, the euthanasia movement gained prominence in the late 1930s with the founding of the Euthanasia Society of America. It had as its agenda "the belief that, with adequate safeguards, it should be made legal to allow incurable sufferers to choose immediate death rather than await it in agony."[12] A bill sponsored by the Euthanasia Society in the New York legislature in 1938 was defeated, but it generated interest and provoked the first article to appear in an American medical journal favoring euthanasia. Abraham Wolbarst, in his "The Doctor Looks at Euthanasia," published in the May 19, 1939 issue of *Medical Record*, wrote: "The vast majority of thinking people favor euthanasia as a humanitarian principle. . . . The human mind revolts at the thought of unnecessary suffering . . . it is not how *long* we humans live, but *how* we live that is important."

The euthanasia movement took a dramatic turn in Germany in the 1920s and 30s which would prove its undoing for decades. With the prevalent notion of *Lebensunwerten* ("life not worthy of life"), it became standard practice beginning in the 1920s for German physicians to terminate "useless" lives. That policy subsequently provided the rationale for the Nazi practice of murdering the mentally and physically handicapped which ultimately culminated in the Holocaust. The horror of that experience so dominated humanitarian thinking in the four decades following the Nuremberg war-crime trials that, as Derek Humphry put it, it "effectively hampered the intellectual and legal progress of the euthanasia movement" in the English-speaking world.

In a 1947 Gallup poll, for example, only 37 percent approved of a physician being authorized to end a patient's life by some painless means if the patient and family requested it. It was not until the 1960s, with Louis Kutner's proposal for a patient-instigated directive—a so-called "living will"—in which a patient stated he would not want medical measures utilized to prolong life, that the "death with dignity" movement revived.

One measure of the shift, particularly interesting in light of Washington State's Initiative 119, was the results of a 1971 survey of medical students at the University of Washington School of Medicine.[13] Ninety percent of fourth-year medical students and 69 percent of first-year students said they would practice passive euthanasia with a signed statement of the patient. Half the students (46 percent in both cases) favored changes in permitting active euthanasia.

In the 1970s and 1980s, the movement took two directions, each of which is represented in the current debate and which culminated in the PSDA and Initiative 119. Legislation recognizing livings wills and health-care proxies, and the court battles over the "right to die" were the vehicles used to protect individuals from unwanted medical treatment. At the same time, such groups as EXIT in England and its American counterpart, the Hemlock Society, pressed for active euthanasia. In 1979, a Scottish EXIT group published the first guide or "suicide recipe book." It gave detailed descriptions of how to end one's life. Derek Humphry soon followed with his guide on "self-deliverance," *Let Me Die Before I Wake.*

Support for physician-assisted suicide remained limited to fringe groups until the publication in 1989 in the prestigious *New England Journal of Medicine* of an article in which ten out of twelve physicians from the leading medical centers of the United States went beyond their earlier support for termination of unwanted medical treatment to endorse physician-assisted suicide. In an article entitled "The Physician's Responsibility Toward Hopelessly Ill Patients," these physicians wrote: "All but two of us . . . believe that it is not immoral for a physician to assist in the rational suicide of a terminally ill patient." The group, somewhat surprisingly, stopped short of a similar endorsement of active euthanasia. The reasoning is illuminating: "The social climate in this country is very litigious, and the likelihood of prosecution if a case of euthanasia were discovered is fairly high—much higher than the likelihood of prosecution after a suicide in which the physician has assisted."[14]

That report by distinguished clinicians from the most reputable institutions in the country followed by just one year the publication in *JAMA* of "It's Over, Debbie,"[15] an anonymous account of a gynecology resident's decision to inject a young cancer patient with a lethal dose of morphine. That action, done at 3:00 a.m. by a physician who had no prior knowledge of the patient, on the basis of her request, "Let's get this over with," provoked a storm of outrage. Willard Gayland and three of his physician colleagues, in a bluntly worded essay entitled "Doctors Must Not Kill,"[16] expressed their horror at what had been done and their incomprehension at *JAMA*'s having published the account. Their incredulity was expressed by their question: "What in the world is going on?" For them, the anonymous author of the "Debbie" essay broke the law, breached medical protocol, and violated the most deeply held and hallowed canon of medical ethics: Doctors must not kill. As they put it, "Generations of physicians and commentators on medical ethics had held fast to the distinction between ceasing useless treatments (or allowing to die) and active, willful taking of life." Since the time of Hippocrates until as recently as a 1989 statement of the Judicial Council of the American Medical Association, Western medicine has regarded the killing of patients, even on request, as a profound violation of the deepest meaning of the medical vocation. Leon Kass undertook to explain the reasons for this prohibition in a deeply probing essay in *The Public Interest*.[17] There he argued that the basis for the shift in attitude, which has already led to some 5,000 cases of active euthanasia or assisted suicide a year in the Netherlands, is an overemphasis on freedom and personal autonomy, expressed in the view that each one has a right to control his or her body and life, including the end of it. In this view, physicians are bound to acquiesce not only to demands for termination of treatment, but also to intentional killing through poison, because the right to choose—freedom—must be respected even more than life itself. The second reason advanced for killing patients is not a concern for choice but the assessment by the patient or others that the patient's life is no longer deemed worth living. It is not autonomy but the miserable or pitiable condition of the body or mind that warrants, in Kass's words, "doing the patient in."

Kass's arguments against those positions constitute a commentary on the now classic essay written in the *Minnesota Law Review*[18] by Yale Kamisar some thirty years earlier. Kamisar asked: Are not the risks and mistakes in authorizing medically assisted voluntary euthanasia too great and, more importantly, the possible radiations from the proposed change too overwhelming? How is one to establish that the patient's choice is "voluntary"? Will we not sweep up in the process some who are not really tired of life, but think others are tired of them? And how much freedom of choice does one really have if he does not want to die, but feels he should not live on because to do so, when there looms the legal alternative of euthanasia, is to be selfish or cowardly?

These realistic problems pale in comparison to the potential difficulties engendered in a society grown indifferent to the taking of life. That indifference would be compounded if the very segment of society committed to saving life were commissioned to destroy it. Once the euthanizing of a patient or two becomes but part of a routine day's work, the brutalization process so vividly described in Leo Alexander's classic essay on "Medical Science Under Dictatorship"[19] (recounting the experience of Nazi Germany) becomes an all too real possibility. And once begun, who sets the limits on "a life not worth living," and how are the limits set?

That such fears are not far-fetched is seen in the actions of Dr. Jack Kevorkian, the Michigan pathologist who in three instances during the past year has used his self-designed "suicide machine" to assist non-dying individuals end their lives.[20] The first of those, Janet Adkins, was a functioning, lucid woman who feared that the debilitating consequences of the early onset of Alzheimer's disease would render her unable to end her life when she chose to. The others were a 43-year-old woman with multiple sclerosis and a 58-year-old woman with a severe, but treatable, pelvic inflammation.

Kevorkian's crude device, the primitive surroundings in which the assisted suicides occurred, and his intransigent attitude offended many. It also led to the Michigan Medical Society summarily revoking his medical license. No such penalty has been attached to the actions of Dr. Timothy Quill, a Rochester, New York physician, who reported in the *New England Journal of Medicine*[21] how he had given instructions and provided adequate supplies of barbiturates so that Diane, a patient he had known and treated for years who was now dying of cervical cancer, could and did end her life. Unlike the outcry over the publication of "It's Over, Debbie" and the negative reaction to Dr. Kevorkian, the response to Dr. Quill's participation in a patient's suicide was mostly approval.[22] Typical was the response of a physician who wrote: "Dr. Quill provided his patient with exactly what was lacking in the more notorious cases involving Dr. Jack Kevorkian and the anonymous author of 'It's Over, Debbie,' comprehensive medical care, with deep concern for the patient's well-being and respect for her choices."

Was the shift in response to these cases of euthanasia or physician-assisted suicide limited to the "mode of disposal"? Is aesthetic sensitivity the only barrier to euthanasia? Is our objection that guns and knives and crude homemade "killing machines" used in the back of rusted-out vans or backwoods cabins are messy or offend our sense of propriety? Do we object to suicide or euthanasia "only if," in J. Roman's phrase, "[the victim] looks disgusting and not just dead?" And what of Roman's proposal in *Exit House*[23] that we should make suicide available to all over eighteen who request it? Derek Humphry's best selling *Final Exit*[24] likewise makes no distinction on who can partake in suicide. With his latest self-help text, all that is required is a desirous individual and a ready source of the lethal potion.

Critique of the Case for Euthanasia

Singer, Kass, and Callahan, as well as the bishops of the State of Washington,[25] use essentially the same public-policy arguments that Kamisar employed in opposition to euthanasia. A splendid special supplement of *Commonweal* devoted to euthanasia[26] contains an essay by Daniel Callahan that succinctly states those public-policy arguments. Callahan writes that the fear of dying is frequently surpassed today by the yet more powerful fear of being forced to endure destructive pain, or to live out a life of unrelieved, pointless suffering. The movement to legalize euthanasia and assisted suicide is a strong and, as he puts it, "historically inevitable response to that fear."[27] He traces that response, as do Kass and Kamisar, in part to the failure of modern medicine to reassure us that it can manage our dying with dignity and comfort and to the fact that, as the Washington bishops put it, "the intense individualism of our culture" leads to the demand that we must be in control, that we be masters of our fate. We resent and reject any kind of dependence as incompatible with human dignity.

In the face of this powerful, almost relentless, dynamic, Callahan asks how we can regain and retain control. He admits that "for many the answer seems obvious and unavoidable, that of active euthanasia and assisted suicide."[28] Callahan rejects that solution, as the bishops do. Though it is ultimately their religious heritage and convictions that buttress that stand, the bishops realize that in a pluralistic secular society, it is public-policy implications and not religious beliefs that must be the basis for their political opposition to Initiative 119. It was Callahan's essay and a subsequent commentary on Initiative 119 by Richard A. McCormick, S.J.[29] that provided the policy arguments used by the bishops.

As Callahan put it, "We should not deceive ourselves into thinking of euthanasia or assisted suicide as merely personal acts, just a slight extension of the already-established right to control our bodies and to have medical treatment terminated . . . [Initiative 119] is a radical move into an entirely different realm of morality: that of the killing of one person by another."[30] As such, it would change the traditional role of the physician from healer to terminator. It would require intrusive regulation and oversight into the most private aspect of life, namely dying. It would also add substantially to the range of permissible killing in our society.

The most notable public-policy implication is the potential for abuse in the authorization of "private killings," i.e., those in which the agreement of one person to kill another "is ratified by the persons themselves, but not by public authorities."[31] How do we control, regulate, or even oversee these killings? What assurance is there or can there be that the limitations enacted in the legislation will be strictly adhered to? The suffering of the person to be killed is, as Callahan notes, "subjective, unmeasurable by, and intangible to an outside observer." If freedom and suffering are to be the norms of euthanasia, there is no logical way in the future (1) to deny euthanasia to anyone who requests it for whatever reason, terminal illness or not; or (2) to deny it to the suffering incompetent, even if they do not request it. The legal safeguards and procedures we specify to prevent that from happening are, as it were, written in smoke—difficult to discern and easily dissipated. Such barriers cannot provide protection over time.

The problem lies in the flawed logic of the moral premise of euthanasia: our right to self-determination and our claim upon the mercy of others, especially physicians, to end our suffering. Consider self-determination, Callahan suggests. If, as it is proposed, the competent adult has a right to euthanasia for the relief of suffering, is it not a restriction on self-determination to limit euthanasia to those who are terminally ill or profoundly pained? "How," he inquires, "can self-determination have any limits?" As for relief of suffering, why should relief be confined to competent patients? Isn't the suffering of the incompetent as great, if not greater? Doesn't it demand as much concern? Further, if the physician who acts to kill the patient does so in the belief that a life marked by some form of suffering is not worth living, how can the physician deny the same relief to a person who cannot request it, or who requests it but whose competence is in doubt?

Our duty to relieve suffering, Callahan notes, cannot justify the introduction of new evils into society. The risk of doing that is simply too great. It is too great because it would take a disproportionate social change to bring it about, one with implications that extend far beyond the sick and dying. It is too great because, in Callahan's powerful words, the history of the twentieth century should demonstrate that "killing is a contagious disease, not easy to stop once unleashed in society."[32]

The Washington bishops adopted those arguments and added the admonition of Richard McCormick that "those who insist that all life-support systems must be used at all times, even though the patient can no longer benefit from them, could well be unwittingly contributing to public acceptance of active euthanasia."[33] What the bishops had in mind is clear from the context in which their caution is placed: "People cringe at the prospect of a dying prolonged by tortuous, aggressive and isolating interventions. They are aware of the Nancy Cruzans of this world as they linger on hopelessly from year to year."[34]

The Washington bishops, joined by their episcopal brethren in Oregon, address the question of the care of the irreversibly comatose or persistent vegetative patient in a pastoral entitled "Living and Dying Well."[35] In language quite at odds with that used by the Massachusetts bishops, who insist "the authentic teaching of the Catholic Church" requires that "nutrition and hydration should always be provided [to irreversibly comatose patients] when they are capable of sustaining human life,"[36] the Catholic bishops of the Pacific Northwest acknowledge that "conscientious Catholic moral theologians and many others in our society have not achieved consensus about this point."[37] Given the lack of agreement on the issues, the Washington and Oregon bishops hold that "decisions regarding artificially administered nutrition and hydration must be made on a case-by-case basis, in light of the benefits and burdens they entail for the individual patient," and then conclude: "In appropriate circumstances, the decision to withhold these means of life support can be in accord with Catholic moral reasoning and ought to be respected by medical caregivers and the laws of the land."[38]

The fears of the Washington bishops that restrictions on active euthanasia, once unleashed, could not be restrained are borne out from studies of euthanasia as practiced in the Netherlands. Though technically illegal, active euthanasia is tolerated in the Netherlands where physicians end the lives of their patients under certain specified conditions: the patient's consent must be free, conscious, explicit and persistent; patient and physician must agree that suffering is intolerable; other measures for relief must have been exhausted; a second physician must concur; these facts must be recorded and the action must be reported to the state prosecutor.[39]

That actual practice in the Netherlands deviates widely from the agreed-upon constraints is documented in two recent studies. Carlos F. Gomez reports that most acts of euthanasia in the Netherlands go unreported and uninvestigated by public authorities.[40] In his own survey of 26 cases of active euthanasia, only 15% had been reported to the prosecutor's office. Despite Initiative 119's assurance of codification into law, Gomez correctly notes that, had it passed, there would be no greater regulation of the private killings in the State of Washington than there is in the Netherlands. If, in instances of euthanasia, the official cause of death is listed as "respiratory arrest," and the massive overdose of narcotics that lead to that arrest is not even mentioned, then cases of physician killing would blend imperceptibly into the larger background of death from natural causes. Under such practice, identification and oversight of euthanasia would prove impossible.

Though exact numbers are difficult to ascertain, a survey which was commissioned by the Dutch government and chaired by the attorney general of the Dutch Supreme Court indicates that "1.8% of deaths in the Netherlands are the result of physician assisted suicide."[41] More revealing is the finding that 54% of physicians interviewed had participated in at least one case of active euthanasia and another 34% stated that, though they had not done so, they would be prepared to do so if asked. Of the 12% who said they would not participate in such an action, more than half said they would refer patients requesting euthanasia to a colleague with a more permissive attitude. In other words, the official Dutch study found that an overwhelming majority of physicians in the Netherlands see euthanasia, under certain circumstances, as an accepted element of medical practice. The circumstances mentioned in the study were "loss of dignity, pain, unworthy dying, being dependent on others, or tiredness of life." In only 10 of 107 cases was pain the only reason.

While most of the cases of euthanasia involved explicit patient requests, the attorney general's survey found that 0.8% of the deaths occurred without the patient's request. In these cases, it occurred "after consultation with the family, nurses, or one or more colleagues." The authors found that in the Netherlands each year more than 25,000 patients seek assurance from their physician that they will assist them if life becomes unbearable. Each year abut 9,000 explicit requests are made, of which less than one-third are agreed to by physicians.

The Dutch apologists for the practice suggest that euthanasia accounts for two to three percent, at most, of all deaths in the Netherlands. In a country with a published mortality rate of 120,000, this would imply from 2,400 to 3,600 cases of euthanasia a year. In the United States, with a rate of approximately two million deaths a year, this would translate into some 40,000 to 60,000 people killed each year by their physician. That not all of these would be voluntary is seen in Gomez's finding that, while most of the cases he studied fit the criteria established by the courts and Dutch medical profession, in four out of the twenty-six cases he investigated it was clear that the patient was incapable of giving consent, or it was doubtful that consent could have been obtained properly. He reports that in none of these cases was the public prosecutor notified.

The Dutch experience shows that to construct the argument for euthanasia in terms of autonomy is to misconstrue the reality of what happens to those who cannot be truly autonomous. If this is true in a nation with universal health-care coverage, how much greater the danger in a society in which 37 percent of the population is uninsured and concern for rising costs dominates the health-care agenda. And how much greater in a system in which there are no safeguards built into the legislation to protect the vulnerable. The practice of euthanasia, at least as envisioned in Initiative 119, would place patients, particularly the most vulnerable of patients, at intolerable risk. As the Washington bishops note, Initiative 119 contained no special requirements for the physicians who would administer lethal injections. There was no requirement for determining the mental state or competency of the patient. There was no waiting period required, no notification of family, no minimum residency, and no notification of euthanasia to public authorities.

The demand for active euthanasia is, in part, a response to the fear of entrapment in a technologically sophisticated, seemingly uncaring world of medicine. Unrestrained freedom to end one's life or to have it ended by a physician ought not to be the only response to that fear; nor is such a response without grave social implications. That legitimate fear does not call for state-sanctioned suicide or euthanasia; it calls for a rejection of the mindset that insists that we utilize *any* intervention capable of sustaining life—indifferent to the pain, suffering and burden to the individual whose life, or dying, is being prolonged.

The Roman Catholic bishops of the State of Washington spent some $1.5 million in their successful campaign against Initiative 119. But the movement for active euthanasia did not end with that ballot. The Hemlock Society has already begun a campaign to place similar initiatives on the Oregon and the California ballots. The success of the Washington bishops is a warning, not a victory. If we fail to be sensitive to people's fear of being trapped by medical technology, that fear will ultimately find its voice in an increased demand for active euthanasia. Unwittingly, then, Catholics, despite their well-developed moral teaching against euthanasia and their sophisticated tradition on the limitations of the moral obligation to prolong life, might contribute to public acceptance of active euthanasia.

For Reflection and Discussion

1. As you begin this text on euthanasia, express your own present position on the subject. Do you have family or personal stories dealing with euthanasia? How have these—or at least stories in the media—shaped your opinion?

2. Some authors distinguish between active and passive euthanasia. What is the basis of this distinction? Do you agree or disagree with this reasoning? Why?

3. What is the difference between "living will" legislation and "aid-in-dying" legislation? Which do you support? Why?

4. Discuss some of the possible risks and mistakes of physician-assisted suicide. What can be learned from the Dutch experience? How do you react to Callahan's comment: "Killing is a contagious disease"?

5. What is the question about artificially administered nutrition and hydration and how is this related to euthanasia?

Notes

1. Proposition 119. An Amendment to Article 1, Section 2, Chapter 112, Laws of 1979; Susan M. Wolf et al., "Sources of Concern About the Patient Self-Determination Act," *New England Journal of Medicine* 325 (1991) 1666-71.
2. 42 U.S.C. 1395 cc(a)(1) et seq. (as amended, Nov. 1990); see John J. Paris, S.J. and Kevin J. O'Connell, "The Patient Self-Determination Act of 1990," *Clinical Ethics Report* (May 5, 1991) 1-10.
3. *In re Quinlan,* 70 N.J. 10, 355 A. 2d 647 (1985).
4. *Cruzan v. Director Missouri Dept. of Health,* 110 S. Ct. 2841 (1990); Lisa Sowle Cahill, "Bioethical Decisions to End Life," *TS* 52 (1991) 107-27.
5. Sacred Congregation for the Doctrine of the Faith, "Declaration on Euthanasia," *Origins* 10 (1980) 154-57.
6. James Rachels, "Active and Passive Euthanasia," *New England Journal of Medicine* 292 (1975) 78-80.
7. Marcia Angell, "Euthanasia," *New England Journal of Medicine* 319 (1990) 1348-50.
8. Peter A. Singer and Mark Siegler, "Euthanasia—A Critique," *New England Journal of Medicine* 322 (1991) 1881-83.
9. Albert R. Jonsen, "What Is at Stake?" *Commonweal* 118 (August 9, 1991) 466-68.
10. Richard A. Knox, "Poll: Americans Favor Mercy Killing," *Boston Globe,* 3 Nov. 1991. A1.
11. Derek Humphry and Ann Wickett, *The Right to Die: Understanding Euthanasia* (New York: Harper & Row, 1986).
12. *New York Times,* 17 Jan. 1938 (reported in Humphry & Wickett 14).
13. E. Harold Laws et al., "Views on Euthanasia," *Journal of Medical Education* 46 (1971) 540-42.
14. Sidney H. Wanzer, David D. Federman, S. James Edelstein, et al., "The Physician's Responsibility Toward Hopelessly Ill Patients: A Second Look," *New England Journal of Medicine* 320 (1984) 844-49, at 845.
15. Anonymous, "It's Over, Debbie," *JAMA* 259 (1988) 272.
16. Willard Gayland, Leon R. Kass, Edmund D. Pellegrino and Mark Siegler, "Doctors Must Not Kill," *JAMA* 259 (1988) 2139-40.
17. Leon R. Kass, "Neither for Love Nor Money: Why Doctors Must Not Kill," *The Public Interest* 94 (1989) 24-45.
18. Yale Kamisar, "Some Non-Religious Views against Proposed Mercy Killing Legislation," *Minnesota Law Review* 42 (1958) 1042-71.
19. Leo Alexander, "Medical Science Under Dictatorship," *New England Journal of Medicine* 214 (1949) 39-47.
20. Israel Wilkerson, "Opponents Weigh Action against Doctor Who Aided Suicides," *New York Times,* 25 Oct. 1991, National Edition, p. 1. See also George Annas, "Killing Machines," *Hastings Center Report* (March/April 1991) 33-35.
21. Timothy Quill, "Death and Dignity: A Case of Individualized Decision Making," *New England Journal of Medicine* 324 (1991) 691-94.
22. Correspondence: "Death and Dignity: The Case of Diane," *New England Journal of Medicine* 325 (1991) 658-60.
23. Jo Roman, *Exit House* (New York: Seaview, 1980).
24. Derek Humphry, *Final Exit* (Eugene, Oreg.: Hemlock Society, 1991).

25. Archbishop Thomas Murphy, "Washington State's November Ballot: Euthanasia and Abortion," *Origins* 21 (1991) 298-302; Washington Bishops, "Initiative 119: The Real Choice," *Origins* 21 (1991) 302.

26. *Commonweal* 118 (Aug. 9, 1991). This Special Supplement, entitled *Euthanasia: Washington State Initiative* 119, included articles by Albert R. Jonsen, "Initiative 119: What Is at Stake?" 466-68; Carlos F. Gomez, "Euthanasia: Consider the Dutch" 46972; Leon R. Kass, "Why Doctors Must Not Kill 472-76; Daniel Callahan, " 'Aid-in-Dying': The Social Dimensions" 476-80.

27. Callahan, "Aid-in-Dying" 476.

28. Ibid.

29. Richard A. McCormick, S.J., "Biomedical Problems in the Nineties," *Catholic World* 234 (1991) 197-201; see also Leo Alexander, "Medical Science under Dictatorship," *New England Journal of Medicine* 241 (1949) 39-47.

30. Callahan, "Aid-in-Dying" 477.

31. Ibid.

32. Ibid., 480.

33. Richard A. McCormick, "Biomedical Problems" 199.

34. Thomas H. Murphy, "Washington State's November Ballot" 300.

35. Oregon and Washington Bishops, "Living and Dying Well," *Origins* 21 (1991) 346-52.

36. The Massachusetts Catholic Conference, *The Health Care Proxy Bill: A Catholic Guide* (Boston: Pilot Publishing Co., Dec. 1, 1990) 1-8, at 3.

37. Oregon and Washington Bishops 349-50.

38. Ibid., 350. Additional support for the Washington and Oregon Bishops' Statement on the moral option to withhold or withdraw nutrition and fluids from dying patients or those in a persistent vegetative condition are found in the Texas Bishops' Statement "On Withdrawing Artificial Nutrition and Hydration," *Origins* 21 (1990) 53 ff.; United States Bishops' Committee for Pro-Life Activities, "The Rights of the Terminally Ill," *Origins* 16 (1987) 222-26; Catholic Health Association of Wisconsin, "Guidelines on the Use of Nutrition and Fluids in Catholic Health Care Facilities" (1989); Richard A. McCormick, S.J., "Nutrition-Hydration: The New Euthanasia?" in *The Critical Calling* (Washington, D.C.: Georgetown Univ., 1989); John J. Pans, S.J., "The Catholic Tradition on the Use of Nutrition and Fluids," in Kevin Wildes, ed., *Birth, Suffering and Death* (Dordrecht: Kluwer, 1991). See also Lisa Sowle Cahill's coverage of the issue in *TS* 52 (1991) 110-19.

39. M. A. M. de Wachter, "Active Euthanasia in the Netherlands," *JAMA* 262 (1989) 3316-19; A. M. J. Ten Have Henk, "Euthanasia in the Netherlands: The Legal Context and the Cases," *Hospital Ethics Committee Forum* 1 (1989) 412-45; R. Fenigsen, "Euthanasia in the Netherlands," *Issues in Law and Medicine* 6 (1990) 229-45; R. Fenigsen, "A Case Against Dutch Euthanasia," *Hastings Center Report* (Special Supplement, January/February, 1989) 22-30.

40. Carlos F. Gomez, *Regulating Death: Euthanasia and the Case of the Netherlands* (New York: Free Press, 1991). Gomez's findings are more readily available in "Euthanasia: Consider the Dutch" (n. 26 above).

41. Cf. the brief report of the survey, Paul J. Van der Maas et al., "Euthanasia and Other Medical Decisions Concerning the End of Life," *Lancet* 338 (September 14, 1991) 669-74, at 672.

Part I:
For Euthanasia

1

Active and Passive Euthanasia

James Rachels, Ph.D.

THE DISTINCTION BETWEEN ACTIVE AND PASSIVE EUTHANA-
sia is thought to be crucial for medical ethics. The idea is that
it is permissible, at least in some cases, to withhold treatment
and allow a patient to die, but it is never permissible to take
any direct action designed to kill the patient. This doctrine
seems to be accepted by most doctors, and it is endorsed in a
statement adopted by the House of Delegates of the American
Medical Association on December 4, 1973:

> The intentional termination of the life of one human
> being by another—mercy killing—is contrary to that for
> which the medical profession stands and is contrary to
> the policy of the American Medical Association.
> The cessation of the employment of extraordinary means
> to prolong the life of the body when there is irrefutable
> evidence that biological death is imminent is the deci-
> sion of the patient and/or his immediate family. The ad-
> vice and judgment of the physician should be freely
> available to the patient and/or his immediate family.

However, a strong case can be made against this doctrine. In what
follows I will set out some of the relevant arguments, and urge
doctors to reconsider their views on this matter.

To begin with a familiar type of situation, a patient who is
dying of incurable cancer of the throat is in terrible pain, which

can no longer be satisfactorily alleviated. He is certain to die within a few days, even if present treatment is continued, but he does not want to go on living for those days since the pain is unbearable. So he asks the doctor for an end to it, and his family joins in the request.

→ Suppose the doctor agrees to withhold treatment, as the conventional doctrine says he may. The justification for his doing so is that the patient is in terrible agony, and since he is going to die anyway, it would be wrong to prolong his suffering needlessly. But now notice this. If one simply withholds treatment, it may take the patient longer to die, and so he may suffer more than he would if more direct action were taken and a lethal injection given. This fact provides strong reason for thinking that, once the initial decision not to prolong his agony has been made, active euthanasia is actually preferable to passive euthanasia, rather than the reverse. To say otherwise is to endorse the option that leads to more suffering rather than less, and is contrary to the humanitarian impulse that prompts the decision not to prolong his life in the first place.

→ Part of my point is that the process of being "allowed to die" can be relatively slow and painful, whereas being given a lethal injection is relatively quick and painless. Let me give a different sort of example. In the United States about one in 600 babies is born with Down's syndrome. Most of these babies are otherwise healthy—that is, with only the usual pediatric care, they will proceed to an otherwise normal infancy. Some, however, are born with congenital defects such as intestinal obstructions that require operations if they are to live. Sometimes, the parents and the doctor will decide not to operate, and let the infant die. Anthony Shaw describes what happens then:

> . . . When surgery is denied [the doctor] must try to keep the infant from suffering while natural forces sap the baby's life away. As a surgeon whose natural inclination is to use the scalpel to fight off death, standing by and watching a salvageable baby die is the most

emotionally exhausting experience I know. It is easy at
a conference, in a theoretical discussion, to decide that
such infants should be allowed to die. It is altogether
different to stand by in the nursery and watch as de-
hydration and infection wither a tiny being over hours
and days. This is a terrible ordeal for me and the hospital staff—much more so than for the parents who never
set foot in the nursery.[1]

→I can understand why some people are opposed to all euthanasia,
and insist that such infants must be allowed to live. I think I can
also understand why other people favor destroying these babies
quickly and painlessly. But why should anyone favor letting "de-
hydration and infection wither a tiny being over hours and days?"
The doctrine that says that a baby may be allowed to dehydrate
and wither but may not be given an injection that would end its life
without suffering, seems so patently cruel as to require no further
refutation. The strong language is not intended to offend, but only
to put the point in the clearest possible way.

→ My second argument is that the conventional doctrine
leads to decisions concerning life and death made on irrelevant
grounds.

Consider again the case of the infants with Down's syndrome who need operations for congenital defects unrelated to
the syndrome in order to live. Sometimes, there is no operation and the baby dies, but when there is no such defect, the
baby lives on. Now, an operation such as that to remove an
intestinal obstruction is not prohibitively difficult. The reason
why such operations are not performed in these cases is,
clearly, that the child has Down's syndrome and the parents
and doctor judge that because of that fact it is better for the
child to die.

But notice that this situation is absurd, no matter what
view one takes of the lives and potentials of such babies. If
the life of such an infant is worth preserving, what does it matter if it needs a simple operation? Or, if one thinks it better
that such a baby should not live on, what difference does it

147582

matter that it happens to have an unobstructed intestinal tract? In either case, the matter of life and death is being decided on irrelevant grounds. It is the Down's syndrome, and not the intestines, that is the issue. The matter should be decided, if at all, on that basis, and not be allowed to depend on the essentially irrelevant question of whether the intestinal tract is blocked.

What makes this situation possible, of course, is the idea that when there is an intestinal blockage, one can "let the baby die," but when there is no such defect there is nothing that can be done, for one must not "kill" it. The fact that this idea leads to such results as deciding life or death on irrelevant grounds is another good reason why the doctrine should be rejected.

One reason why so many people think that there is an important moral difference between active and passive euthanasia is that they think killing someone is morally worse than letting someone die. But is it? Is killing, in itself, worse than letting someone die? To investigate this issue, two cases may be considered that are exactly alike except that one involves killing whereas the other involves letting one die. Then, it can be asked whether this difference makes any difference to the moral assessments. It is important that the cases be exactly alike except for this one difference since otherwise one cannot be confident that it is this difference and not some other that accounts for any variation in the assessments of the two cases. So, let us consider this pair of cases:

In the first, Smith stands to gain a large inheritance if anything should happen to his six-year-old cousin. One evening while the child is taking his bath, Smith sneaks into the bathroom and drowns the child, and then arranges things so that it will look like an accident.

In the second, Jones also stands to gain if anything should happen to his six-year-old cousin. Like Smith, Jones sneaks in planning to drown the child in his bath. However, just as he enters the bathroom Jones sees the child slip and hit his head, and fall face down in the water. Jones is delighted; he stands by, ready to push the child's head back under if it is necessary, but it is not necessary. With only a little thrashing about, the child drowns all by himself, "accidentally," as Jones watches and does nothing.

Now Smith killed the child, whereas Jones "merely" let the child die. That is the only difference between them. Did either man behave better, from a moral point of view? If the difference between killing and letting die were in itself a morally important matter, one should say that Jones's behavior was less reprehensible than Smith's. But does one really want to say that? I think not. In the first place, both men acted from the same motive, personal gain, and both had exactly the same end in view when they acted. It may be inferred from Smith's conduct that he is a bad man, although that judgment may be withdrawn or modified if certain further facts are learned about him—for example, that he is mentally deranged. But would not the very same thing be inferred about Jones from his conduct? And would not the same further considerations also be relevant to any modification of this judgment? Moreover, suppose Jones pleaded, in his own defense, "After all, I didn't do anything except just stand there and watch the child drown. I didn't kill him; I only let him die." Again, if letting die were in itself less bad than killing, this defense should have at least some weight. But it does not. Such a "defense" can only be regarded as a grotesque perversion of moral reasoning. Morally speaking, it is no defense at all.

Now, it may be pointed out, quite properly, that the cases of euthanasia with which doctors are concerned are not like this at all. They do not involve personal gain or the destruction of normal healthy children. Doctors are concerned only with cases in which the patient's life is of no further use to him, or in which the patient's life has become or will soon become a terrible burden. However, the point is the same in these cases: the bare difference between killing and letting die does not, in itself, make a moral difference. If a doctor lets a patient die, for humane reasons, he is in the same moral position as if he had given the patient a lethal injection for humane reasons. If his decision was wrong—if, for example, the patient's illness was in fact curable—the decision would be equally regrettable no matter which method was used to carry it out. And if the doctor's decision was the right one, the method used is not in itself important.

The AMA policy statement isolates the crucial issue very well; the crucial issue is "the intentional termination of the life of one human being by another." But after identifying this issue, and forbidding "mercy killing," the statement goes on to deny that the cessation of treatment is the intentional termination of a life. This is where the mistake comes in, for what is the cessation of treatment, in these circumstances, if it is not "the intentional termination of the life of one human being by another?" Of course it is exactly that, and if it were not, there would be no point to it.

Many people will find this judgment hard to accept. One reason, I think, is that it is very easy to conflate the question of whether killing is, in itself, worse than letting die, with the very different question of whether most actual cases of killing are more reprehensible than most actual cases of letting die. Most actual cases of killing are clearly terrible (think, for example, of all the murders reported in the newspapers), and one hears of such cases every day. On the other hand, one hardly ever hears of a case of letting die, except for the actions of doctors who are motivated by humanitarian reasons. So one learns to think of killing in a much worse light than of letting die. But this does not mean that there is something about killing that makes it in itself worse than letting die, for it is not the bare difference between killing and letting die that makes the difference in these cases. Rather, the other factors—the murderer's motive of personal gain, for example, contrasted with the doctor's humanitarian motivation—account for different reactions to the different cases.

I have argued that killing is not in itself any worse than letting die; if my contention is right, it follows that active euthanasia is not any worse than passive euthanasia. What arguments can be given on the other side? The most common, I believe, is the following: "The important difference between active and passive euthanasia is that, in passive euthanasia, the doctor does not do anything to bring about the patient's death. The doctor does nothing, and the patient dies of whatever ills already afflict him. In active euthanasia, however, the doctor does something to bring about the patient's death: he kills him. The doctor who gives the patient with cancer a lethal injection has himself caused his patient's death; whereas if he merely ceases treatment, the cancer is the cause of the death."

A number of points need to be made here. The first is that it is not exactly correct to say that in passive euthanasia the doctor does nothing, for he does do one thing that is very important: he lets the patient die. "Letting someone die" is certainly different, in some respects, from other types of action—mainly in that it is a kind of action that one may perform by way of not performing certain other actions. For example, one may let a patient die by way of not giving medication, just as one may insult someone by way of not shaking his hand. But for any purpose of moral assessment, it is a type of action nonetheless. The decision to let a patient die is subject to moral appraisal in the same way that a decision to kill him would be subject to moral appraisal: it may be assessed as wise or unwise, compassionate or sadistic, right or wrong. If a doctor deliberately let a patient die who was suffering from a routinely curable illness, the doctor would certainly be to blame for what he had done, just as he would be to blame if he had needlessly killed the patient. Charges against him would then be appropriate. If so, it would be no defense at all for him to insist that he didn't "do anything." He would have done something very serious indeed, for he let his patient die.

Fixing the cause of death may be very important from a legal point of view, for it may determine whether criminal charges are brought against the doctor. But I do not think that this notion can be used to show a moral difference between active and passive euthanasia. The reason why it is considered bad to be the cause of someone's death is that death is regarded as a great evil—and so it is. However, if it has been decided that euthanasia—even passive euthanasia—is desirable in a given case, it has also been decided that in this instance death is no greater an evil than the patient's continued existence. And if this is true, the usual reason for not wanting to be the cause of someone's death simply does not apply.

Finally, doctors may think that all of this is only of academic interest—the sort of thing that philosophers may worry about but that has no practical bearing on their own work. After all, doctors must be concerned about the legal consequences of what they do, and active euthanasia is clearly forbidden by the law. But even so, doctors should also be concerned with the fact that the law is forcing upon them a moral doctrine that may well be indefensible, and has a considerable effect on their practices. Of course, most doctors are not now in the position of being coerced in this matter, for they do not regard themselves as merely going along with what the law requires. Rather, in statements such as the AMA policy statement that I have quoted, they are endorsing this doctrine as a central point of medical ethics. In that statement, active euthanasia is condemned not merely as illegal but as "contrary to that for which the medical profession stands," whereas passive euthanasia is approved. However, the preceding considerations suggest that there is really no moral difference between the two, considered in themselves (there may be important moral differences in some cases in their *consequences,* but, as I pointed out, these differences "may make active euthanasia, and not passive euthanasia, the morally preferable option). So, whereas doctors may have to discriminate between active and passive euthanasia to satisfy the law, they should not do any more than that. In particular, they should not give the distinction any added authority and weight by writing it into official statements of medical ethics.

For Reflection and Discussion

1. What is meant by the traditional distinction between active and passive euthanasia? What is the significance of the phrase, "at least in some cases," regarding passive euthanasia?

2. The author's first point stresses his desire not to prolong agony, stating that allowing to die is "so patently cruel as to require no further refutation." Do you agree? What is the meaning and significance for the physician of ending someone's life by lethal injection? (Concerning the author's example of babies with Down syndrome, see James Gustafson's careful analysis of such a tragic case in *Perspectives in Biology and Medicine* 16 [Summer 1973]: 529-57.)

3. If passive euthanasia is permissible "at least in some cases," the implication seems to be that allowing to die is *not* permissible in some other cases. Into which category does the author's drowning example fall? Why?

4. The AMA statement claims that euthanasia is "contrary to that for which the medical profession stands." What is your sense of the meaning of the medical profession? Would euthanasia be contrary to that? How would legalized euthanasia affect the medical profession and patients?

Notes

1. A. Shaw, "Doctor, Do We Have A Choice?" *New York Times Magazine* (January 30, 1972), 54.

2

Euthanasia

Marcia Angell, M.D.

OVER THE PAST DECADE THE ISSUE OF WHETHER IT IS
ever permissible to withhold life-sustaining treatment has been
debated by doctors and ethicists and in the courts and state
legislatures. Gradually, a consensus has emerged that it is indeed permissible and even mandatory to withhold life-sustaining treatment under certain circumstances.[1-3] Now attention
has begun to turn toward the issue of euthanasia. Euthanasia
means purposely terminating the life of a patient to prevent
further suffering, and it is illegal. Thus, it is different from
withholding life-sustaining treatment. It is also different from
administering a drug, such as morphine, that may hasten death
but has another purpose. For many, the beginning of a debate
about euthanasia is ominous—a step down a slippery slope
leading to widespread disregard for the value of human life.
For others, it signifies an opportunity to deal more humanely
and rationally with prolonged meaningless suffering. My purpose here is to provide some background on this issue and to
present arguments for and against euthanasia.

In the Netherlands, euthanasia officially remains a crime,
punishable by up to 12 years in prison, but it is practiced fairly
commonly and openly there, protected by a body of case law
and by strong public support. Estimates are that 5,000 to 8,000
Dutch lives are ended by euthanasia each year.[4] The Dutch
Medical Association in 1984 suggested guidelines for perform-

ing euthanasia,[5] and in 1985 a government-appointed Commission on Euthanasia issued a report[6] that in essence endorsed the guidelines and recommended a change in the criminal code to permit euthanasia. Although a change is unlikely during the tenure of the present government, it will almost certainly be an important issue in the next general election. The guidelines under which euthanasia is performed in the Netherlands are stringent. Four essential conditions must be met: (1) The patient must be competent. This requirement excludes many groups of patients for whom the question of withholding life-sustaining treatment has been most contentious in the United States—such as patients with advanced Alzheimer's disease, retarded patients, handicapped newborns, and patients, such as Karen Quinlan, who are in a persistent vegetative state. (2) The patient must request euthanasia voluntarily, consistently, and repeatedly over a reasonable time, and the request must be well documented. This requirement prevents euthanasia in response to an ill-considered or impulsive request. (3) The patient must be suffering intolerably, with no prospect of relief, although there needn't be a terminal disease. Thus, depression, for which there is treatment, would not be a reason for euthanasia, but amyotrophic lateral sclerosis might be. (4) Euthanasia must be performed by a physician in consultation with another physician not involved in the case; the usual method is to induce sleep with a barbiturate, followed by a lethal injection of curare.

In California this year, an unsuccessful effort was made to collect enough signatures on a petition to place a proposed law on the fall ballot that would legalize euthanasia.[7] This initiative was sponsored by Americans Against Human Suffering, the political arm of the Hemlock Society, an organization devoted to promoting the idea of appropriate euthanasia. In two important ways the provisions of the proposed law in California differed from the Dutch guidelines. First, they were more stringent than the Dutch guidelines in that they required a candidate for euthanasia to be terminally ill, with a life expectancy of less than six months with or without medical treatment. Second, they were more lax than the Dutch guidelines in that they permitted euthanasia by advance directive. A competent adult, healthy or not, could assign a durable power of attorney to authorize euthanasia if he became terminally ill and incompetent within seven years. Thus, unlike the situation in the Netherlands, euthanasia would be possible for incompetent as well as competent patients, provided they had once been competent; only children and those born mentally retarded would be excluded. Note that both the Dutch guidelines and the California proposal would preclude performing euthanasia at the sole discretion of a physician, as purportedly occurred in the case of Debbie.[8]

Most observers believe that the California initiative failed because of organizational problems, not voter sentiment. Public opinion polls have shown fairly consistently that about three fifths of the American public favor legalizing euthanasia under certain conditions (compared with about three-quarters of the Dutch public).[9] Americans Against Human Suffering intends to repeat its effort to place the issue on the ballot in California in 1990 and also to make similar efforts in Washington, Oregon, and Florida.

What are the arguments for and against legalizing euthanasia? And where do doctors fit in? Arguments against euthanasia are more familiar than those for it. First, we have strong legal, religious, and cultural taboos against taking human life, almost regardless of the circumstances (wars, self-defense, and legal executions being the notable exceptions). These reflect the supreme value we place on human life, as well as a concern that any compromise of this position might lead to a general erosion of our respect for life. Thus, many would acknowledge that there may be circumstances in which euthanasia would be appropriate for an individual patient, but would oppose it because it would tend to devalue life. Related to this argument is the fear that the devaluation would be selective, that euthanasia might occur too often among the weak and powerless in our society—that is, among the very old, the poor, or the handicapped. Lessons learned from the Nazis fuel this fear.

There is also concern that euthanasia could be abused not only by society at large, but by individuals. Inevitably, despite safeguards (even as stringent as those in the Netherlands), there must be some vagueness in any language permitting euthanasia. For example, how do we define intolerable suffering? Exactly what is a voluntary, repeated, and consistent request? This vagueness reflects the variations and subtleties of the circumstances, as well as the inadequacies of language. However, it makes it easy to imagine the ne'er-do-well nephew persuading his rich old uncle to request euthanasia.

Finally, doctors have their own set of special concerns about euthanasia. Many of us believe that euthanasia is appropriate under certain conditions and that it should, indeed, be legalized, but that we should not perform it ourselves. According to this view, doctors should only extend life, never shorten it, and patients must be in no doubt about what our function is. A poll of doctors released June 2 by the University of Colorado at Denver Center for Health Ethics and Policy showed that three-fifths of them favored legalizing euthanasia, but nearly half of those would not perform it themselves.

—— The principal argument in favor of euthanasia is that it is more humane than forcing a patient to continue a life of unmitigated suffering. According to this view, there is no moral difference under some circumstances between euthanasia and withholding life-sustaining treatment. In both situations, the purpose is a merciful death, and the only practical difference is that withholding life-sustaining treatment entails more suffering because it takes longer. Furthermore, it requires an element of happenstance, such as the development of pneumonia, for which there is treatment that could be withheld. Proponents of euthanasia also argue that it furthers the principle of individual self-determination, and that this enhances rather than diminishes respect for human life. They believe that it is contradictory to permit patients to refuse life-sustaining treatment, while not honoring their request for euthanasia.

If euthanasia were permissible, the best way to minimize the possibility of abuse would be to limit its availability, as in the Netherlands, to competent patients who request it because of their current situation and not because of a hypothetical future one. This would mean denying euthanasia to incompetent patients, even with an advance directive, and would thus sharply limit its use. Nevertheless, such a limitation may be the price of preventing abuse. Furthermore, it could be argued that the suffering of incompetent patients, certainly those in a persistent vegetative state, is experienced more by their families than by themselves.

If euthanasia were legalized, doctors morally opposed to it should not, of course, be required to perform it. On the other hand, doctors who believe in the desirability of euthanasia under certain conditions, but who would refuse to perform it, raise a different issue. Can they appropriately excuse themselves from a difficult part of what they consider good patient care? Would they favor the creation of a profession especially dedicated to performing euthanasia (a problematic and, I think, unsavory prospect)?

Whatever their view of the morality and appropriateness of legalizing euthanasia and of performing it, doctors should be prepared for its emergence as an important issue in the years ahead and should be ready to debate it. Perhaps, also, those who favor legalizing euthanasia but would not perform it should rethink their position. Our ability to extend life through new technologies will certainly grow, and with it will grow the dilemmas created by the extension of intractable suffering.

For Discussion and Reflection

1. What is meant by the "slippery-slope" argument regarding euthanasia? Do you share this kind of concern? Why/why not?

2. What are the advantages and disadvantages of the guidelines for euthanasia in the Netherlands? Do you think there should be any guidelines at all?

3. In what ways is Angell's argument for euthanasia similar to that of Rachels'? What is your reaction to their position?

4. Would it be fair to limit euthanasia only to competent patients? How do you react to doctors who approve legalizing euthanasia but who refuse to perform it? How would you react to doctors who are willing to perform euthanasia?

Notes

1. President's Commission for the Study of Ethical Problems in Medicine and Biomedical and Behavioral Research, "Deciding to Forego Life-sustaining Treatment: A Report on the Ethical, Medical, and Legal Issues in Treatment Decisions," Washington, D.C.: Government Printing Office, 1983.

2. G.J. Annas, L.H. Glantz, "The Right of Elderly Patients to Refuse Life-sustaining Treatment," *Milbank Q* 64 (1986) 95-162.

3. Current Opinions of the Council on Ethical and Judicial Affairs of the AMA—1986. "Withholding or Withdrawing Life-prolonging Treatment" (Chicago: American Medical Association, 1986).

4. G.E. Pence, "Do Not Go Slowly into that Dark Night: Mercy Killing in Holland." *American Journal of Medicine* 84 (1988) 139-41.

5. Central Committee of the Royal Dutch Medical Association, "Vision on Euthanasia," *Med. Contact*, 39 (1984) 990-8.

6. Final report of the Netherlands State Commission on Euthanasia: an English Summary. *Bioethics* 1 (1987) 163-74.

7. The Humane and Dignified Death Act. California Civil Code, Title 10.5.

8. "It's Over, Debbie," *JAMA* 259 (1988) 272.

9. Roper Organization of New York City, "The 1988 Roper Poll on Attitudes toward Active Voluntary Euthanasia" (Los Angeles: National Hemlock Society, 1988).

3

The Physician's Responsibility Toward Hopelessly Ill Patients: A Second Look

Sidney H. Wanzer, M.D., Daniel D. Federman, M.D., S. James Adelstein, M.D., Christine K. Cassel, M.D., Edwin H. Cassem, M.D., Ronald E. Cranford, M.D., Edward W. Hook, M.D., Bernard Lo, M.D., Charles G. Moertel, M.D., Peter Safar, M.D., Alan Stone, M.D., Jan Van Eys, Ph.D., M.D.

SOME OF THE PRACTICES THAT WERE CONTROVERSIAL FIVE years ago[1] in the care of the dying patient have become accepted and routine. Do-not-resuscitate (DNR) orders, nonexistent only a few years ago, are now commonplace. Many physicians and ethicists now agree that there is little difference between nasogastric or intravenous hydration and other life-sustaining measures. They have concluded, therefore, that it is ethical to withdraw nutrition and hydration from certain dying, hopelessly ill, or permanently unconscious patients. The public and the courts have tended to accept this principle. Most important, there has been an increase in sensitivity to the desires of dying patients on the part of doctors, other health professionals, and the public. The entire subject is now discussed openly. Various studies and reports from governmental bodies, private foundations, the American Medical Association, and state medical societies reflect these advances in thinking.[2-9] The increased awareness of the rights of dying patients has also been translated into new laws. Thirty-eight states now have legislation covering advance directives ("living wills"), and fifteen states specifically provide that a patient's health-care spokesperson, or proxy, can authorize the withholding or withdrawal of life support.[10,11]

The courts have continued to support patients' rights and have expanded the legal concept of the right to refuse medical treatment, upholding this right in more than 80 court decisions.[12] As a general rule, the cases in the early 1980s involved terminally ill patients whose death was expected whether or not treatment was continued, and the treatment at issue—for instance, prolonged endotracheal intubation, mechanical ventilation, dialysis, or chemotherapy—was often intrusive or burdensome. The courts recognized the patient's common-law right to autonomy (to be left alone to make one's own choices) as well as the constitutional right to privacy (to be protected from unwanted invasive medical treatment).

Currently, the courts are moving closer to the view that patients are entitled to be allowed to die, whether or not they are terminally ill or suffering. Many recent cases have permitted treatment to be terminated in patients who are permanently unconscious, indicating that the right to refuse treatment can be used to put an end to unacceptable conditions even if the patients are not perceptibly suffering or close to death. In such court opinions, many of which have dealt with artificial feeding, the cause of the patient's death continues to be attributed to the underlying disease, rather than to the withholding or withdrawal of treatment.[13]

Popular attitudes about the rights of dying patients have also changed, often in advance of the attitudes of health-care providers, legislators, and the courts. The results of one public-opinion poll indicated that 68 percent of the respondents believed that "people dying of an incurable painful disease should be allowed to end their lives before the disease runs its course."[14]

Health professionals have also become much more aware of patients' rights. In states with laws legitimizing living wills, hospitals have become responsive to patients' wishes as expressed in their advance directives, and hospital accreditation by the Joint Commission on Accreditation of Health Care Organizations now requires the establishment of formal DNR policies. The frequency with which DNR orders are used in nursing homes has also increased. In 1987 the California Department of Health Services became the first state agency to develop clear guidelines for the removal of life support, including tube feeding, in the state's 1,500 nursing homes and convalescent hospitals.[15]

Gaps Between Accepted Policies and Their Implementation

Many patients are aware of their right to make decisions about their health care, including the refusal of life-sustaining measures, yet few actually execute living wills or appoint surrogates through a health care proxy. Although such documents can be very helpful in clarifying the patient's wishes, they are all too infrequently discussed in standard medical practice. Furthermore, at present, advance directives do not exert enough influence on either the patient's ability to control medical decision making at the end of life or the physician's behavior with respect to such issues in hospitals, emergency rooms, and nursing homes. There remains a considerable gap between the acceptance of the directive and its implementation. There is also a large gap between what the courts now allow with respect to withdrawal of treatment and what physicians actually do. All too frequently, physicians are reluctant to withdraw aggressive treatment from hopelessly ill patients, despite clear legal precedent.

Physicians have a responsibility to consider timely discussions with patients about life-sustaining treatment and terminal care. Only a minority of physicians now do so consistently.[16] The best time to begin such discussions is during the course of routine, nonemergency care, remembering that not all patients are emotionally prepared, by virtue of their stage in life, their psychological makeup, or the stage of their illness. Nevertheless, as a matter of routine, physicians should become acquainted with their patients' personal values and wishes and should document them just as they document information about medical history, family history, and sociocultural background. Such discussions and the resultant documentation should be considered a part of the minimal standard of acceptable care. The physician should take the initiative in obtaining the documentation and should enter it in the medical record.

These issues are not sufficiently addressed in medical schools and residency programs. Medical educators need to recognize that practitioners may not sufficiently understand or value the patient's role in medical decision making or may be unwilling to relinquish control of the decision-making process. The interests of patients and physicians alike are best served when decisions are made jointly, and medical students and residents should learn to pursue this goal. These topics ought to be specifically included as curriculums are revised.

In general, health-care institutions must recognize their obligation to inform patients of their right to participate in decisions about their medical care, including the right to refuse treatment, and should formulate institutional policies about the use of advance directives and the appointment of surrogate decision makers. Hospitals, health-maintenance organizations, and nursing homes should ask patients on admission to indicate whether they have prepared a living will or designated a surrogate. It seems especially important that nursing homes require a regular review of patient preferences, with each patient's physician taking responsibility for ensuring that such information is obtained and documented. In the case of patients who lack decision-making capacity, surrogate decision-makers should be identified and consulted appropriately. (We prefer the term "decision-making capacity" to "competency" because in the medical context, the patient either has or does not have the capacity to make decisions, whereas competency is a legal determination that can be made only by the courts.)

Although we advocate these approaches, we recognize that the mechanisms of appointing a surrogate and executing a living will do present certain problems. Obviously, it may happen that a surrogate appointed previously is unavailable for consultation when problems arise in the treatment of a patient who lacks decision-making capacity. In addition, there is the problem of determining what constitutes an outdated living will or surrogate appointment and how often they need to be reaffirmed. Laws in most states provide that a living will is valid until it is revoked, but patients need to be encouraged to update and reconfirm such directives from time to time.

Settings for Dying

Home

Dying at home can provide the opportunity for quiet and privacy, dignity, and family closeness that may make death easier for the patient and provide consolation for the bereaved. Assuming that a stable and caring home environment exists, emotional and physical comfort is most often greatest at home, with family and friends nearby.

Patients and their families need reassurance that dying at home will not entail medical deprivation. They should be carefully instructed in the means of coping with possible problems, and appropriate community resources should be mobilized to assist them. The provision of care should be guided by the physician and implemented with the help of well-trained, highly motivated personnel from the hospice units that now serve many communities in this country, since home care often becomes too difficult for the family to handle alone. Hospice, a form of care in which an interdisciplinary team provides palliative and support services to both patient and family, is a concept whose time has come.

Recent cost-containment measures for expensive hospital care have given the home hospice movement considerable impetus, resulting in an emphasis on alternatives such as home care.[17] On the other hand, hospice care at home, which should be adequately financed by insurance as a cost-effective way to care for the patient, is often poorly reimbursed, and many hospice programs struggle to stay solvent. There is too much emphasis on reimbursement for high-technology care in the home, as opposed to hands-on nursing care. More adequate financing is clearly indicated for hospice and other home care providers, since it is clear that, overall, care at home usually costs much less than in other settings.

Nursing Home

When an admission to a nursing home is planned for a terminally ill patient, it is important to specify the treatment plans and goals at the outset. The nursing home should inquire about the patient's wishes with regard to life-sustaining procedures, including DNR orders and artificial nutrition and hydration. The patient should be encouraged to execute an advance directive, appoint a surrogate, or both. The possibility that it may be necessary to transfer the patient to a general hospital should be discussed in advance (transfer may become indicated, but usually it is not). All parties should anticipate that the final phases of the dying process will occur in the nursing home without a transfer to the hospital, unless the patient cannot be kept reasonably comfortable in the nursing home.

Even though care can clearly be given more cost effectively in the nursing home setting than in the general hospital, a major drawback to using the nursing home as a place for dying is that often insurance does not cover the cost of the nursing home care (just as it often does not cover the cost of care at home). Currently, there is almost no private insurance for nursing home care, and Medicare now covers only about 3 percent of nursing home days. The rest must be covered by a combination of Medicaid, to be eligible for which a patient must be pauperized, and private pay. It is essential that federal and private health-care plans be modified to make nursing home care more accessible to patients of limited means.

Hospital

As much as one-third of the patients cared for at home and expected to die there actually die in the hospital, even when hospice techniques of home care are used. The symptoms or anxiety generated by an impending death may overwhelm the family, and recourse to the hospital is appropriate whenever any treatment program, including a psychosocial one, cannot palliate the distress felt by the patient, the family, or both.

To accommodate such families and patients, hospitals should consider the development of specialized units, with rooms appointed so as to provide pleasant surroundings that will facilitate comfortable interchange among patient, family, and friends. The presence of life-sustaining equipment would be inappropriate in such an environment.

The intensive care unit should generally be discouraged as a treatment setting for the hospitalized patient who is dying, unless intensive palliative measures are required that cannot be done elsewhere. Too often, life-sustaining measures are instituted in the intensive care unit without sufficient thought to the proper goals of treatment. Although the courts have held that in the treatment of the hopelessly ill there is no legal distinction between stopping treatment and not starting it in the first place, there is a bias in the intensive care unit toward continuing aggressive measures that may be inappropriate. Though difficult, it is possible for a patient to die in the intensive care unit with dignity and comfort, since medical hardware itself has no capacity to dehumanize anyone. The important point is that the physician set a tone of caring and support, no matter what the setting.

Although the physicians and nurses in intensive care units may be less prepared than other professionals to switch from aggressive curative care to palliation and the provision of comfort only, they have all seen many situations in which clear decisions to limit treatment have brought welcome relief. Since these caregivers often have considerable emotional energy invested in patients who have previously been receiving aggressive curative treatment, they may need consultation with colleagues from outside the intensive care unit to decide when to change the treatment goals.

Treating the Dying Patient—The Importance of Flexible Care

The care of the dying is an art that should have its fullest expression in helping patients cope with the technologically complicated medical environment that often surrounds them at the end of life. The concept of a good death does not mean simply the withholding of technological treatments that serve only to prolong the act of dying. It also requires the art of deliberately creating a medical environment that allows a peaceful death. Somewhere between the unacceptable extremes of failure to treat the dying patient and intolerable use of aggressive life-sustaining measures, the physician must seek a level of care that optimizes comfort and dignity.

In evaluating the burdens and benefits of treatment for the dying patient—whether in the hospital, in a nursing home, or at home—the physician needs to formulate a flexible and adjustable care plan, tailoring treatment to the patient's changing needs as the disease progresses. Such plans contrast sharply with the practice, frequent in medicine, in which the physician makes rounds and prescribes, leaving orders for nurses and technicians, but not giving continual feedback and adjustment. The physician's actions on behalf of the patient should be appropriate, with respect to both the types of treatments and the location in which they are given. Such actions need to be adjusted continually to the individual patient's needs, with the physician keeping primarily in mind that the benefits of treatment must outweigh the burdens imposed.

When the patient lacks decision-making capacity, discussing the limitation of treatment with the family becomes a major part of the treatment plan. The principle of continually adjusted care should guide all these decisions.

Pain and Suffering

The principle of continually adjusted care is nowhere more important than in the control of pain, fear, and suffering. The hopelessly ill patient must have whatever is necessary to control pain. One of the most pervasive causes of anxiety among patients, their families, and the public is the perception that physicians' efforts toward the relief of pain are sadly deficient. Because of this perceived professional deficiency, people fear that needless suffering will be allowed to occur as patients are dying.[18] To a large extent, we believe such fears are justified.

In the patient whose dying process is irreversible, the balance between minimizing pain and suffering and potentially hastening death should be struck clearly in favor of pain relief. Narcotics or other pain medications should be given in whatever dose and by whatever route is necessary for relief. It is morally correct to increase the dose of narcotics to whatever dose is needed, even though the medication may contribute to the depression of respiration or blood pressure, the dulling of consciousness, or even death, provided the primary goal of the physician is to relieve suffering. The proper dose of pain medication is the dose that is sufficient to relieve pain and suffering, even to the point of unconsciousness.

Dying patients often feel isolated and doubt seriously that their physician will be there to relieve their pain when the terminal phase is near. Early in the course of fatal disease, patients should be offered strong reassurance that pain will be controlled and that their physician will be available when the need is greatest. Both the patient and the family should be told that addiction need not be a source of concern and that the relief of pain will have nothing but a salutary effect from both the physical and the emotional standpoint. When possible, pain medication should be given orally to maximize patient autonomy, but usually a continuous parenteral route is needed for the adequate medication of patients in the near-terminal or terminal state. Under no circumstances should medication be "rationed." For episodic pain, patients should be encouraged to take medication as soon as they are conscious of pain, instead of waiting until it becomes intense and far more difficult to control. For continuous or frequently recurring pain, the patient should be placed on a regular schedule of administration. Some patients will choose to endure a degree of pain rather than experience any loss of alertness or control from taking narcotics—a choice that is consistent with patient autonomy and the concept of continually adjusted care.

If pain cannot be controlled with the commonly used analgesic regimens of mild or moderate strength, the patient should be switched quickly to more potent narcotics. It is important that doses be adequate; the textbook doses recommended for short-term pain are often grossly inadequate for long-term pain in the patient dying of cancer. The physician should be familiar with two or three narcotics and their side effects and appropriate starting dosages. Doses should be brought promptly to levels that provide a reliable pain-free state. Since adequate narcotic management seems to be an unfamiliar area to many physicians, we urge that educational material be distributed to them from a noncommercial source.[19] To allow a patient to experience unbearable pain or suffering is unethical medical practice.

Legal Concerns

The principles of medical ethics are formulated independent of legal decisions, but physicians may fear that decisions about the care of the hopelessly ill will bring special risks of criminal charges and prosecution. Although no medical decision can be immune from legal scrutiny, courts in the United States have generally supported the approaches advocated here.[20-23] The physician should follow these principles without exaggerated concern for legal consequences, doing whatever is necessary to relieve pain and bring comfort, and adhering to the patient's wishes as much as possible. To withhold any necessary measure of pain relief in a hopelessly ill person out of fear of depressing respiration or of possible legal repercussions is unjustifiable. Good medical practice is the best protection against legal liability.

Preparing for Death

As sickness progresses toward death, measures to minimize suffering should be intensified. Dying patients may require palliative care of an intensity that rivals even that of curative efforts. Keeping the patient clean, caring for the skin, preventing the formation of bed sores, treating neuropsychiatric symptoms, controlling peripheral and pulmonary edema, aggressively reducing nausea and vomiting, using intravenous medications, fighting the psychosocial forces that can lead to family fragmentation—all can tax the ingenuity and equanimity of the most skilled health professionals. Even though aggressive curative techniques are no longer indicated, professionals and families are still called on to use intensive measures—extreme responsibility, extraordinary sensitivity, and heroic compassion.

In training programs for physicians, more attention needs to be paid to these aspects of care. Progress has been made in persuading house staff and attending physicians to discuss DNR orders and to include clear orders and notes in the chart about limits on life-sustaining therapies, but patients are too rarely cared for directly by the physician at or near the time of death. Usually it is nurses who care for patients at this time. In a few innovative training programs, most notably at the University of Oregon, the hands-on aspects of care of the dying are addressed,[24] and such techniques should be presented at all training institutions.

Assisted Suicide

If care is administered properly at the end of life, only the rare patient should be so distressed that he or she desires to commit suicide. Occasionally, however, all fails. The doctor, the nurse, the family, and the patient may have done everything possible to relieve the distress occasioned by a terminal illness, and yet the patient perceives his or her situation as intolerable and seeks assistance in bringing about death. Is it ever justifiable for the physician to assist suicide in such a case?

Some physicians, believing it to be the last act in a continuum of care provided for the hopelessly ill patient, do assist patients who request it, either by prescribing sleeping pills with knowledge of their intended use or by discussing the required doses and methods of administration with the patient. The frequency with which such actions are undertaken is unknown, but they are certainly not rare. Suicide differs from euthanasia in that the act of bringing on death is performed by the patient, not the physician.

The physician who considers helping a patient who requests assistance with suicide must determine first that the patient is indeed beyond all help and not merely suffering from a treatable depression of the sort common in people with terminal illnesses. Such a depression requires therapeutic intervention. If there is no treatable component to the depression and the patient's pain or suffering is refractory to treatment, then the wish for suicide may be rational. If such a patient acts on the wish for death and actually commits suicide, it is ethical for a physician who knows the patient well to refrain from an attempt at resuscitation.

Even though suicide itself is not illegal, helping a person commit suicide is a crime in many states, either by statute or under common law. Even so, we know of no physician who has ever been prosecuted in the United States for prescribing pills in order to help a patient commit suicide.[25] However, the potential illegality of this act is a deterrent, and apart from that, some physicians simply cannot bring themselves to assist in suicide or to condone such action.

Whether it is bad medical practice or immoral to help a hopelessly ill patient commit a rational suicide is a complex issue, provoking a number of considerations. First, as their disease advances, patients may lose their decision-making capacity because of the effects of the disease or the drug treatment. Assisting such patients with suicide comes close to performing an act of euthanasia. Second, patients who want a doctor's assistance with suicide may be unwilling to endure their terminal illness because they lack information about what is ahead. Even when the physician explains in careful detail the availability of the kind of flexible, continually adjusted care described here, the patient may still opt out of that treatment plan and reject the physician's efforts to ease the dying process. Also, what are the physician's obligations if a patient who retains decision-making capacity insists that family members not be told of a suicide plan? Should the physician insist on obtaining the family's consent? Finally, should physicians acknowledge their role in a suicide in some way—by obtaining consultation, or in writing? Physicians who act in secret become isolated and cannot consult colleagues or ethics committees for confirmation that the patient has made a rational decision. If contacted, such colleagues may well object and even consider themselves obligated to report the physician to the Board of Medical Licensure or to the prosecutor. The impulse to maintain secrecy gives the lie to the moral intuition that assistance with suicide is ethical.

It is difficult to answer such questions, but all but two of us (J.v.E. and E.H.C.) believe that it is not immoral for a physician to assist in the rational suicide of a terminally ill person. However, we recognize that such an act represents a departure from the principle of continually adjusted care that we have presented. As such, it should be considered a separate alternative and not an extension of the flexible approach to care that we have recommended. Clearly, the subject of assisted suicide deserves wide and open discussion.

Euthanasia

Some patients who cannot carry out suicide plans themselves, with or without assistance, may ask their physicians to take a more active part in ending their lives. In the case of suicide, the final act is performed by the patient, even when the physician provides indirect assistance in the form of information and means. By contrast, euthanasia requires the physician to perform a medical procedure that causes death directly. It is therefore even more controversial than assisted rational suicide, and various arguments have been mustered through the years for and against its use.[26,27]

In the Netherlands, the practice of euthanasia has gained a degree of social acceptance. As a result of a 1984 decision by the Dutch Supreme Court, euthanasia is no longer prosecuted in certain approved circumstances. The Dutch government authorized the State Commission on Euthanasia to study the issue, and the commission's report favored permitting doctors to perform euthanasia with certain safeguards, but the Dutch parliament, the States-General, has not yet acted to change the law.

Many Dutch physicians believe, however, that the medical treatments and actions needed to keep dying patients comfortable may at times be extended to include the act of euthanasia. Some of them hold that a continuum of measures can be brought into play to help the patient, and occasionally the injection of a lethal dose of a drug (usually a short-acting barbiturate, followed by a paralyzing agent) becomes necessary, representing the extreme end of that continuum. This occurs between 5,000 and 10,000 times a year in the Netherlands, according to van der Werf[28] (and Admiral P: personal communication).

The medical community in the Netherlands has developed criteria that must be met for an act of euthanasia to be considered medically and ethically acceptable.[29] The patient's medical situation must be intolerable, with no prospect of improvement. The patient must be rational and must voluntarily and repeatedly request euthanasia of the physician. The patient must be fully informed. There must be no other means of relieving the suffering, and two physicians must concur with the request.

In recent years, euthanasia has been discussed more openly in the United States, and the public response has been increasingly favorable. When a Roper poll asked in 1988 whether a physician should be lawfully able to end the life of a terminally ill patient at the patient's request, 58 percent said yes, 27 percent said no, and 10 percent were undecided. (This poll, taken for the National Hemlock Society by the Roper Organization of New York City, surveyed 1,982 adult Americans in March 1988.)

Presumably, the majority of physicians in the United States do not favor the Dutch position. Many physicians oppose euthanasia on moral or religious grounds, and indeed it raises profound theological questions. All religions address the matter of whether it is proper to decide the time of one's death. Whatever attitudes society may develop toward assisted suicide or euthanasia, individual physicians should not feel morally coerced to participate in such approaches. Many physicians oppose euthanasia because they believe it to be outside the physician's role, and some fear that it may be subject to abuse. (Some physicians and laypersons fear that active voluntary euthanasia, as practiced in the Netherlands, could lead to involuntary euthanasia and to murder, as practiced by the Nazis. Ethically, however, the difference is obvious.) In addition, the social climate in this country is very litigious, and the likelihood of prosecution if a case of euthanasia were discovered is fairly high—much higher than the likelihood of prosecution after a suicide in which the physician has assisted. Thus, the prospect of criminal prosecution deters even the hardiest advocates of euthanasia among physicians. Nevertheless, the medical profession and the public will continue to debate the role that euthanasia may have in the treatment of the terminally or hopelessly ill patient.[30]

For Reflection and Discussion

1. How has care for the dying patient changed in recent years? What ethical dilemmas are part of this change? Have you had any personal experience of this type of situation? If so, how has that influenced your views?

2. What are "advance directives"? How can they be helpful in the care of dying patients? What are their limitations? Do you have an advance directive? Has your physician discussed this with you?

3. Discuss the three settings for dying, with their pros and cons. What changes in health-care plans do the authors recommend concerning these settings? Why?

4. Discuss the meaning of "continually adjusted care." Is such an approach feasible in today's health care? How does the control of pain fit into this form of care? Are there ethical limits in the use of pain-relieving medications? What? Why?

5. What are the connections between pain and the extensive use of medical technology with physician-assisted suicide and euthanasia? Why do a majority of the authors support assisted

suicide? Do you agree with them? Why/why not? What about their position on euthanasia?"

Notes

1. S.H. Wanzer, S.J. Adelstein, R.E. Cranford, et. al., "The Physician's Responsibility toward Hopelessly Ill Patients: A Second Look," *New England Journal of Medicine* 310 (1984) 955-9.
2. President's Commission for the Study of Ethical Problems in Medicine and Biomedical and Behavioral Research, "Deciding to Forego Life-sustaining Treatment: A Report on the Ethical, Medical and Legal Issues in Treatment Decisions" (Washington, DC: Government Printing Office, 1983).
3. Office of Technology Assessment, "Life-sustaining Technologies and the Elderly" (Washington, DC: Government Printing Office, 1987).
4. Senate Special Committee on Aging, "A Matter of Choice: Planning Ahead for Health Care Decisions" (Washington, DC: Government Printing Office, 1987).
5. *Guidelines on the Termination of Life-sustaining Treatment and the Care of the Dying: A Report by the Hastings Center* (Briarcliff Manor, NY: Hastings Center, 1987).
6. Current Opinions of the Council on Ethical and Judicial Affairs of the American Medical Association—1986, *Withholding or Withdrawing Life-prolonging Treatment* (Chicago: American Medical Association, 1986).
7. Executive Board of the American Academy of Neurology, *Position of the American Academy of Neurology on Certain Aspects of the Care and Management of the Persistent Vegetative State Patient* (Minneapolis: American Academy of Neurology, 1988).
8. J.E. Ruark, and T.A. Raffin, Stanford University Medical Center Committee on Ethics, "Initiating and Withdrawing Life Support," *New England Journal of Medicine* 318 (1988) 25-30.
9. P. Safar, N. Bircher, *Cardiopulmonary Cerebral Resuscitation: An Introduction to Resuscitation Medicine*, 3rd ed. (Philadelphia: W. B. Saunders, 1988).
10. Society for the Right to Die, *Handbook of Living Will Laws*. (New York: Society for the Right to Die, 1987).
11. *Appointing a Proxy for Health Care Decisions* (New York: Society for the Right to Die, 1988).
12. *Adult Right to Die Case Citations* (New York: Society for the Right to Die, 1988).
13. Right to Die Court Decisions: Artificial Feeding (New York: Society for the Right to Die, 1988).
14. Associated Press/Media General, Poll no. 4 (Richmond, VA: Media General, February 1985).
15. *Guidelines Regarding Withdrawal or Withholding of Life-sustaining Procedure(s) in Long-term Care Facilities* (California Department of Health Services, August 7, 1987).
16. S. E. Bedell, D. Pelle, P.L. Maher, P.D. Cleary, "Do-Not-Resuscitate Orders for Critically Ill Patients in the Hospital: How Are They Used and What Is Their Impact?" *JAMA* 256 (1986) 233-7.

17. W. Bulkin, H. Lukashok, "Rx for Dying: the Case for Hospice," *New England Journal of Medicine* 318 (1988) 376-8.

18. M. Angell, "The Quality of Mercy," *New England Journal of Medicine* 306 (1982) 98-9.

19. R. Payne, K.M. Foley, eds., "Cancer Pain," *Medical Clinics of North America* 71 (1987) 153-352.

20. Bartling v. Superior Court (Glendale Adventist Medical Center), 163 Cal. App. 3d 186, 209 Cal. Rptr. 220 (Ct. App. 1984).

21. Bouvia v. Superior Court (Glenchur), 179 Cal. App. 3d 1127, 225 Cal. Rptr. 297 (Ct. App. 1986), review denied (Cal. June 5, 1986).

22. Brophy v. New England Sinai Hosp., Inc., 398 Mass. 417, 497, N.E. 2d 626 (1986).

23. In re Culham, No. 87-340537-AC (Mich. Cir. Ct., Oakland County, Dec. 15, 1987) (Breck, J.).

24. S.W. Tolle, D.H. Hickham, E.B. Larson, and J.A. Benson, "Patient Death and House-staff Stress, *Clinical Research* 35 (1987) 762A abstract.

25. L.H. Glantz. "Withholding and Withdrawing Treatment: The Role of the Aminal Law," *Law, Medicine and Health Care* 15 (1987-88) 231-41.

26. H. Van Bommel, *Choices for People Who have a Terminal Illness, Their Families and Their Caregivers* (Toronto: NC Press, 1986).

27. M. Angell, *Euthanasia, New England Journal of Medicine* 319 (1988) 1348-50.

28. G.T. van der Werf, "Huisarts en Euthanasie," *Medisch Contact* 43 (1986) 1389.

29. The Central Committee of the Royal Dutch Medical Association, *Vision on Euthanasia* (Utrecht, the Netherlands, 1986).

30. We are indebted to Marjorie B. Zuckerman, Ph.D., and Peg Cameron for assistance in the preparation of the manuscript.

4

It's Over, Debbie

Anonymous

THE CALL CAME IN THE MIDDLE OF THE NIGHT. AS A GYNECO-
logy resident rotating through a large, private hospital, I had
come to detest telephone calls, because invariably I would be
up for several hours and would not feel good the next day.
However, duty called, so I answered the phone. A nurse informed me that a patient was having difficulty getting rest,
could I please see her. She was on 3 North. That was the
gynecologic oncology unit, not my usual duty station. As I
trudged along, bumping sleepily against walls and corners and
not believing I was up again, I tried to imagine what I might
find at the end of my walk. Maybe an elderly woman with an
anxiety reaction, or perhaps something particularly horrible.

I grabbed the chart from the nurses station on my way to
the patient's room, and the nurse gave me some hurried details:
a 20-year-old girl named Debbie was dying of ovarian cancer.
She was having unrelenting vomiting, apparently as the result
of an alcohol drip administered for sedation. Hmmm, I
thought. Very sad. As I approached the room I could hear
loud, labored breathing. I entered and saw an emaciated, dark-
haired woman who appeared much older than 20. She was receiving nasal oxygen, had an IV, and was sitting in bed suffering from what was obviously severe air hunger. The chart
noted her weight at 80 pounds. A second woman, also dark-

haired but of middle age, stood at her right, holding her hand. Both looked up as I entered. The room seemed filled with the patient's desperate effort to survive. Her eyes were hollow, and she had suprasternal and intercostal retractions with her rapid inspirations. She had not eaten or slept in two days. She had not responded to chemotherapy and was being given supportive care only. It was a gallows scene, a cruel mockery of her youth and unfulfilled potential. Her only words to me were, "Let's get this over with."

I retreated with my thoughts to the nurses station. The patient was tired and needed rest. I could not give her health, but I could give her rest. I asked the nurse to draw 20 mg of morphine sulfate into a syringe. Enough, I thought, to do the job. I took the syringe into the room and told the two women I was going to give Debbie something that would let her rest and to say good-bye. Debbie looked at the syringe, then laid her head on the pillow with her eyes open, watching what was left of the world. I injected the morphine intravenously and watched to see if my calculations on its effects would be correct. Within seconds her breathing slowed to a normal rate, her eyes closed, and her features softened as she seemed restful at last. The older woman stroked the hair of the now-sleeping patient. I waited for the inevitable next effect of depressing the respiratory drive. With clocklike certainty, within four minutes the breathing rate slowed even more, then became irregular, then ceased. The dark-haired woman stood erect and seemed relieved.

It's over, Debbie.

For Reflection and Discussion

1. Discuss all the circumstances influencing the physician's judgment. Would you consider his decision-making sufficient and proper?

2. Would the case be different if the physician had been Debbie's regular physician? How?

3. Can you suggest other steps that could have been taken? That ought to have been taken?

4. Medical ethics frequently discusses such topics as autonomy, freedom, informed consent, patient's best interests, suffering and pain. How are these realities expressed in this case? How ought they to be weighed in the decision-making?

(See "Doctors Must Not Kill" elsewhere in this text for another view of this case.)

5

Death and Dignity: A Case of Individualized Decision-Making

Timothy E. Quill, M.D.

DIANE WAS FEELING TIRED AND HAD A RASH. A COM-
mon scenario, though there was something subliminally worri-
some that prompted me to check her blood count. Her
hematocrit was 22, and the white-cell count was 4.3 with some
metamyelocytes and unusual white cells. I wanted it to be
viral, trying to deny what was staring me in the face. Perhaps
in a repeated count it would disappear. I called Diane and told
her it might be more serious than I had initially thought—that
the test needed to be repeated and that if she felt worse, we
might have to move quickly. When she pressed for the possibilities, I reluctantly opened the door to leukemia. Hearing the
word seemed to make it exist. "Oh, shit!" she said. "Don't
tell me that." Oh, shit! I thought, I wish I didn't have to.

Diane was no ordinary person (although no one I have
ever come to know has been really ordinary). She was raised
in an alcoholic family and had felt alone for much of her life.
She had vaginal cancer as a young woman. Through much of
her adult life, she had struggled with depression and her own
alcoholism. I had come to know, respect, and admire her over

the previous eight years as she confronted these problems and gradually overcame them. She was an incredibly clear, at times brutally honest, thinker and communicator. As she took control of her life, she developed a strong sense of independence and confidence. In the previous three and a half years, her hard work had paid off. She was completely abstinent from alcohol, she had established much deeper connections with her husband, college-age son, and several friends, and her business and her artistic work were blossoming. She felt she was really living fully for the first time.

Not surprisingly, the repeated blood count was abnormal, and detailed examination of the peripheral blood smear showed myelocytes. I advised her to come into the hospital, explaining that we needed to do a bone marrow biopsy and make some decisions relatively rapidly. She came to the hospital knowing what we would find. She was terrified, angry, and sad. Although we knew the odds, we both clung to the thread of possibility that it might be something else.

The bone marrow confirmed the worst: acute mye-lomonocytic leukemia. In the face of this tragedy, we looked for signs of hope. This is an area of medicine in which technological intervention has been successful, with cures 25 percent of the time—long-term cures. As I probed the costs of these cures, I heard about induction chemotherapy (three weeks in the hospital, prolonged neutropenia, probable infectious complications, and hair loss; 75 percent of patients respond, 25 percent do not). For the survivors, this is followed by consolidation chemotherapy (with similar side effects; another 25 percent die, for a net survival of 50 percent). Those still alive, to have a reasonable chance of long-term survival, then need bone marrow transplantation (hospitalization for two months and wholebody irradiation, with complete killing of the bone marrow, infectious complications, and the possibility for graft-versus-host disease—with a survival of approximately 50 percent, or 25 percent of the original group). Though hematologists may argue over the exact percentages, they do not argue about the outcome of no treatment—certain death in days, weeks, or at most a few months.

Believing that delay was dangerous, our oncologist broke the news to Diane and began making plans to insert a Hickman catheter and begin induction chemotherapy that afternoon. When I saw her shortly thereafter, she was enraged at his presumption that she would want treatment, and devastated by the finality of the diagnosis. All she wanted to do was go home and be with her family. She had no further questions about treatment and, in fact, had decided that she wanted none. Together we lamented her tragedy and the unfairness of life. Before she left, I felt the need to be sure that she and her husband understood that there was some risk in delay, that the problem was not going to go away, and that we needed to keep considering the options over the next several days. We agreed to meet in two days.

She returned in two days with her husband and son. They had talked extensively about the problem and the options. She remained very clear about her wish not to undergo chemotherapy and to live whatever time she had left outside the hospital. As we explored her thinking further, it became clear that she was convinced she would die during the period of treatment and would suffer unspeakably in the process (from hospitalization, from lack of control over her body, from the side effects of chemotherapy, and from pain and anguish). Although I could offer support and my best effort to minimize her suffering if she chose treatment, there was no way I could say any of this would not occur. In fact, the last four patients with acute leukemia at our hospital had died very painful deaths in the hospital during various stages of treatment (a fact I did not share with her). Her family wished she would choose treatment but sadly accepted her decision. She articulated very clearly that it was she who would be experiencing all the side effects of treatment and that odds of 25 percent were not good enough for her to undergo so toxic a course of therapy, given her expectations of chemotherapy and hospitalization and the absence of a closely matched bone marrow donor. I had her repeat her understanding of the treatment, the odds, and what to expect if there were no treatment. I clarified a few misunderstandings, but she had a remarkable grasp of the options and implications.

I have been a long-time advocate of active, informed patient choice of treatment or nontreatment, and of a patient's right to die with as much control and dignity as possible. Yet there was something about her giving up a 25-percent chance of long-term survival in favor of almost certain death that disturbed me. I had seen Diane fight and use her considerable inner resources to overcome alcoholism and depression, and I half expected her to change her mind over the next week. Since the window of time in which effective treatment can be initiated is rather narrow, we met several times that week. We obtained a second hematology consultation and talked at length about the meaning and implications of treatment and nontreatment. She talked to a psychologist she had seen in the past. I gradually understood the decision from her perspective and became convinced that it was the right decision for her. We arranged for home hospice care (although at that time Diane felt reasonably well, was active, and looked healthy), left the door open for her to change her mind, and tried to anticipate how to keep her comfortable in the time she had left.

Just as I was adjusting to her decision, she opened up another area that would stretch me profoundly. It was extraordinarily important to Diane to maintain control of herself and her own dignity during the time remaining to her. When this was no longer possible, she clearly wanted to die. As a former director of a hospice program, I know how to use pain medicines to keep patients comfortable and lessen suffering. I explained the philosophy of comfort care, which I strongly believe in. Although Diane understood and appreciated this, she had known of people lingering in what was called relative comfort, and she wanted no part of it. When the time came, she wanted to take her life in the least painful way possible.

Knowing of her desire for independence and her decision to stay in control, I thought this request made perfect sense. I acknowledged and explored this wish, but also thought that it was out of the realm of currently accepted medical practice and that it was more than I could offer or promise. In our discussion, it became clear that preoccupation with her fear of a lingering death would interfere with Diane's getting the most out of the time she had left until she found a safe way to ensure her death. I feared the effects of a violent death on her family, the consequences of an ineffective suicide that would leave her lingering in precisely the state she dreaded so much, and the possibility that a family member would be forced to assist her, with all the legal and personal repercussions that would follow. She discussed this at length with her family. They believed that they should respect her choice. With this in mind, I told Diane that information was available from the Hemlock Society that might be helpful to her.

A week later she phoned me with a request for barbiturates for sleep. Since I knew that this was an essential ingredient in a Hemlock Society suicide, I asked her to come to the office to talk things over. She was more than willing to protect me by participating in a superficial conversation about her insomnia, but it was important to me to know how she planned to use the drugs and to be sure that she was not in despair or overwhelmed in a way that might color her judgment.

In our discussion, it was apparent that she was having trouble sleeping, but it was also evident that the security of having enough barbiturates available to commit suicide when and if the time came would leave her secure enough to live fully and concentrate on the present. It was clear that she was not despondent and that in fact she was making deep, personal connections with her family and close friends. I made sure that she knew how to use the barbiturates for sleep, and, also, that she knew the amount needed to commit suicide. We agreed to meet regularly, and she promised to meet with me before taking her life, to ensure that all other avenues had been exhausted. I wrote the prescription with an uneasy feeling about the boundaries I was exploring—spiritual, legal, professional, and personal. Yet I also felt strongly that I was setting her free to get the most out of the time she had left, and to maintain dignity and control on her own terms until her death.

The next several months were very intense and important for Diane. Her son stayed home from college, and they were able to be with one another and say much that had not been said earlier. Her husband did his work at home so that he and Diane could spend more time together. She spent time with her closest friends. I had her come into the hospital for a conference with our residents, at which she illustrated in a most profound and personal way the importance of informed decision making, the right to refuse treatment, and the extraordinarily personal effects of illness and interaction with the medical system. There were emotional and physical hardships as well. She had periods of intense sadness and anger. Several times she became very weak, but she received transfusions as an outpatient and responded with marked improvement of symptoms. She had two serious infections that responded surprisingly well to empirical courses of oral antibiotics. After three tumultuous months, there were two weeks of relative calm and well-being, and fantasies of a miracle began to surface.

Unfortunately, we had no miracle. Bone pain, weakness, fatigue, and fevers began to dominate her life. Although the hospice workers, family members, and I tried our best to minimize the suffering and promote comfort, it was clear that the end was approaching. Diane's immediate future held what she feared the most—increasing discomfort, dependence, and hard choices between pain and sedation. She called up her closest friends and asked them to come over to say goodbye, telling them that she would be leaving soon. As we had agreed, she let me know as well. When we met, it was clear that she knew what she was doing, that she was sad and frightened to be leaving, but that she would be even more terrified to stay and suffer. In our tearful goodbye, she promised a reunion in the future at her favorite spot on the edge of Lake Geneva, with dragons swimming in the sunset.

Two days later her husband called to say that Diane had died. She had said her final goodbyes to her husband and son that morning, and asked them to leave her alone for an hour. After an hour, which must have seemed an eternity, they found her on the couch, lying very still and covered by her favorite shawl. There was no sign of struggle. She seemed to be at peace. They called me for advice about how to proceed. When I arrived at their house, Diane, indeed, seemed peaceful. Her husband and son were quiet. We talked about what a remarkable person she had been. They seemed to have no doubts about the course she had chosen or about their cooperation, although the unfairness of her illness and the finality of her death were overwhelming to us all.

I called the medical examiner to inform him that a hospice patient had died. When asked about the cause of death, I said, "acute leukemia." He said that was fine and that we should call a funeral director. Although acute leukemia was the truth, it was not the whole story. Yet, any mention of suicide would have given rise to a police investigation and probably brought the arrival of an ambulance crew for resuscitation. Diane would have become a "coroner's case," and the decision to perform an autopsy would have been made at the discretion of the medical examiner. The family or I could have been subject to criminal prosecution, and I to professional review, for our roles in support of Diane's choices. Although I truly believe that the family and I gave her the best care possible, allowing her to define her limits and directions as much as possible, I am not sure the law, society, or the medical profession would agree. So I said "acute leukemia" to protect all of us, to protect Diane from an invasion into her past and her body, and to continue to shield society from the knowledge of the degree of suffering that people often undergo in the process of dying. Suffering can be lessened to some extent, but in no way eliminated or made benign, by the careful intervention of a competent, caring physician, given current social constraints.

Diane taught me about the range of help I can provide if I know people well and if I allow them to say what they really want. She taught me about life, death, and honesty, and about taking charge and facing tragedy squarely when it strikes. She taught me that I can take small risks for people that I really know and care about. Although I did not assist in her suicide directly, I helped indirectly to make it possible, successful, and relatively painless. Although I know we have measures to help control pain and lessen suffering, to think that people do not suffer in the process of dying is an illusion. Prolonged dying can occasionally be peaceful, but more often the role of the physician and family is limited to lessening, but not eliminating, severe suffering.

I wonder how many families and physicians secretly help patients over the edge into death in the face of such severe suffering. I wonder how many severely ill or dying patients secretly take their lives, dying alone in despair. I wonder whether the image of Diane's final aloneness will persist in the minds of her family, or if they will remember more the intense, meaningful months they had together before she died. I wonder whether Diane struggled in that last hour, and whether the Hemlock Society's way of death by suicide is the most benign. I wonder why Diane, who gave so much to so many of us, had to be alone for the last hour of her life. I wonder whether I will see Diane again, on the shore of Lake Geneva at sunset, with dragons swimming on the horizon.

For Reflection and Discussion

1. Summarize the most important facts of Diane's case. What were the most significant values expressed in the case? Were some values rejected? Was the physician's extensive and time-consuming involvement appropriate? Typical?

2. Two major decisions are described: first, to take no treatment; second, to prepare for and then carry out suicide. Discuss the ethical dimensions of these two decisions, both for Diane and for her physician.

3. Does the author's description of Diane's death—"favorite shawl . . . no sign of struggle . . . at peace"—influence your reactions and your judgment about physician-assisted suicide? Would a different, less tranquil scene change the reality? Would it change your judgment?

4. Given your life's experience, how do you react to and find meaning in suffering? How do you value independence and control? What is the meaning of human dignity? Do religious beliefs—salvation, grace, providence—play a part in your life? How do all these realities fit together for you?

5. Compare Diane's story with Debbie's. What are the major similarities? The major differences? Would you judge either to be justified ethically?

Part II:
Against Euthanasia

6

Medical Science Under Dictatorship

Leo Alexander, M.D.

SCIENCE UNDER DICTATORSHIP BECOMES SUBORDINATED to the guiding philosophy of the dictatorship. Irrespective of other ideologic trappings, the guiding philosophic principle of recent dictatorships, including that of the Nazis, has been Hegelian in that what has been considered "rational utility" and corresponding doctrine and planning has replaced moral, ethical and religious values. Nazi propaganda was highly effective in perverting public opinion and public conscience, in a remarkably short time. In the medical profession this expressed itself in a rapid decline in standards of professional ethics. Medical science in Nazi Germany collaborated with this Hegelian trend particularly in the following enterprises: the mass extermination of the chronically sick in the interest of saving "useless" expenses to the community as a whole; the mass extermination of those considered socially disturbing or racially and ideologically unwanted; the individual, inconspicuous extermination of those considered disloyal within the ruling group; and the ruthless use of "human experimental material" for medico-military research.

This paper discusses the origins of these activities, as well as their consequences upon the body social, and the motivation of those participating in them.

Preparatory Propaganda

Even before the Nazis took open charge in Germany, a propaganda barrage was directed against the traditional compassionate nineteenth-century attitudes toward the chronically ill, and for the adoption of a utilitarian, Hegelian point of view. Sterilization and euthanasia of persons with chronic mental illnesses was discussed at a meeting of Bavarian psychiatrists in 1931.[1] By 1936, extermination of the physically or socially unfit was so openly accepted that its practice was mentioned incidentally in an article published in an official German medical journal.[2]

Lay opinion was not neglected in this campaign. Adults were propagandized by motion pictures, one of which, entitled "I Accuse," deals entirely with euthanasia. This film depicts the life history of a woman suffering from multiple sclerosis; in it her husband, a doctor, finally kills her to the accompaniment of soft piano music rendered by a sympathetic colleague in an adjoining room.

Acceptance of this ideology was implanted even in the children. A widely used high-school mathematics text, "Mathematics in the Service of National Political Education,"[3] included problems stated in distorted terms of the cost of caring for and rehabilitating the chronically sick and crippled. One of the problems asked, for instance, how many new housing units could be built and how many marriage-allowance loans could be given to newly wedded couples for the amount of money it cost the state to care for "the crippled, the criminal and the insane."

Euthanasia

The first direct order for euthanasia was issued by Hitler on September 1, 1939, and an organization was set up to execute the program. Dr. Karl Brandt headed the medical section, and Phillip Bouhler the administrative section. All state institutions were required to report on patients who had been ill five years or more and who were unable to work, by filling out questionnaires giving name, race, marital status, nationality, next of kin, whether regularly visited and by whom, who bore financial responsibility and so forth. The decision regarding which patients should be killed was made entirely on the basis of this brief information by expert consultants, most of whom were professors of psychiatry in the key universities. These consultants never saw the patients themselves. The thoroughness of their scrutiny can be appraised by the work of one expert, who between November 14 and December 1, 1940 evaluated 2109 questionnaires.

These questionnaires were collected by a "Realm's Work Committee of Institutions for Cure and Care."[4] A parallel organization devoted exclusively to the killing of children was known by the similarly euphemistic name of "Realm's Committee for Scientific Approach to Severe Illness Due to Heredity and Constitution." The "Charitable Transport Company for the Sick" transported patients to the killing centers, and the "Charitable Foundation for Institutional Care" was in charge of collecting the cost of the killings from the relatives, without, however, informing them what the charges were for; in the death certificates the cause of death was falsified.

What these activities meant to the population at large was well expressed by a few hardy souls who dared to protest. A member of the court of appeals at Frankfurt-am-Main wrote in December, 1939:

> There is constant discussion of the question of the destruction of socially unfit life—in the places where there are mental institutions, in neighboring towns, sometimes

over a large area, throughout the Rhineland, for example. The people have come to recognize the vehicles in which the patients are taken from their original institution to the intermediate institution and from there to the liquidation institution. I am told that when they see these buses even the children call out: "They're taking some more people to be gassed." From Limburg it is reported that every day from one to three buses with shades drawn pass through on the way from Weilmunster to Hadamar, delivering inmates to the liquidation institution there. According to the stories the arrivals are immediately stripped to the skin, dressed in paper shirts, and forthwith taken to a gas chamber, where they are liquidated with hydrocyanic acid gas and an added anesthetic. The bodies are reported to be moved to a combustion chamber by means of a conveyor belt, six bodies to a furnace. The resulting ashes are then distributed into six urns which are shipped to the families. The heavy smoke from the crematory building is said to be visible over Hadamar every day. There is talk, furthermore, that in some cases heads and other portions of the body are removed for anatomical examination. The people working at this liquidation job in the institutions are said to be assigned from other areas and are shunned completely by the populace. This personnel is described as frequenting the bars at night and drinking heavily. Quite apart from these overt incidents that exercise the imagination of the people, they are disquieted by the question of whether old folk who have worked hard all their lives and may merely have come into their dotage are also being liquidated. There is talk that the homes for the aged are to be cleaned out too. The people are said to be waiting for legislative regulation providing some orderly method that will ensure especially that the aged feeble-minded are not included in the program.

Here one sees what "euthanasia" means in actual practice. According to the records, 275,000 people were put to death in these killing centers. Ghastly as this seems, it should be realized that this program was merely the entering wedge for exterminations of far greater scope in the political program for genocide of conquered nations and the racially unwanted. The methods used and personnel trained in the killing centers for the chronically sick became the nucleus of the much larger centers in the East, where the plan was to kill all Jews and Poles and to cut down the Russian population by 30,000,000.

The original program developed by Nazi hotheads included also the genocide of the English, with the provision that the English males were to be used as laborers in the vacated territories in the East, there to be worked to death, whereas the English females were to be brought into Germany to improve the qualities of the German race. (This was indeed a peculiar admission on the part of the German eugenists.)

In Germany the exterminations included the mentally defective, psychotics (particularly schizophrenics), epileptics and patients suffering from infirmities of old age and from various organic neurologic disorders such as infantile paralysis, Parkinsonism, multiple sclerosis and brain tumors. The technical arrangements, methods and training of the killer personnel were under the direction of a committee of physicians and other experts headed by Dr. Karl Brandt. The mass killings were first carried out with carbon monoxide gas, but later cyanide gas ("cyclon B") was found to be more effective. The idea of camouflaging the gas chambers as shower baths was developed by Brack, who testified before Judge Sebring that the patients walked in calmly, deposited their towels and stood with their little pieces of soap under the shower outlets, waiting for the water to start running. This statement was ample rebuttal of his claim that only the most severely regressed patients among the mentally sick and only the moribund ones among the physically sick were exterminated. In truth, all those unable to work and considered nonrehabilitable were killed.

All but their squeal was utilized. However, the program grew so big that even scientists who hoped to benefit from the treasure of material supplied by this totalitarian method were disappointed. A neuropathologist, Dr. Hallervorden, who had obtained 500 brains from the killing centers for the insane, gave me a vivid first-hand account.[5] The Charitable Transport Company for the Sick brought the brains in batches of 150 to 250 at a time. Hallervorden stated:

> There was wonderful material among those brains, beautiful mental defectives, malformations and early infantile diseases. I accepted those brains of course. Where they came from and how they came to me was really none of my business.

In addition to the material he wanted, all kinds of other cases were mixed in, such as patients suffering from various types of Parkinsonism, simple depressions, involutional depressions and brain tumors, and all kinds of other illnesses, including psychopathy that had been difficult to handle:

> These were selected from the various wards of the institutions according to an excessively simple and quick method. Most institutions did not have enough physicians and what physicians there were were either too busy or did not care, and they delegated the selection to the nurse and attendants. Whoever looked sick or was otherwise a problem was put on a list and was transported to the killing center. The worst thing about this business was that it produced a certain brutalization of the nursing personnel. They got to simply picking out those whom they did not like, and the doctors had so many patients that they did not even know them, and put their names on the list.

Of the patients thus killed, only the brains were sent to Dr. Hallervorden; they were killed in such large numbers that autopsies of the bodies were not feasible. That, in Dr. Hallervorden's opinion, greatly reduced the scientific value of the material. The brains, however, were always well fixed and suspended in formalin, exactly according to his instructions.

He thinks that the cause of psychiatry was permanently injured by these activities, and that psychiatrists have lost the respect of the German people forever. Dr. Hallervorden concluded: "Still, there were interesting cases in this material."

In general only previously hospitalized patients were exterminated for reasons of illness. An exception was a program carried out in a northwestern district of Poland, the "Warthegau," where a health survey of the entire population was made by an "S.S. X-Ray Battalion" headed by Professor Hohlfelder, radiologist at the University of Frankfurt-am-Main. Persons found to be infected with tuberculosis were carted off to special extermination centers.

It is rather significant that the German people were considered by their Nazi leaders more ready to accept the exterminations of the sick than exterminations for political reasons. It was for that reason that the first of the latter group were carried out under the guise of sickness. So-called "psychiatric experts" were dispatched to survey the inmates of camps with the specific order to pick out members of racial minorities and political offenders from occupied territories and to dispatch them to killing centers with specially made diagnoses such as that of "inveterate German hater" applied to a number of prisoners who had been active in the Czech underground.

Certain classes of patients with mental diseases who were capable of performing labor, particularly members of the armed forces suffering from psychopathy or neurosis, were sent to concentration camps to be worked to death, or to be reassigned to punishment battalions and to be exterminated in the process of removal of mine fields.[6]

A large number of persons marked for death for political or racial reasons were made available for "medical" experiments involving the use of involuntary human subjects. From 1942 on, such experiments carried out in concentration camps were openly presented at medical meetings. This program included "terminal human experiments," a term introduced by Dr. Rascher to denote an experiment so designed that its successful conclusion depended upon the test person's being put to death.

The Science of Annihilation

A large part of this research was devoted to the science of destroying and preventing life, for which I have proposed the term "ktenology," the science of killing[7-9] In the course of this ktenologic research, methods of mass killing and mass sterilization were investigated and developed for use against non-German peoples or Germans who were considered useless.

Sterilization methods were widely investigated but proved impractical in experiments conducted in concentration camps. A rapid method developed for sterilization of females, which could be accomplished in the course of a regular health examination, was the intra-uterine injection of various chemicals. Numerous mixtures were tried, some with iodopine and others containing barium; another was most likely silver nitrate with iodized oil, because the result could be ascertained by X-ray examination. The injections were extremely painful, and a number of women died in the course of the experiments. Professor Karl Clauberg reported that he had developed a method at the Auschwitz concentration camp by which he could sterilize 1,000 women in one day.

Another method of sterilization, or rather castration, was proposed by Viktor Brack especially for conquered populations. His idea was that X-ray machinery could be built into desks at which the people would have to sit, ostensibly to fill out a questionnaire requiring five minutes, during which time they would be sterilized without being aware of it. This method failed because experiments carried out on 100 male prisoners brought out the fact that severe X-ray burns were produced on all subjects. In the course of this research, which was carried out by Dr. Horst Schuman, the testicles of the victims were removed for histologic examination two weeks later. I myself examined four castrated survivors of this ghastly experiment.

Three had extensive necrosis of the skin near the genitalia, and one had extensive necrosis of the urethra. Other experiments in sterilization used an extract of the plant *Caladium seguinum*, which had been shown in animal studies by Madaus and his co-workers[10,11] to cause selective necrosis of the germinal cells of the testicles as well as the ovary.

The development of methods for rapid and inconspicuous execution of individuals was the objective of another large part of the ktenologic research. These methods were to be applied to members of the ruling group, including the SS itself, who were suspected of disloyalty. This, of course, is an essential requirement in a dictatorship, in which "cut-throat competition" becomes a grim reality, and any hint of faintheartedness or lack of enthusiasm for the methods of totalitarian rule is considered a threat to the entire group. Poisons were the subject of many of these experiments. A research team at the Buchenwald concentration camp, consisting of Drs. Joachim Mrugowsky, Erwin Ding-Schuler and Waldemar Hoven, developed the most widely used means of individual execution under the guise of medical treatment—namely, the intravenous injection of phenol or gasoline. Several alkaloids were also investigated, among them aconitine, which was used by Dr. Hoven to kill several imprisoned former fellow SS men who were potential witnesses against the camp commander, Koch, then under investigation by the SS. At the Dachau concentration camp Dr. Rascher developed the standard cyanide capsules, which could be easily bitten through, either deliberately or accidentally, if mixed with certain foods, and which, ironically enough, later became the means with which Himmler and Goering killed themselves. In connection with these poison experiments there is an interesting incident of characteristic sociologic significance. When Dr. Hoven was under trial by the SS, the investigating SS judge, Dr. Morgen, proved Hoven's guilt by feeding the poison found in Dr. Hoven's possession to a number of Russian prisoners of war; these men died with the same symptoms as the SS men murdered by Dr. Hoven. This worthy judge was rather proud of this efficient method of proving Dr. Hoven's guilt and appeared entirely unaware of the fact that in the process he had committed murder himself.

Poisons, however, proved too obvious or detectable to be used for the elimination of high-ranking Nazi party personnel who had come into disfavor, or of prominent prisoners whose deaths should appear to result from natural causes. Phenol or gasoline, for instance, left a telltale odor with the corpse. For this reason, a number of more subtle methods were devised. One of these was the artificial production of septicemia. An intramuscular injection of 1 cc. of pus, containing numerous chains of streptococci, was the first step. The pus was usually injected into the inside of the thigh, close to the adductor canal. When an abscess formed it was tapped, and 3 cc. of the creamy pus removed was injected intravenously into the patient's opposite arm. If the patient then died from septicemia, the autopsy proved that death was caused by the same organism that had caused the abscess. These experiments were carried out in many concentration camps. At the Dachau camp the subjects were almost exclusively Polish Catholic priests. However, since this method did not always cause death—sometimes resulting merely in a local abscess—it was considered inefficient, and research was continued with other methods along the same lines.

The final triumph on the part of ktenologic research aimed at finding a method of inconspicuous execution that would produce autopsy findings indicative of death from natural causes was the development of repeated intravenous injections of suspensions of live tubercle bacilli, which brought on acute miliary tuberculosis within a few weeks. This method was produced by Professor Dr. Heissmeyer, who was one of Dr. Gebhardt's associates at the SS hospital of Hohenlychen. As a means of further camouflage, so that the SS at large would not suspect the purpose of these experiments, the preliminary tests for the efficacy of this method were performed exclusively on children imprisoned in the Neuengamme concentration camp.

For use in "medical" executions of prisoners and of members of the SS and other branches of the German armed forces the use of simple lethal injections, particularly phenol injections, remained the instrument of choice. Whatever methods he used, the physician gradually became the unofficial executioner, for the sake of convenience, informality and relative secrecy. Even on German submarines it was the physician's duty to execute the troublemakers among the crew by lethal injections.

Medical science has for some time been an instrument of military power in that it preserved the health and fighting efficiency of troops. This essentially defensive purpose is not inconsistent with the ethical principles of medicine. During World War I the German empire had enlisted medical science as an instrument of aggressive military power by putting it to use in the development of gas warfare. It was left to the Nazi dictatorship to make medical science into an instrument of political power—a formidable, essential tool in the complete and effective manipulation of totalitarian control. This should be a warning to all civilized nations, and particularly to individuals who are blinded by the "efficiency" of a totalitarian rule, under whatever name.

This entire body of research as reported so far served the master crime to which the Nazi dictatorship was committed— namely, the genocide of non-German peoples and the elimination by killing, in groups or singly, of Germans who were considered useless or disloyal. In effecting the two parts of this program, Himmler demanded and received the cooperation of physicians and of German medical science. The result was a significant advance in the science of killing, or ktenology.

Medicomilitary Research

Another chapter in Nazi scientific research was that aimed to aid the military forces. Many of these ideas originated with Himmler, who fancied himself a scientist.

When Himmler learned that the cause of death of most SS men on the battlefield was hemorrhage, he instructed Dr. Sigmund Rascher to search for a blood coagulant that might be given before the men went into action. Rascher tested this coagulant when it was developed by clocking the number of drops emanating from freshly cut amputation stumps of living and conscious prisoners at the crematorium of Dachau concentration camp and by shooting Russian prisoners of war through the spleen.

Live dissections were a feature of another experimental study designed to show the effects of explosive decompression.[12-14] A mobile decompression chamber was used. It was found that when subjects were made to descend from altitudes of 40,000 to 60,000 feet without oxygen, severe symptoms of cerebral dysfunction occurred—at first, convulsions; then unconsciousness, in which the body was hanging limp; and later, after wakening, temporary blindness, paralysis or severe confusional twilight states. Rascher, who wanted to find out whether these symptoms were due to anoxic changes or to other causes, did what appeared to him the most simple thing: he dissected the subject under water, while the heart was still beating, thereby demonstrating air embolism in the blood vessels of the heart, liver, chest wall and brain.

Another part of Dr. Rascher's research, carried out in collaboration with Holzloehner and Finke, concerned shock from exposure to cold.[15] It was known that military personnel generally did not survive immersion in the North Sea for more than 60-100 minutes. Rascher therefore attempted to duplicate these conditions at Dachau concentration camp and used about 300 prisoners in experiments on shock from exposure to cold; of these 80 or 90 were killed. (The figures do not include persons killed during mass experiments on exposure to cold outdoors.) In one report on this work, Rascher asked permission to shift these experiments from Dachau to Auschwitz, a larger camp where they might cause less disturbance because the subjects shrieked from pain when their extremities froze white. The results, like so many of those obtained in the Nazi research program, are not dependable. In his report Rascher stated that it took from fifty-three to a hundred minutes to kill a human being by immersion in ice water—a time closely in agreement with the known survival period in the North Sea. Inspection of his own experimental records and statements made to me by his close associates showed that it actually took from 80 minutes to five or six hours to kill an undressed person in such a manner, whereas a man in full aviator's dress took six or seven hours to kill. Obviously, Rascher dressed up his findings to forestall criticism, although any scientist should have known that during actual exposure many other factors, including greater convection of heat due to the motion of water, would affect the time of survival.

Another series of experiments gave results that might have been an important medical contribution if an important lead had not been ignored. The efficacy of various vaccines and drugs against typhus was tested at the Buchenwald and Natzweiler concentration camps. Prevaccinated persons and nonvaccinated controls were injected with live typhus rickettsias, and the death rates of the two groups were compared. After a certain number of passages, the Matelska strain of typhus rickettsia proved to become avirulent for humans. Instead of seizing upon this as a possibility to develop a live vaccine, the experimenters, including the chief consultant, Professor Gerhard Rose, who should have known better, were merely annoyed at the fact that the controls did not die either. They discarded this strain and continued testing their relatively ineffective dead vaccines against a new virulent strain. This incident shows that the basic unconscious motivation and attitude has a great influence in determining the scientist's awareness of the phenomena that pass through his vision.

Sometimes human subjects were used for tests that were totally unnecessary, or whose results could have been predicted by simple chemical experiments. For example, 90 gypsies were given unaltered sea water and sea water whose taste was camouflaged as their sole source of fluid, apparently to test the well-known fact that such hypertonic saline solutions given as the only source of supply of fluid will cause severe physical disturbance or death within six to twelve days. These persons were subjected to the tortures of the damned, with death resulting in at least two cases.

Heteroplastic transplantation experiments were carried out by Professor Dr. Karl Gebhardt at Himmler's suggestion. Whole limbs—shoulder, arm or leg—were amputated from live prisoners at Ravensbrueck concentration camp, wrapped in sterile moist dressings and sent by automobile to the SS hospital at Hohenlychen, where Professor Gebhardt busied himself with a futile attempt at heteroplastic transplantation. In the meantime the prisoners deprived of a limb were usually killed by lethal injection.

One would not be dealing with German science if one did not run into manifestations of the collector's spirit. By February, 1942, it was assumed in German scientific circles that the Jewish race was about to be completely exterminated, and alarm was expressed over the fact that only very few specimens of skulls and skeletons of Jews were at the disposal of science. It was therefore proposed that a collection of 150 body casts and skeletons of Jews be preserved for perusal by future students of anthropology. Dr. August Hirt, professor of anatomy at the University of Strassburg, declared himself interested in establishing such a collection at his anatomical institute. He suggested that captured Jewish officers of the Russian armed forces be included, as well as females from Auschwitz concentration camp; that they be brought alive to Natzweiler concentration camp near Strassburg; and that after "their subsequently induced *death*—care should be taken that the heads not be damaged [sic]"—the bodies be turned over to him at the anatomical institute of the University of Strassburg. This was done. The entire collection of bodies and the correspondence pertaining to it fell into the hands of the United States Army.

One of the most revolting experiments was the testing of sulfonamides against gas gangrene by Professor Gebhardt and his collaborators, for which young women captured from the

Polish Resistance Movement served as subjects. Necrosis was produced in a muscle of the leg by ligation and the wound was infected with various types of gas-gangrene bacilli; frequently, dirt, pieces of wood and glass splinters were added to the wound. Some of these victims died, and others sustained severe mutilating deformities of the leg.

Motivation

An important feature of the experiments performed in concentration camps was the fact that they not only represented a ruthless and callous pursuit of legitimate scientific goals but also were motivated by rather sinister practical ulterior political and personal purposes, arising out of the requirements and problems of the administration of totalitarian rule.

Why did men like Professor Gebhardt participate in such experiments? The reasons are fairly simple and practical, no surprise to anyone familiar with the evidence of fear, hostility, suspicion, rivalry and intrigue, the fratricidal struggle euphemistically termed the "self-selection of leaders," that went on within the ranks of the ruling Nazi party and the SS. The answer was fairly simple and logical. Dr. Gebhardt performed these experiments to clear himself of the suspicion that he had been contributing to the death of SS General Reinhard ("The Hangman") Heydrich, either negligently or deliberately, by failing to treat his wound infection with sulfonamides. After Heydrich died from gas gangrene, Himmler himself told Dr. Gebhardt that the only way in which he could prove that Heydrich's death was "fate determined" was by carrying out a "large-scale experiment" in prisoners, which would prove or disprove that people died from gas gangrene irrespective of whether they were treated with sulfonamides or not.

Dr. Sigmund Rascher did not become the notorious vivisectionist of Dachau concentration camp and the willing tool of Himmler's research interests until he had been forbidden to use the facilities of the Pathological Institute of the University of Munich because he was suspected of having Communist sympathies. Then he was ready to go all out and to do anything merely to regain acceptance by the Nazi party and the SS.

These cases illustrate a method consciously and methodically used in the SS, an age-old method used by criminal gangs everywhere: that of making suspects of disloyalty clear themselves by participation in a crime that would definitely and irrevocably tie them to the organization. In the SS, this process of reinforcement of group cohesion was called "Blutkitt" (blood-cement), a term that Hitler himself is said to have obtained from a book on Genghis Khan in which this technique was emphasized.

The important lesson here is that this motivation, with which one is familiar in ordinary crimes, applies also to war crimes and to ideologically conditioned crimes against humanity—namely, that fear and cowardice, especially fear of punishment or of ostracism by the group, are often more important motives than simple ferocity or aggressiveness.

The Early Change in Medical Attitudes

Whatever proportions these crimes finally assumed, it became evident to all who investigated them that they had started from small beginnings. The beginnings at first were merely a subtle shift in emphasis in the basic attitude of the physicians. It started with the acceptance of the attitude, basic in the euthanasia movement, that there is such a thing as life not worthy to be lived. This attitude in its early stages concerned itself merely with the severely and chronically sick. Gradually the sphere of those to be included in this category was enlarged to encompass the socially unproductive, the ideologically unwanted, the racially unwanted and finally all non-Germans. But it is important to realize that the infinitely small wedged-in lever from which this entire trend of mind received its impetus was the attitude toward the nonrehabilitable sick.

It is, therefore, this subtle shift in emphasis of the physicians' attitude that one must thoroughly investigate. It is a recent significant trend in medicine, including psychiatry, to regard prevention as more important than cure. Observation and recognition of early signs and symptoms have become the basis for prevention of further advance of disease.[8]

In looking for these early signs one may well retrace the early steps of propaganda on the part of the Nazis in Germany as well as in the countries that they overran and in which they attempted to gain supporters by means of indoctrination, seduction and propaganda.

The Example of Successful Resistance by the Physicians of the Netherlands

There is no doubt that in Germany itself the first and most effective step of propaganda within the medical profession was the propaganda barrage against the useless, incurably sick described above. Similar, even more subtle efforts were made in some of the occupied countries. It is to the everlasting honor of the medical profession of Holland that they recognized the earliest and most subtle phases of this attempt and rejected it. When Seiss-Inquart, Reich Commissar for the Occupied Netherlands Territories, wanted to draw the Dutch physicians into the orbit of the activities of the German medical profession, he did not tell them "You must send your chronic patients to death factories" or "You must give lethal injections at Government request in your offices," but he couched his order in most careful and superficially acceptable terms. One of the paragraphs in the order of the Reich Commissar of the Netherlands Territories concerning the Netherlands doctors, dated 19 December 1941, reads as follows: "It is the duty of the doctor, through advice and effort, conscientiously and to his best ability, to assist as helper the person entrusted to his care in the maintenance, improvement and re-establishment of his vitality, physical efficiency and health. The accomplishment of this duty is a public task."[16] The physicians of Holland rejected this order unanimously because they saw what it actually meant—namely, the concentration of their efforts on mere rehabilitation of the sick for useful labor, and abolition of medical secrecy. Although on the surface the new order appeared not too grossly unacceptable, the Dutch physicians decided that it was the first, although slight, step away from principle that was the most important one. The Dutch physicians declared that they would not obey this order. When Seiss-Inquart threatened them with revocation of their licenses, they returned their licenses, removed their shingles and, while seeing their own patients secretly, no longer wrote death or birth certificates. Seiss-Inquart retraced his steps and tried to cajole them—still to no effect. Then he arrested 100 Dutch physicians and sent them to concentration camps. The medical profession remained adamant and quietly took care of their widows and orphans, but would not give in. Thus it came about that not a single euthanasia or nontherapeutic sterilization was recommended or participated in by any Dutch physician. They had the foresight to resist before the first step was taken, and they acted unanimously and won out in the end. It is obvious that if the medical profession of a small nation under the conqueror's heel could resist so effectively the German medical profession could likewise have resisted had they not taken the fatal first step. It is the first seemingly innocent step away from principle that frequently decides a career of crime. Corrosion begins in microscopic proportions.

The Situation in the United States

The question that this fact prompts is whether there are any danger signs that American physicians have also been infected with Hegelian, cold-blooded, utilitarian philosophy and whether early traces of it can be detected in their medical thinking that may make them vulnerable to departures of the type that occurred in Germany. Basic attitudes must be examined dispassionately. The original concept of medicine and nursing was not based on any rational or feasible likelihood that they could actually cure and restore but rather on an essentially maternal or religious idea. The Good Samaritan had no thought of nor did he actually care whether he could restore working capacity. He was merely motivated by the compassion in alleviating suffering. Bernal[17] states that prior to the advent of scientific medicine, the physician's main function was to give hope to the patient and to relieve his relatives of responsibility. Gradually, in all civilized countries, medicine has moved away from this position, strangely enough in direct proportion to the actual ability to perform feats that would have been plain miracles in days of old. However, with this increased efficiency based on scientific development went a subtle change in attitude. Physicians have become dangerously close to being mere technicians of rehabilitation. This essentially Hegelian rational attitude has led them to make certain distinctions in the handling of acute and chronic diseases. The patient with a chronic illness carries an obvious stigma as the one less likely to be fully rehabilitable for social usefulness. In an increasingly utilitarian society these patients are being looked down upon with increasing definiteness as unwanted ballast. A certain amount of rather open contempt for the people who cannot be rehabilitated with present knowledge has developed. This is probably due to a good deal of unconscious hostility, because these people for whom there seem to be no effective remedies have become a threat to newly acquired delusions of omnipotence.

Hospitals like to limit themselves to the care of patients who can be fully rehabilitated, and the patient whose full rehabilitation is unlikely finds himself, at least in the best and most advanced centers of healing, as a second-class patient faced with a reluctance on the part of both the visiting and the house staff to suggest and apply therapeutic procedures that are not likely to bring about immediately striking results in terms of recovery. I wish to emphasize that this point of view did not arise primarily within the medical profession, which has always been outstanding in a highly competitive economic society for giving freely and unstintingly of its time and efforts, but was imposed by the shortage of funds available, both private and public. From the attitude of easing patients with chronic diseases away from the doors of the best types of treatment facilities available to the actual dispatching of such patients to killing centers is a long but nevertheless logical step. Resources for the so-called incurable patient have recently become practically unavailable.

There has never in history been a shortage of money for the development and manufacture of weapons of war; there is and should be none now. The disproportion of monetary support for war and that available for healing and care is an anachronism in an era that has been described as the "enlightened age of the common man" by some observers. The comparable cost of jet planes and hospital beds is too obvious for any excuse to be found for a shortage of the latter. I trust that these remarks will not be misunderstood. I believe that armament, including jet planes, is vital for the security of the republic, but adequate maintenance of standards of health and alleviation of suffering are equally vital, both from a practical point of view and from that of morale. All who took part in induction-board examinations during the war realize that the maintenance and development of national health is of as vital importance as the maintenance and development of armament.

The trend of development in the facilities available for the chronically ill outlined above will not necessarily be altered by public or state medicine. With provision of public funds in any setting of public activity the question is bound to come up, "Is it worthwhile to spend a certain amount of effort to restore a certain type of patient?" This rationalistic point of view has insidiously crept into the motivation of medical effort, supplanting the old Hippocratic point of view. In emergency situations, military or otherwise, such grading of effort may be pardonable. But doctors must beware lest such attitudes creep into the civilian public administration of medicine entirely outside emergency situations, because once such considerations are at all admitted, the more often and the more definitely the question is going to be asked, "Is it worth while to do this or that for this type of patient?" Evidence of the existence of such an attitude stared at me from a report on the activities of a leading public hospital unit, which stated rather proudly that certain treatments were given only when they appeared promising: "Our facilities are such that a case load of 20 patients is regularly carried . . . in selecting cases for treatment careful consideration is given to the prognostic criteria, and in no instance have we instituted treatment merely to satisfy relatives or our own consciences." If only those whose treatment is worth while in terms of prognosis are to be treated, what about the other ones? The doubtful patients are the ones whose recovery appears unlikely, but frequently if treated energetically, they surprise the best prognosticators. And what shall be done during that long time lag after the disease has been called incurable and the time of death and autopsy? It is that period during which it is most difficult to find hospitals and other therapeutic organizations for the welfare and alleviation of suffering of the patient.

Under all forms of dictatorship the dictating bodies or individuals claim that all that is done is being done for the best of the people as a whole, and that for that reason they look at health merely in terms of utility, efficiency and productivity. It is natural in such a setting that eventually Hegel's principle that "what is useful is good" wins out completely. The killing center is the *reductio ad absurdum* of all health planning based only on rational principles and economy and not on humane compassion and divine law. To be sure, American physicians are still far from the point of thinking of killing centers, but they have arrived at a danger point in thinking, at which likelihood of full rehabilitation is considered a factor that should determine the amount of time, effort and cost to be devoted to a particular type of patient on the part of the social body upon which this decision rests. At this point Americans should remember that the enormity of a euthanasia movement is present in their own midst. To the psychiatrist it is obvious that this represents the eruption of unconscious aggression on the part of certain administrators alluded to above, as well as on the part of relatives who have been understandably frustrated by the tragedy of illness in its close interaction upon their own lives. The hostility of a father erupting against his feebleminded son is understandable and should be considered from the psychiatric point of view, but it certainly should not influence social thinking. The development of effective analgesics and pain-relieving operations has taken even the last rationalization away from the supporters of euthanasia.

The case, therefore, that I should like to make is that American medicine must realize where it stands in its fundamental premises. There can be no doubt that in a subtle way the Hegelian premise of "what is useful is right" has infected society, including the medical portion. Physicians must return to the older premises, which were the emotional foundation and driving force of an amazingly successful quest to increase powers of healing and which are bound to carry them still farther if they are not held down to earth by the pernicious attitudes of an overdone practical realism.

What occurred in Germany may have been the inexorable historic progression that the Greek historians have described as the law of the fall of civilizations and that Toynbee[18] has convincingly confirmed—namely, that there is a logical sequence from Koros to Hybris to Ate, which means from surfeit to disdainful arrogance to disaster, the surfeit being increased scientific and practical accomplishments, which, however, brought about an inclination to throw away the old motivations and values by disdainful arrogant pride in practical efficiency. Moral and physical disaster is the inevitable consequence.

Fortunately, there are developments in this democratic society that counteract these trends. Notable among them are the organizations of patients afflicted with various chronic diseases that have sprung up and are dedicating themselves to guidance and information for their fellow sufferers and for the support and stimulation of medical research. Among the earliest was the mental-hygiene movement, founded by a former patient with mental disease, followed by the National Foundation for

Infantile Paralysis, the tuberculosis societies, the American Epilepsy League, the National Association to Control Epilepsy, the American Cancer Society, the American Heart Association, "Alcoholics Anonymous" and, most recently, the National Multiple Sclerosis Society. All these organizations, which are coordinated with special medical societies and which received inspiration and guidance from outstanding physicians, are having an extremely wholesome effect in introducing fresh motivating power into the ivory towers of academic medicine. It is indeed interesting and an assertion of democratic vitality that these societies are activated by and for people suffering from illnesses who, under certain dictatorships, would have been slated for euthanasia.

It is thus that these new societies have taken over one of the ancient functions of medicine—namely, to give hope to the patient and to relieve his relatives. These groups need the whole-hearted support of the medical profession. Unfortunately, this support is by no means yet unanimous. A distinguished physician, investigator and teacher at an outstanding university recently told me that he was opposed to these special societies and clinics because they had nothing to offer to the patient. It would be better to wait until someone made a discovery accidentally and then start clinics. It is my opinion, however, that one cannot wait for that. The stimulus supplied by these societies is necessary to give stimulus both to public demand and to academic medicine, which at times grows stale and unproductive even in its most outstanding centers, and whose existence did nothing to prevent the executioner from having logic on his side in Germany.

Another element of this free democratic society and enterprise that has been a stimulus to new developments is the pharmaceutical industry, which, with great vision, has invested considerable effort in the sponsorship of new research.

Dictatorships can indeed be defined as systems in which there is a prevalence of thinking in destructive rather than in ameliorative terms in dealing with social problems. The ease

with which destruction of life is advocated for persons considered either socially useless or socially disturbing instead of educational or ameliorative measures may be the first danger sign
of loss of creative liberty in thinking, which is the hallmark of
democratic society. All destructiveness ultimately leads to self-
destruction; the fate of the SS and of Nazi Germany is an eloquent example. The destructive principle, once unleashed, is
bound to engulf the whole personality and to occupy all its relationships. Destructive urges and destructive concepts arising
therefrom cannot remain limited or focused upon one subject or
several subjects alone, but must inevitably spread and be directed against one's entire surrounding world, including one's
own group and ultimately the self. The ameliorative point of
view maintained in relation to all others is the only real means
of self-preservation.

A most important need in this country is for the development of active and alert hospital centers for the treatment of
chronic illnesses. They must have active staffs similar to those
of the hospitals for acute illnesses, and these hospitals must be
fundamentally different from the custodial repositories for dere-
licts, of which there are too many in existence today. Only
thus can one give the right answer to divine scrutiny: Yes, we
are our brothers' keepers.

For Reflection and Discussion

1. Describe your strongest reactions to this article. Do you
   know of doctors and scientists who cooperate with oppres-
   sive governments in today's world?

2. What major points of this article, written more than 40 years
   ago, do you consider still valid? Which do not apply to the
   euthanasia discussion in our society today?

3. Discuss the implications of the following quotation for the
   present debate about euthanasia: "It is rather significant that
   the German people were considered by their Nazi leaders

more ready to accept the exterminations of the sick than those for political reasons." How is this comment related to the "slippery-slope" argument?

4. Do you see any irony in the author's account of the Dutch resistance?

5. Discuss the author's concerns about utilitarianism and rationalism. What motivations and values does he support? After reading the article by Leon Kass, return to this article and compare their fundamental similarities and concerns.

Notes

1. O. Bumke, "Discussion of Faltlhauser, K. Zur Frage der Sterilisierung geistig Abnormer," *Allg. Ztsch. f. Psychiat.* 96 (1932) 372.

2. R. Dierichs, "Beitrag zur psychischen Anstaltsbehandlung Tuberkulöser," *Ztschr. f Tuberk* 74 (1936) 21-28.

3. A. Dorner, *Mathematik in Dienste der Nationalpolitischen Erziehung: Ein Handbuch für Lehrer, herausgegeben in Auftrage des Reischsverbandes Deutscher mathematischer Gesellschaften und Vereine,* 3d. ed., rev. (Frankfurt: Moritz Diesterweg, 1935). 1-118.

4. L. Alexander, "Public Mental Health Practices in Germany, Sterilization and Execution of Patients Suffering from Nervous or Mental Disease," Combined Intelligence Objectives Subcommittee, Item No. 24. File No. XXVIII-50 (August 1945) 1-173.

5. *Idem.*, "Neuropathology and Neurophysiology, Including Electro-encephalography in Wartime Germany." Combined Intelligence Objectives Subcommittee Item No. 24, File No. XXVII-1 (July, 1945) 1-65.

6. *Idem.*, "German Military Neuropsychiatry and Neurosurgery," Combined Intelligence Objectives Subcommittee, Item No. 24, File No. XXVIII-49 (August, 1945) 1-138.

7. *Idem.*, "Sociopsychologic Structure of SS: Psychiatric Report of Nurnberg Trials for War Crimes," *Arch. Neurol. & Psychiat.* 59 (1948) 622-634.

8. *Idem.*, "War Crimes: Their Social-psychological Aspects," *American Journal of Psychiatry* 105 (1948), 170-177.

9. *Idem.*, "War Crimes and Their Motivation: Socio-psychological Structure of SS and Criminalization of Society," *Journal of Criminal Law & Criminology* 39 (1948) 298-326.

10. G. Madaus, and F.E. Koch, "Tierexperimentelle Studien zur Frage der medikamentösen Sterilisierung (durch Caladium seguinum) (Dieffenbachia seguina)," *Ztschr. f.d. ges. exper. Med.* 109 (1941) 68-87.

11. G. Madaus, "Zauberpflanzen im Lichte experimenteller Forschung, Das Schweigrohr- Caladium seguinum," *Umschau* 24 (1941) 600-602.

12. L. Alexander, "Miscellaneous Aviation Medical Matters," Combined Intelligence Objectives Subcommittee, Item No. 24, File No. XXIX-21. (August, 1945) 1-163.

13. Document 1971 a PS.

14. Document NO 220.

15. L. Alexander, "Treatment of Shock from Prolonged Exposure to Cold, Especially in Water," Combined Intelligence Objectives Subcommittee, Item No. 24, File No. XXVI-37. (July, 1945) 1-128.

16. Seiss-Inquart, "Order of the Reich Commissar for the Occupied Netherlands Territories Concerning the Netherlands Doctors," Gazette containing the orders for the Occupied Netherlands Territories, (December, 1941) 1004-1026.

17. J.D. Bernal, *The Social Function of Science*, 6th ed. (London: George Routledge & Sons, 1946) 482.

18. A.J. Toynbee, *A Study of History*, abridgement of Vol. I-VI by D. C. Somervell (New York and London: Oxford University Press, 1947) 617.

7

Neither for Love
nor Money:
Why Doctors Must Not Kill

Leon R. Kass, M.D.

IS THE PROFESSION OF MEDICINE ETHICALLY NEUTRAL? IF SO,
whence shall we derive the moral norms or principles to govern its practices? If not, how are the norms of professional
conduct related to the rest of what makes medicine a profession?

These difficult questions, now much discussed, are in fact
very old, indeed as old as the beginnings of Western medicine.
According to an ancient Greek myth, the goddess Athena procured two powerful drugs in the form of blood taken from the
Gorgon Medusa, the blood drawn from her left side providing
protection against death, that from her right side a deadly poison. According to one version of the myth, Athena gave to As-
clepius, the revered founder of medicine, vials of both drugs;
according to the other version, she gave him only the life-pre-
serving drug, reserving the power of destruction for herself.
There is force in both accounts: the first attests to the moral
neutrality of medical means, and of technical power generally;
the second shows that wisdom would constitute medicine an
unqualifiedly benevolent—i.e., intrinsically ethical—art.

Today, we doubt that medicine is an intrinsically ethical activity, but we are quite certain that it can both help and harm. In fact, today, help and harm flow from the same vial. The same respirator that brings a man back from the edge of the grave also senselessly prolongs the life of an irreversibly comatose young woman. The same morphine that reverses the respiratory distress of pulmonary edema can, in higher doses, arrest respiration altogether. Whether they want to or not, doctors are able to kill—quickly, efficiently, surely. And what is more, it seems that they may soon be licensed and encouraged to do so.

Last year in Holland some 5,000 patients were intentionally put to death by their physicians, while authorities charged with enforcing the law against homicide agreed not to enforce it. Not satisfied with such hypocrisy, and eager to immunize physicians against possible prosecution, American advocates of active euthanasia are seeking legislative changes in several states that would legalize so-called mercy killing by physicians. A year ago [Ed., Jan. 1988], the editor of the *Journal of the American Medical Association* published an outrageous (and perhaps fictitious) case of mercy killing, precisely to stir professional and public discussion of direct medical killing—perhaps, some have said, as a trial balloon.[1] So-called active euthanasia practiced by physicians seems to be an idea whose time has come. But, in my view, it is a bad idea whose time must not come—not now, not ever. This essay is in part an effort to support this conclusion. But it is also an attempt to explore the ethical character of the medical profession, using the question of killing by doctors as a probe. Accordingly, I will be considering these interrelated questions: What are the norms that all physicians, *as physicians* should agree to observe, whatever their personal opinions? What is the basis of such a medical ethic? What does it say—and what should we think—about doctors intentionally killing?

Contemporary Ethical Approaches

The question about physicians killing is a special case of—but not thereby identical to—this general question: May or ought one kill people who ask to be killed? Among those who answer this general question in the affirmative, two reasons are usually given. Because these reasons also reflect the two leading approaches to medical ethics today, they are especially worth noting. First is the reason of *freedom* or *autonomy*. Each person has a right to control his or her body and his or her life, including the end of it; some go so far as to assert a right to die, a strange claim in a liberal society, founded on the need to secure and defend the unalienable right to life. But strange or not, for patients with waning powers too weak to oppose potent life-prolonging technologies wielded by aggressive physicians, the claim based on choice, autonomy, and self-determination is certainly understandable. On this view, physicians (or others) are bound to acquiesce in demands not only for termination of treatment but also for intentional killing through poison, because the right to choose—freedom—must be respected, even more than life itself, and even when the physician would never recommend or concur in the choices made. When persons exercise their right to choose against their continuance as embodied beings, doctors must not only cease their ministrations to the body; as keepers of the vials of life and death, they are also morally bound actively to dispatch the embodied person, out of deference to the autonomous personal choice that is, in this view, most emphatically the patient to be served.

The second reason for killing the patient who asks for death has little to do with choice. Instead, death is to be directly and swiftly given because the patient's life is deemed no longer worth living, according to some substantive or "objective" measure. Unusually great pain or a terminal condition or an irreversible coma or advanced senility or extreme degradation is the disqualifying quality of life that pleads—choice or no choice—for merciful termination. Choice may enter indirectly to confirm the judgment: if the patient does not speak up, the doctor (or the relatives or some other proxy) may be asked to affirm that he would not himself choose—or that his patient, were he *able* to choose, *would* not choose—to remain alive with one or more of these stigmata. It is not his autonomy but rather the miserable and pitiable condition of his body or mind that justifies doing the patient in. Absent such substantial degradations, requests for assisted death would not be honored. Here the body itself offends and must be plucked out, from compassion or mercy, to be sure. Not the autonomous will of the patient, but the doctor's benevolent and compassionate love for suffering humanity justifies the humane act of mercy killing.

As I have indicated, these two reasons advanced to justify the killing of patients correspond to the two approaches to medical ethics most prominent in the literature today: the school of autonomy and the school of general benevolence and compassion (or love). Despite their differences, they are united in their opposition to the belief that medicine is intrinsically a moral profession, with its own immanent principles and standards of conduct that set limits on what physicians may properly do. Each seeks to remedy the ethical defect of a profession seen to be in itself amoral, technically competent but morally neutral.

For the first ethical school, morally neutral technique is morally used only when it is used according to the wishes of the patient as client or consumer. The implicit (and sometimes explicit) model of the doctor-patient relationship is one of *contract*: the physician—a highly competent hired syringe, as it were—sells his services on demand, restrained only by the law (though he is free to refuse his services if the patient is unwilling or unable to meet his fee). Here's the deal: for the patient, autonomy and service; for the doctor, money, graced by the pleasure of giving the patient what he wants. If a patient wants to fix her nose or change his gender, determine the sex of unborn children, or take euphoriant drugs just for kicks, the physician can and will go to work—provided that the price is right and that the contract is explicit about what happens if the customer isn't satisfied.[2]

For the second ethical school, morally neutral technique is morally used only when it is used under the guidance of general benevolence or loving charity. Not the will of the patient, but the humane and compassionate motive of the physician— not as physician but as human *being*—makes the doctor's actions ethical. Here, too, there can be strange requests and stranger deeds, but if they are done from love, nothing can be wrong—again, providing the law is silent. All acts—including killing the patient—done lovingly are licit, even praiseworthy. Good and humane intentions can sanctify any deed.

In my opinion, each of these approaches should be rejected as a basis for medical ethics. For one thing, neither can make sense of some specific duties and restraints long thought absolutely inviolate under the traditional medical ethic—e.g., the proscription against having sex with patients. Must we now say that sex with patients is permissible if the patient wants it and the price is right, or, alternatively, if the doctor is gentle and loving and has a good bedside manner? Or do we glimpse in this absolute prohibition a deeper understanding of the medical vocation, which the prohibition both embodies and protects? Indeed, as I will now try to show, using the taboo against doctors killing patients, the medical profession has its own instrinsic ethic, which a physician true to his calling will not violate, either for love or for money.

Professing Ethically

Let me propose a different way of thinking about medicine as a profession. Consider medicine not as a mixed marriage between its own value-neutral technique and some extrinsic moral principles, but as an inherently ethical activity, in which technique and conduct are both ordered in relation to an overarching good, the naturally given end of health. This once traditional view of medicine I have defended at length in four chapters of my book, *Toward a More Natural Science.*[3] Here I will present the conclusions without the arguments. It will suffice, for present purposes, if I can render this view plausible.

A profession, as etymology suggests, is an activity or occupation to which its practitioner publicly professes—that is, confesses—his devotion. Learning may, of course, be required of, and prestige may, of course, be granted to, the professional, but it is the profession's *goal* that calls, that learning serves, and that prestige honors. Each of the ways of life to which the various professionals profess their devotion must be a way of life worthy of such devotion—and so they all are. The teacher devotes himself to assisting the learning of the young, looking up to truth and wisdom; the lawyer (or the judge) devotes himself to rectifying injustice for his client (or for the parties before the court), looking up to what is lawful and right; the clergyman devotes himself to tending the souls of his parishioners, looking up to the sacred and the divine; and the physician devotes himself to healing the sick, looking up to health and wholeness.

Being a professional is thus more than being a technician. It is rooted in our moral nature; it is a matter not only of the mind and hand but also of the heart, not only of intellect and skill but also of character. For it is only as a being willing and able to devote himself to others and to serve some high good that a person makes a public profession of his way of life. To profess is an ethical act, and it makes the professional qua *professional* a moral being who prospectively affirms the moral nature of his activity.

Professing oneself a professional is an ethical act for many reasons. It is an articulate public act, not merely a private and silent choice—a confession before others who are one's witnesses. It freely promises continuing devotion, not merely announces present preferences, to a way of life, not just a way to a livelihood, a life of action, not only of thought. It serves some high good, which calls forth devotion because it is both good and high, but which requires such devotion because its service is most demanding and difficult, and thereby engages one's character, not merely one's mind and hands.

The good to which the medical profession is devoted is health, a naturally given although precarious standard or norm, characterized by "wholeness" and "well-working," toward which the living body moves on its own. Even the modern physician, despite his great technological prowess, is but an assistant to natural powers of self-healing. But health, though a goal tacitly sought and explicitly desired, is difficult to attain and preserve. It can be ours only provisionally and temporarily, for we are finite and frail. Medicine thus finds itself in between: the physician is called to serve the high and universal goal of health while also ministering to the needs and relieving the sufferings of the frail and particular patient. Moreover, the physician must respond not only to illness but also to its meaning for each individual, who, in addition to his symptoms, may suffer from self-concern—and often fear and shame—about weakness and vulnerability, neediness and dependence, loss of self-esteem, and the fragility of all that matters to him. Thus, the inner meaning of the art of medicine is derived from the pursuit of health and the care for the ill and suffering, guided by the self-conscious awareness, shared (even if only tacitly) by physician and patient alike, of the delicate and dialectical tension between wholeness and necessary decay.

When the activity of healing the sick is thus understood, we can discern certain virtues requisite for practicing medicine—among them, moderation and self-restraint, gravity, patience, sympathy, discretion, and prudence. We can also discern specific positive duties, addressed mainly to the patient's vulnerability and self-concern—including the demands for truthfulness, patient instruction, and encouragement. And, arguably, we can infer the importance of certain negative duties, formulable as absolute and unexceptionable rules. Among these, I submit, is this rule: Doctors must not kill. The rest of this essay attempts to defend this rule and to show its relation to the medical ethic, itself understood as growing out of the inner meaning of the medical vocation.

I confine my discussion solely to the question of direct, intentional killing of patients by *physicians*—so-called mercy killing. Though I confess myself opposed to such killing even by nonphysicians, I am not arguing here against euthanasia p*er se*. More importantly, I am not arguing against the cessation of medical treatment when such treatment merely prolongs painful or degraded dying, nor do I oppose the use of certain measures to relieve suffering that have, as an unavoidable consequence, an increased risk of death. Doctors may and must allow to die, even if they must not intentionally kill.

I appreciate the danger in offering arguments against killing: even at best, they are unlikely to be equal to the task. Most taboos operate immediately and directly, through horror and repugnance; discursive arguments against, say, incest or cannibalism can never yield the degree of certitude intuitively and emotionally felt by those who know such practices to be abominable, nor are they likely to persuade anyone who is morally blind. It is not obvious that any argument can demonstrate, once and for all, why murder is bad or why doctors must not kill. No friend of decency wants to imperil sound principles by attempting to argue, unsuccessfully, for their soundness. Yet we have no other choice. Some moral matters, once self-evident, are no longer self-evident to us. When physicians themselves—as in Holland—undertake to kill patients, with public support, intuition and revulsion have fallen asleep. Only argument, with all its limitations, can hope to reawaken them.

Assessing the Consequences

Although the bulk of my argument will turn on my understanding of the special meaning of professing the art of healing, I begin with a more familiar mode of ethical analysis: assessing needs and benefits versus dangers and harms. To do this properly is a massive task. Here, I can do little more than raise a few of the relevant considerations. Still the best discussion of this topic is a now-classic essay by Yale Kamisar, written thirty years ago.[4] Kamisar makes vivid the difficulties in assuring that the choice for death will be *freely* made and adequately *informed*, the problems of physician error and abuse, the troubles for human relationships within families and between doctors and patients, the difficulty of preserving the boundary between voluntary and involuntary euthanasia, and the risks to the whole social order from weakening the absolute prohibition against taking innocent life. These considerations are, in my view, alone sufficient to rebut any attempt to weaken the taboo against medical killing; their relative importance for determining public policy far exceeds their relative importance in this essay. But here they serve also to point us to more profound reasons why doctors must not kill.

There is no question that fortune deals many people a very bad hand, not least at the end of life. All of us, I am sure, know or have known individuals whose last weeks, months, or even years were racked with pain and discomfort, degraded by dependency or loss of self-control, isolation or insensibility, or who lived in such reduced humanity that it cast a deep shadow over their entire lives, especially as remembered by the survivors. All who love them would wish to spare them such an end, and there is no doubt that an earlier death could do it. Against such a clear benefit, attested to by many a poignant and heartrending true story, it is difficult to argue, especially when the arguments are necessarily general and seemingly abstract. Still, in the aggregate, the adverse consequences—including real suffering—of being governed solely by mercy and compassion may far outweigh the aggregate benefits of relieving agonal or terminal distress.

The "Need" for Mercy Killing

The first difficulty emerges when we try to gauge the so-called "need" or demand for medically assisted killing. This question, to be sure, is in part empirical. But evidence can be gathered only if the relevant categories of "euthanizable" people are clearly defined. Such definition is notoriously hard to accomplish—and it is not always honestly attempted. On careful inspection, we discover that if the category is precisely defined, the need for mercy killing seems greatly exaggerated, and if the category is loosely defined, the poisoners will be working overtime.

The category always mentioned first to justify mercy killing is the group of persons suffering from incurable and fatal illnesses, with intractable pain and with little time left to live but still fully aware, who freely request a release from their distress—e.g., people rapidly dying from disseminated cancer with bony metastases, unresponsive to chemotherapy. But as experts in pain control tell us, the number of such people with truly intractable and untreatable pain is in fact rather low. Adequate analgesia is apparently possible in the vast majority of cases, provided that the physician and patient are willing to use strong enough medicines in adequate doses and with proper timing.[5]

But, it will be pointed out, full analgesia induces drowsiness and blunts or distorts awareness. How can that be a desired outcome of treatment? Fair enough. But then the rationale for requesting death begins to shift from relieving experienced suffering to ending a life no longer valued by its bearer or, let us be frank, by the onlookers. If this becomes a sufficient basis to warrant mercy killing, now the category of euthanizable people cannot be limited to individuals with incurable or fatal painful illnesses with little time to live. Now persons in all sorts of greatly reduced and degraded conditions—from persistent vegetative state to quadriplegia, from severe depression to the condition that now most horrifies, Alzheimer's disease—might have equal claim to have their suffering mercifully halted. The trouble, of course, is that most of these people can no longer request for themselves the dose of poison. Moreover, it will be difficult—if not impossible—to develop the requisite calculus of degradation or to define the threshold necessary for ending life.

From Voluntary to Involuntary

Since it is so hard to describe precisely and "objectively" what kind and degree of pain, suffering, or bodily or mental impairment, and what degree of incurability or length of anticipated remaining life, could justify mercy killing, advocates repair (at least for the time being) to the principle of volition: the request for assistance in death is to be honored because it is freely made by the one whose life it is, and who, for one reason or another, cannot commit suicide alone. But this too is fraught with difficulty: How free or informed is a choice made under debilitated conditions? Can consent long in advance be sufficiently informed about all the particular circumstances that it is meant prospectively to cover? And, in any case, are not such choices easily and subtly manipulated, especially in the vulnerable? Kamisar is very perceptive on this subject:

> Is this the kind of choice, assuming that it can be made in a fixed and rational manner, that we want to offer a gravely ill person? Will we not sweep up, in the process, some who are not really tired of life, but think others are tired of them; some who do not really want to die, but who feel they should not live on, because to do so when there looms the legal alternative of euthanasia is to do a selfish or a cowardly act? Will not some feel an obligation to have themselves "eliminated" in order that funds allocated for their terminal care might be better used by their families or, financial worries aside, in order to relieve their families of the emotional strain involved?

Even were these problems soluble, the insistence on voluntariness as the justifying principle cannot be sustained. The enactment of a law legalizing mercy killing on voluntary request will certainly be challenged in the courts under the equal-protection clause of the Fourteenth Amendment. The law, after all, will not legalize assistance to suicides in general, but only mercy killing. The change will almost certainly occur not as an exception to the criminal law proscribing homicide but as a new "treatment option" as part of a right to "A Humane and Dignified Death."[6] Why, it will be argued, should the comatose or the demented be denied such a right or such a "treatment," just because they cannot claim it for themselves? This line of reasoning has already led courts to allow substituted judgment and proxy consent in termination-of-treatment cases since *Quinlan,* the case that, Kamisar rightly says, first "badly smudged, if it did not erase, the distinction between the right to choose one's own death and the right to choose someone else's." When proxies give their consent, they will do so on the basis not of autonomy but of a substantive judgment—namely, that for these or those reasons, the life in question is not worth living. Precisely because most of the cases that are candidates for mercy killing are of this sort, the line between voluntary and involuntary euthanasia cannot hold, and will be effaced by the intermediate case of the mentally impaired or comatose who are declared no longer willing to live because someone else wills that result for them. In fact, the more honest advocates of euthanasia openly admit that it is these nonvoluntary cases that they especially hope to dispatch, and that their plea for *voluntary* euthanasia is just a first step. It is easy to see the trains of abuses that are likely to follow the most innocent cases, especially because the innocent cases cannot be precisely and neatly separated from the rest.

Everyone is, of course, aware of the danger of abuses. So procedures are suggested to prevent their occurrence. But to provide real safeguards against killing the unwilling or the only half-heartedly willing, and to provide time for a change of mind, they must be intrusive, cumbersome, and costly. As Kamisar points out, the scrupulous euthanasiasts seek a goal "which is *inherently inconsistent*: a procedure for death which *both* (1) provides ample safeguards against abuse and mistake; and (2) is 'quick' and 'easy' in operation." Whatever the procedure adopted, moreover, blanket immunity from lawsuits and criminal prosecution cannot be given in advance, especially because of ineradicable suspicions of coercion or engineered consent, and the likelihood of mixed motives and potential conflict, post mortem, among family members.

Damaging the Doctor-Patient Relationship

Abuses and conflicts aside, legalized mercy killing by doctors will almost certainly damage the doctor-patient relationship. The patient's trust in the doctor's wholehearted devotion to the patient's best interests will be hard to sustain once doctors are licensed to kill. Imagine the scene: you are old, poor, in failing health, and alone in the world; you are brought to the city hospital with fractured ribs and pneumonia. The nurse or intern enters late at night with a syringe full of yellow stuff for your intravenous drip. How soundly will you sleep? It will not matter that your doctor has never yet put anyone to death; that he is legally entitled to do so—even if only in some well-circumscribed areas—will make a world of difference.

And it will make a world of psychic difference too for conscientious physicians. How easily will they be able to care wholeheartedly for patients when it is always possible to think of killing them as a "therapeutic option"? Shall it be penicillin and a respirator one more time, or perhaps just an overdose of morphine this time? Physicians get tired of treating patients who are hard to cure, who resist their best efforts, who are on their way down—"gorks," "gomers," and "vegetables" are only some of the less than affectionate names they receive from the house officers. Won't it be tempting to think that death is the best treatment for the little old lady "dumped" again on the emergency room by the nearby nursing home?

Even the most humane and conscientious physician psychologically needs protection against himself and his weaknesses, if he is to care fully for those who entrust themselves to him. A physician friend who worked many years in a hospice caring for dying patients explained it to me most convincingly: "Only because I knew that I could not and would not kill my patients was I able to enter most fully and intimately into caring for them as they lay dying." The psychological burden of the license to kill (not to speak of the brutalization of the physician-killers) could very well be an intolerably high price to pay for physician-assisted euthanasia, especially if it also leads to greater remoteness, aloofness, and indifference as defenses against the guilt associated with harming those we care for.

The point, however, is not merely psychological and consequentialist: it is also moral and essential. My friend's horror at the thought that he might be tempted to kill his patients, were he not enjoined from doing so, embodies a deep understanding of the medical ethic and its intrinsic limits. We move from assessing the consequences to looking at medicine itself.

The Limits of Medicine

Every activity can be distinguished, more or less easily, from other activities. Sometimes the boundaries are indistinct; it is not always easy, especially today, to distinguish some music from noise or some teaching from indoctrination. Medicine and healing are no different; it is sometimes hard to determine the boundaries, both with regard to ends and means. Is all cosmetic surgery healing? Are placebos—or food and water—drugs?

There is, of course, a temptation to finesse these questions of definition or to deny the existence of boundaries altogether:

medicine is whatever doctors *do*, and doctors do whatever doctors *can*. Technique and power alone define the art. Put this way, we see the need for limits: Technique and power are ethically neutral, usable for both good and ill. The need for finding or setting limits to the use of power is especially important when the power is dangerous; it matters more that we know the proper limits on the use of medical power—or military power—than, say, the proper limits on the use of a paint brush or violin.

The beginning of ethics regarding power generally lies in naysaying. Small children coming into their powers must be taught restraint, both for their own good and for the good of others. The wise setting of boundaries is based on discerning the excesses to which the power, unrestrained, is prone. Applied to the professions, this principle would establish strict outer limits—indeed, inviolable taboos—against those "occupational hazards" to which each profession is especially prone. *Within* these outer limits, no fixed rules of conduct apply; instead, prudence—the wise judgment of the man on the spot— finds and adopts the best course of action in light of the circumstances. But the outer limits themselves are fixed, firm, and nonnegotiable.

What are those limits for medicine? At least three are set forth in the venerable Hippocratic Oath: no breach of confidentiality; no sexual relations with patients; no dispensing of deadly drugs.[7] These unqualified, self-imposed restrictions are readily understood in terms of the temptations to which the physician is most vulnerable, temptations in each case regarding an area of vulnerability and exposure that the practice of medicine requires of patients. Patients necessarily divulge and reveal private and intimate details of their personal lives; patients necessarily expose their naked bodies to the physician's objectifying gaze and investigating hands; patients necessarily entrust their very lives to the physician's skill, technique, and judgment. The exposure is, in all cases, one-sided and asymmetric: the doctor does not reveal his intimacies, display his nakedness, offer up his embodied life to the patient. The patient is vulnerable and exposed; the physician is neither, or, rather, his own vulnerabilities are not exposed to the patient. Mindful of the meaning of such nonmutual exposure, the physician voluntarily sets limits on his own conduct, pledging not to take advantage of or to violate the patient's intimacies, sexuality, or life itself.

The reason for these restraints is not just the asymmetry of power and the ever-present hazard of its abuse. The relationship between doctor and patient transforms the ordinary human meaning of exposure. Medical nakedness is not erotic nakedness; palpation is not caressing; frank speech is not shared intimacy and friendship; giving out diets and drugs is not hospitality. The physician necessarily objectifies, reduces, and analyzes, as he probes, pokes, and looks for latent clues and meanings, while curbing his own sentiments and interests, so as to make a diagnosis and find a remedy. The goal that constitutes the relationship requires the detachment of the physician and the asymmetry of exposure and communication, and legitimates the acquisition and exercise of power. Yet it also informs the limits on how the power should be used and the manner in which the patient should be treated.

The prohibition against killing patients rests also on a narrower ground, related not only to the meaning of the doctor-patient relationship, but also, once again, to the potentially deadly moral neutrality of medical technique—the problem of the two vials. For this reason, it stands as the *first* promise of self-restraint sworn to in the Hippocratic Oath, as medicine's primary taboo: "I will neither give a deadly drug to anybody if asked for it, nor will I make a suggestion to this effect. . . . In purity and holiness I will guard my life and my art." In forswearing the giving of poison, the physician recognizes and restrains the godlike power he wields over patients, mindful that his drugs can both cure and kill. But in forswearing the giving of poison *when asked for it*, the Hippocratic physician rejects the view that the patient's choice for death can make killing him right. For the physician, at least, human life in living bodies commands respect and reverence—*by its very nature*. As its respectability does not depend upon human agreement or patient consent, revocation of one's consent to live does not deprive one's living body of respectability. The deepest ethical principle restraining the physician's power is not the autonomy or freedom of the patient; neither is it his own compassion or good intention. Rather, it is the dignity and mysterious power of human life itself, and, therefore, also what the Oath calls the purity and holiness of the life and art to which he has sworn devotion. A person can choose to be a physician, but he cannot choose what physicianship means.

The Essence of Medicine

One way to define medicine—or anything else—is to delimit its boundaries, to draw the line separating medicine from nonmedicine, or its ethical from its unethical practice. Another way to define medicine—or anything else—is to capture its center, to discern its essence. In the best case, the two kinds of definitions will be related: the outer boundary will at least reflect, and will at best be determined by, what is at the center. Some practices are beyond the pale precisely because they contradict what is at the center.

To seek the center, one begins not with powers but with goals, not with means but with ends. In the Hippocratic Oath, the physician states his goal this way: "I will apply dietetic measures *for the benefit of the sick* according to my ability and judgment. I will keep them from harm and injustice." In a more thorough explication of the Oath in my book, I have argued that this little paragraph, properly unpacked, reveals the core of medicine. For example, the emphasis on dietetics indicates that medicine is a cooperative rather than a transformative art, and the physician an assistant to the immanent healing powers of the body. And because a body possessed of reason is a body whose "possessor" may lead it astray through ignorance or self-indulgence, the physician, as servant of the patient's good, must teach, advise, and exhort to keep him from *self*-harm and injustice. Here I focus only on the modest little phrase, "the benefit of the sick."

The physician as physician serves only the sick. He does not serve the relatives or the hospital or the national debt inflated due to Medicare costs. Thus he will never sacrifice the well-being of the sick to the convenience or pocketbook or feelings of the relatives or society. Moreover, the physician serves the sick not because they have rights or wants or claims, but because they are sick. The benefit needed by the sick qua sick is health. The healer works with and for those who need to be healed, in order to make them whole.

Healing is thus the central core of medicine: to heal, to make whole, is the doctor's primary business. The sick, the ill, the unwell present themselves to the physician in the hope that he can help them become well—or, rather, as well as they can become, some degree of well-ness being possible always, this side of death. The physician shares that goal; his training has been devoted to making it possible for him to serve it. Despite enormous changes in medical technique and institutional practice, despite enormous changes in nosology and therapeutics, the center of medicine has not changed: it is as true today as it was in the days of Hippocrates that the ill desire to be whole; that wholeness means a certain well-working of the enlivened body and its unimpaired powers to sense, think, feel, desire, move, and maintain itself; and that the relationship between the healer and the ill is constituted, essentially even if only tacitly, around the desire of both to promote the wholeness of the one who is ailing.

Human Wholeness

The wholeness and well-working of a human being is, of course, a rather complicated matter, much more so than for our animal friends and relations. Because of our powers of mind, our partial emancipation from the rule of instinct, our self-consciousness, and the highly complex and varied ways of life we follow as individuals and as members of groups, health and fitness seem to mean different things to different people, or even to the same person at different times of life. Moreover, departures from health have varying importance depending on the way of life one follows. Yet not everything is relative and contextual; beneath the variable and cultural lies the constant and organic, the well-regulated, properly balanced, and fully empowered human body. Indeed, only the existence of this natural and universal subject makes possible the study of medicine. The cornerstone of medical education is the analytic study of the human body, *universally* considered: anatomy, physiology, biochemistry and molecular biology, genetics, microbiology, pathology, and pharmacology—all these sciences of somatic function, disorder, and remedy are the first business of medical schools, and they must be learned before one can hope to heal particular human beings.

But *human* wholeness goes beyond the kind of somatic wholeness abstractly and reductively studied by these various sciences. Whether or not doctors are sufficiently prepared by their training to recognize it, those who seek medical help in search of wholeness are not *to themselves* just bodies or organic machines. Each person intuitively knows himself to be a center of thoughts and desires, deeds and speeches, loves and hates, pleasures and pains, but a center whose workings are none other than the workings of his enlivened and mindful body. The patient presents himself to the physician, tacitly to be sure, as a psychophysical unity, as a *one*, not just as a body, but also not just as a separate disembodied entity that simply *has* or *owns* a body. The person and the body are self-identical. To be sure, the experience of psychophysical unity is often disturbed by illness, indeed, by bodily illness; it becomes hard to function as a unity if part of oneself is in revolt, is in pain, is debilitated. Yet the patient aspires to have the disturbance quieted, to restore the implicit feeling and functional fact of oneness with which we freely go about our business in the world. The sickness may be experienced largely as belonging to the body as something other; but the healing one wants is the wholeness of one's entire embodied being. Not the wholeness of *soma*, not the wholeness of *psyche*, but the wholeness of *anthropos* as a (puzzling) concretion of *soma-psyche* is the benefit sought by the sick. This human wholeness is what medicine is finally all about.

Wholeness and Killing

Can wholeness and healing ever be compatible with intentionally killing the patient? Can one benefit the patient as a whole by making him dead? There is, of course, a logical difficulty: how can any good exist for a being that is not? "Better off dead" is logical nonsense—unless, of course, death is not death at all but instead a gateway to a new and better life beyond. But the error is more than logical: to intend and to act for someone's good requires his continued existence to receive the benefit.

Certain attempts to benefit may in fact turn out, unintentionally, to be lethal. Giving adequate morphine to control pain might induce respiratory depression leading to death. But the intent to relieve the pain of the living presupposes that the living still live to be relieved. This must be the starting point in discussing all medical benefits: no benefit without a beneficiary.

Against this view of healing the whole human being, someone will surely bring forth the hard cases: patients so ill-served by their bodies that they can no longer bear to live, bodies riddled with cancer and racked with pain, against which their "owners" protest in horror and from which they insist on being released. It is argued that it just isn't true that we are psychophysical unities; rather, we are some hard-to-specify duality (or multiplicity) of impersonal organic body plus supervening consciousness, what the professionals dub personhood:

awareness, intellect, will. Cannot the person "in the body" speak up against the rest, and request death for "personal" reasons?

However sympathetically we listen to such requests, we must see them as incoherent. Strict person-body dualism cannot be sustained. "Personhood" is manifest on earth only in living bodies, our highest mental functions are held up by, and are inseparable from, lowly metabolism, respiration, circulation, excretion. There may be blood without consciousness, but there is never consciousness without blood. The body is the living ground of all so-called higher functions. Thus, one who calls for death in the service of personhood is like a tree seeking to cut its roots for the sake of growing its highest fruit. No physician devoted to the benefit of the sick can serve the patient as person by denying and thwarting his personal embodiment.

To say it plainly, to bring nothingness is incompatible with serving wholeness: one cannot heal—or comfort—by making nil. The healer cannot annihilate if he is truly to heal. The boundary condition, "No deadly drugs," flows directly from the center, "Make whole."

Analogies

The reasonableness of this approach to medical ethics is supported by analogies with other professions. For example, we can clearly discover why suborning perjury and contempt of court are taboos for lawyers, why falsifying data is taboo for a scientist, or why violating the confessional is taboo for a priest, once we see the goals of these professions to be, respectively, justice under law, truth about nature, and purification of the soul before God. Let me expand two other analogies, somewhat closer to our topic.

Take the teacher. His business: to encourage, and to provide the occasion for, learning and understanding. Recognizing this central core, we see that the teacher ought never to oppose himself to the student's effort to learn, or even to his prospects for learning. This means, among other things, never ridiculing an honest effort, never crushing true curiosity or thoughtfulness; it also means opposing firmly the temptations that face students to scramble their minds through drugs. And even when the recalcitrant student refuses to make the effort, the teacher does not abandon his post, but continues to look for a way to arouse, to cajole, to inspire, to encourage. The teacher will perhaps not *pursue* the unwilling student, but as long as the student keeps coming to class, the true teacher will not participate in or assist him with his mental self-neglect.

Now consider the parent. These days only a fool would try to state precisely what the true business of a father or mother is, qua father or mother. Yet it must be something like protection, care, nurture, instruction, exhortation, chastisement, encouragement, and support, all in the service of the growth and development of a mature, healthy, competent, and decent adult, capable of an independent and responsible life of work and love and participation in community affairs—no easy task, especially now. What will the true parent do when teenagers rise in revolt and try to reject not only the teachings of their homes but even the parents themselves, when sons and daughters metaphorically kill their parents as parents by un-sonning and un-daughtering themselves? Should fathers acquiesce and willingly unfather themselves; should mothers stand against their life-work of rearing and abandon the child? Or does not the true parent "hang in there" in one way or another, despite the difficulty and sense of failure, and despite the need, perhaps, for great changes in his or her conduct? Does not the true parent refuse to surrender or to abandon the child, knowing that it would be deeply self-contradictory to deny the fact of one's parenthood, whatever the child may say or do? Again, one may freely choose or refuse to become a parent, but one cannot fully choose what parenthood means. The inner meaning of the work has claims on our hearts and minds, and sets boundaries on what we may do without self-contradiction and self-violation.

When Medicine Fails

Being a physician, teacher, or parent has a central inner meaning that characterizes it essentially, and that is independent both of the demands of the "clients" and of the benevolent motives of the practitioners. For a physician, to be sure, things go better when the patient is freely willing and the physician is virtuous and compassionate. But the physician's work centers on the goal of healing, and he is thereby bound not to behave in contradiction to that central goal.

But there is a difficulty. The central goal of medicine— health—is, in each case, a perishable good: inevitably, patients get irreversibly sick, patients degenerate, patients die. Unlike—at least on first glance—teaching or rearing the young, healing the sick is *in principle* a project that must at some point fail. And here is where all the trouble begins: How does one deal with "medical failure"? What does one seek when restoration of wholeness—or "much" wholeness—is by and large out of the question?

There is much that can and should be said on this topic, which is, after all, the root of the problems that give rise to the call for mercy killing. In my book I have argued for the primacy of easing pain and suffering, along with supporting and comforting speech, and, more to the point, the need to draw back from some efforts at prolongation of life that prolong or increase only the patient's pain, discomfort, and suffering. Although I am mindful of the dangers and aware of the impossibility of writing explicit rules for ceasing treatment— hence the need for prudence—considerations of the individual's health, activity, and state of mind must enter into decisions of *whether* and *how vigorously* to treat if the decision is indeed to be for the patient's good. Ceasing treatment and allowing death to occur when (and if) it will seem to be quite compatible with the respect that life itself commands for itself. For life is to be revered not only as manifested in physiological powers, but also as these powers are organized in the form of a life, with its beginning, middle, and end. Thus life can be revered not only in its preservation, but also in the manner in which we allow a given life to reach its terminus. For physicians to adhere to efforts at indefinite prolongation not only reduces them to slavish technicians without any intelligible goal, but also degrades and assaults the gravity and solemnity of a life in its close.

Ceasing medical intervention, allowing nature to take its course differs fundamentally from mercy killing. For one thing, death does not necessarily follow the discontinuance of treatment—Karen Ann Quinlan lived more than ten years after the court allowed the "life-sustaining" respirator to be removed. Not the physician, but the underlying fatal illness becomes the true cause of death. More important morally, in ceasing treatment the physician need not *intend* the death of the patient, even when the death follows as a result of his omission. His intention should be to avoid useless and degrading medical *additions* to the already sad end of a life. In contrast, in active, direct mercy killing the physician must, necessarily and indubitably, intend *primarily* that the patient be made dead. And he must knowingly and indubitably cast himself in the role of the agent of death.

Being Humane and Being Human

Yet one may still ask: Is killing the patient, even on request, compatible with respecting the life that is failing or nearing its close? Obviously, the euthanasia movement thinks it is. Yet one of the arguments most often advanced by proponents of mercy killing seems to me rather to prove the reverse. Why, it is argued, do we put animals out of their misery but insist on compelling fellow human beings to suffer to the bitter end? Why, if it is not a contradiction for the veterinarian, does the medical ethic absolutely rule out mercy killing? Is this not simply inhumane?

Perhaps inhumane, but not thereby inhuman. On the contrary, it is precisely because animals are not human that we must treat them (merely) humanely. We put dumb animals to sleep because they do not know that they are dying, because they can make nothing of their misery or mortality, and, therefore, because they cannot live deliberately—i.e., humanly—in the face of their own suffering or dying. They cannot live out a fitting end. Compassion for their weakness and dumbness is our only appropriate emotion, and given our responsibility for their care and well-being, we do the only humane thing we can. But when a conscious human being asks us for death, by that very action he displays the presence of something that precludes our regarding him as a dumb animal. Humanity is owed humanity, not humaneness. Humanity is owed the bolstering of the human, even or especially in its dying moments, in resistance to the temptation to ignore its presence in the sight of suffering.

What humanity needs most in the face of evils is courage, the ability to stand against fear and pain and thoughts of nothingness. The deaths we most admire are those of people who, knowing that they are dying, face the fact frontally and act accordingly: they set their affairs in order, they arrange what could be final meetings with their loved ones, and yet, with strength of soul and a small reservoir of hope, they continue to live and work and love as much as they can for as long as they can. Because such conclusions of life require courage, they call for our encouragement—and for the many small speeches and deeds that shore up the human spirit against despair and defeat.

Many doctors are in fact rather poor at this sort of encouragement. They tend to regard every dying or incurable patient as a failure, as if an earlier diagnosis or a more vigorous intervention might have avoided what is, in truth, an inevitable collapse. The enormous successes of medicine these past

50 years have made both doctors and laymen less prepared than ever to accept the fact of finitude. Doctors behave, not without some reason, as if they have godlike powers to revive the moribund; laymen expect an endless string of medical miracles. It is against this background that terminal illness or incurable disease appears as medical failure, an affront to medical pride. Physicians today are not likely to be agents of encouragement once their technique begins to fail.

It is, of course, partly for these reasons that doctors will be pressed to kill—and many of them will, alas, be willing. Having adopted a largely technical approach to healing, having medicalized so much of the end of life, doctors are being asked—often with thinly veiled anger—to provide a final technical solution for the evil of human finitude and for their own technical failure: if you cannot cure me, kill me. The last gasp of autonomy or cry for dignity is asserted against a medicalization and institutionalization of the end of life that robs the old and the incurable of most of their autonomy and dignity: intubated and electrified, with bizarre mechanical companions, helpless and regimented, once proud and independent people find themselves cast in the roles of passive, obedient, highly disciplined children. People who care for autonomy and dignity should try to reverse this dehumanization of the last stages of life instead of giving dehumanization its final triumph by welcoming the desperate goodbye-to-all-that contained in one final plea for poison.

The present crisis that leads some to press for active euthanasia is really an opportunity to learn the limits of the medicalization of life and death and to recover an appreciation of living with and against mortality. It is an opportunity for physicians to recover an understanding that there remains a residual human wholeness—however precarious—that can be cared for even in the face of incurable and terminal illness. Should doctors cave in, should doctors become technical dispensers of death, they will not only be abandoning their posts, their patients, and their duty to care; they will set the worst sort of example for the community at large—teaching technicism and so-called humaneness where encouragement and humanity are both required and sorely lacking. On the other hand, should physicians hold fast, should they give back to Athena her deadly vial, should medicine recover the latent anthropological knowledge that alone can vindicate its venerable but now threatened practice, should doctors learn that finitude is no disgrace and that human wholeness can be cared for to the very end, medicine may serve not only the good of its patients, but also, by example, the failing moral health of modern times.[8]

For Reflection and Discussion

1. Discuss the author's statement: "A person can choose to be a physician, but he cannot choose what physicianship means." How is this view related to his conviction that the medical profession has its own intrinsic ethic?

2. What ethical systems (schools) in today's culture would disagree with this "intrinsic ethic" approach? Which do you find convincing? How do you make moral decisions, that is, what grounds and directs your own process of deciding what you ought to do?

3. Does the author's description of the patient-physician relationship ring true with your own experience? Also his concerns if euthanasia were legalized—"How soundly would you sleep?" What about his emphasis on nonmutual, intimate exposure?

4. Discuss the distinction between being humane and being human. How would some of the authors who support euthanasia respond to this distinction? How do you? Are Kass's recommendations for dealing with the end of life sufficient? Why/why not?

5. If "doctors must not kill," may others? Or can his argument be expanded to include all people? How?

Notes

1. "It's Over, Debbie," *Journal of the American Medical Association,* 259 (January 8, 1988) 272. See, in response, Willard Gaylin, Leon R. Kass, Edmund D. Pellegrino, Mark Siegler, "'Doctors Must Not Kill,'" *Journal of the American Medical Association* 259 (April 8, 1988) 2139-40.
2. Of course, any physician with *personal* scruples against one or another of these practices may "write" the relevant exclusions into the service contract he offers his customers.
3. Leon R. Kass, M.D., *Toward a More Natural Science: Biology and Human Affairs* (New York: The Free Press, 1985) Paperback, 1988. See Chapters Six to Nine.
4. Yale Kamisar, "Some Non-Religious Views Against Proposed 'Mercy-Killing' Legislation," *Minnesota Law Review* 42 (May, 1958) 969-1042. Reprinted, with a new preface by Professor Kamisar, in "The Slide Toward Mercy-Killing," *Child and Family Reprint Booklet Series* (1987).
5. The inexplicable failure of many physicians to provide the proper—and available— relief of pain is surely part of the reason why some people now insist that physicians (instead) should give them death.
6. This was the title of the recently proposed California voter initiative that barely failed to gather enough signatures to appear on the November 1988 ballot. It will almost certainly be back. [Ed., Proposition 161 (physician-assisted death) on the ballot for 11/3/92.]
7. For a fuller discussion of these prohibitions, both in relation to the Hippocratic Oath and to the meaning of the doctor-patient relationship, see my essays, "Is There a Medical Ethic? The Hippocratic Oath and the Sources of Ethical Medicine," and "Professing Ethically: The Place of Ethics in Defining Medicine," in *Toward a More Natural Science: Biology and Human Affairs* (New York: The Free Press, 1985).
8. This article is dedicated to the memory of my father-in-law, Kalman Apfel, M.D., physician extraordinaire (1907-1988), and my mother-in-law, Polly Apfel (1911-1987), who exemplified even with her last breath the noblest possibilities of the human soul. Earlier versions of this essay were presented as lectures delivered for the Program in Ethics and the Professions, Harvard University, March 16, 1988, and for the Kennedy Institute of Ethics, Georgetown University, May 6, 1988.

8

Doctors Must Not Kill

Willard Gaylin, M.D., Leon R. Kass, M.D., Edmund D. Pellegrino, M.D., Mark Siegler, M.D.

IN THE MIDDLE OF THE NIGHT, A SLEEPY GYNECOLOGY RESI-dent is called to attend a young woman, dying of cancer, whom he has never seen before. Horrified by her severe distress, and proceeding alone without consultation with anyone, he gives her a lethal injection of morphine, clearly intending the death that promptly ensues. The resident submits a first-person account of his killing to the *Journal of the American Medical Association.* Without any editorial comment, *JAMA* publishes the account, withholding the author's name at his request. What in the world is going on?

Before the sophisticated obscure our vision with clouds of arguments and subtle qualifications, we must fix our gaze on the brute facts.

First, on his own admission, the resident appears to have committed a felony: premeditated murder. Direct intentional homicide is a felony in all American jurisdictions, for which the plea of merciful motive is no excuse. That the homicide was clearly intentional is confirmed by the resident's act of unrepentant publication.

Second, law aside, the physician behaved altogether in a scandalously unprofessional and unethical manner. He did not know the patient: he had never seen her before, he did not study her chart, he did not converse with her or her family. He never spoke to *her* physician. He took as an unambiguous command her only words to him, "Let's get this over with": he did not bother finding out what precisely she meant or whether she meant it wholeheartedly. He did not consider alternative ways of bringing her relief or comfort; instead of comfort, he gave her death. This is no humane and thoughtful physician succumbing with fear and trembling to the pressures and well-considered wishes of a patient well known to him, for whom there was truly no other recourse. This is, by his own account, an impulsive yet cold technician, arrogantly masquerading as a knight of compassion and humanity. (Indeed, so cavalier is the report and so cold-blooded the behavior, it strains our credulity to think that the story is true.)

Third, law and professional manner both aside, the resident violated one of the first and most hallowed canons of the medical ethic: doctors must not kill. Generations of physicians and commentators on medical ethics have underscored and held fast to the distinction between ceasing useless treatments (or allowing to die) and active, willful taking of life; at least since the Oath of Hippocrates, Western medicine has regarded the killing of patients, even on request, as a profound violation of the deepest meaning of the medical vocation. As recently as 1986, the Judicial Council of the American Medical Association, in an opinion regarding treatment of dying patients, affirmed the principle that a physician "should not intentionally cause death." Neither legal tolerance nor the best bedside manner can ever make medical killing medically ethical.

The conduct of the physician is inexcusable. But the conduct of the editor of *JAMA* is incomprehensible. By publishing this report, he knowingly publicizes a felony and shields the felon. He deliberately publicizes the grossest medical malfeasance and shields the malefactor from professional scrutiny and judgment, presumably allowing him to continue his practices without possibility of rebuke and remonstrance, not even from the physician whose private patient he privately dispatched.

Why? For what possible purpose central to *JAMA*'s professional mission?

According to newspaper reports, the editor of *JAMA* published the article "to promote discussion" of a timely and controversial topic. But is this a responsible way for the prestigious voice of our venerable profession to address the subject of medical killing? Is it morally responsible to promulgate challenges to our most fundamental moral principles without editorial rebuke or comment, "for the sake of discussion"? Decent folk do not deliberately stir discussion of outrageous practices, like slavery, incest, or killing those in our care.

What is to be done? Regarding the case at hand, the proper course is clear: *JAMA* should voluntarily turn all the information it has regarding the case over to the legal authorities in the pertinent jurisdictions. The physician's name should also be reported to his hospital directors and to his state and county medical societies for their scrutiny and action. The Council on Ethical and Judicial Affairs of the American Medical Association should examine the case, as well as the decision to publish it. Justice requires nothing less.

But much more is at stake than punishing an offender. The very soul of medicine is on trial. For this is not one of those peripheral issues about which pluralism and relativism can be tolerated, about which a value-free stand on the substance can be hedged around with procedural safeguards to ensure informed consent or "sound decision-making." Nor is this an issue, like advertising, fee-splitting, or cooperation with chiropractors, that touches medicine only as a trade. This issue touches medicine at its very moral center; if this moral center collapses, if physicians become killers or are even merely licensed to kill, the profession—and, therewith, each physician—will never again be worthy of trust and respect as healer and comforter and protector of life in all its frailty. For if medicine's power over life may be used equally to heal or to kill, the doctor is no more a moral professional but rather a morally neutered technician.

These are perilous times for our profession. The Hemlock Society and others are in the courts and legislatures trying to legalize killing by physicians at patient request. Such a proposal is almost certainly going to be on the ballot in California next November [Ed., 1988]. High costs of care for the old and incurable already tempt some physicians to regard as "dispensable" some patients who never express the wish to die. In the Netherlands, where the barriers to physician killing are gone, there are now many well-documented cases of such cryptic and "uninvited" killing by doctors.[1]

Now is not the time for promoting neutral discussion. Rather, now is the time for the medical profession to rally in defense of its fundamental moral principles, to repudiate any and all acts of direct and intentional killing by physicians and their agents. We call on the profession and its leadership to obtain the best advice, regarding both theory and practice, about how to defend the profession's moral center and to resist growing pressures both from without and from within. We call on fellow physicians to say that we will not deliberately kill. We must say, also, to each of our fellow physicians that we will not tolerate killing of patients and that we shall take disciplinary action against doctors who kill. And we must say to the broader community that if it insists on tolerating or legalizing active euthanasia, it will have to find nonphysicians to do its killing.

For Reflection and Discussion

1. These physicians take a clear stand on this case (see "It's Over, Debbie"). Discuss their opinion. Do you agree or disagree with them? Why?

2. They also take a strong stand first about the journal's publishing the account and then about what ought to be done now. Do you agree or disagree with the authors on these points?

3. How is the "very soul of medicine" on trial? What is the meaning of pluralism and relativism—and why can they not be tolerated in this situation? Do you support these physicians' views on euthanasia?

4. Reflect on your relationships with your physicians. Are descriptions such as "healer and comforter and protector of life" appropriate for these physicians? Would the relationships change if they had the power to kill?

Notes

1. R. Fenigsen, *Euthanasie: Een Weldaad (Charitable Euthanasia)* (Deventer, the Netherlands, Van Loghum Slaterus, 1987).

9

Euthanasia—A Critique

Peter A. Singer, M.D., F.R.C.P.C.
Mark Siegler, M.D.

A VIGOROUS MEDICAL AND POLITICAL DEBATE HAS BEGUN
again on euthanasia, a practice proscribed 2,500 years ago in
the Hippocratic oath.[1-4] The issue has been publicized recently in three widely divergent settings: a journal article, a
legislative initiative in California, and public policy in the
Netherlands.

The case of "Debbie" shows that euthanasia can be discussed openly in a respected medical journal. "It's Over, Debbie" was an anonymous, first-person account of euthanasia,
published on January 8, 1988, in the *Journal of the American
Medical Association*,[5-8] that stimulated widespread discussion
and elicited spirited replies. Later in 1988, perhaps as a result,
the Council on Ethical and Judicial Affairs of the American
Medical Association reaffirmed its opposition to euthanasia.[9]

In California, a legislative initiative[10,11] has shown that in
the near future euthanasia may be legalized in certain U.S. jurisdictions. A bill proposing a California Humane and Dignified Death Act was an attempt to legalize euthanasia through
the referendum process, which allows California voters to
approve controversial issues directly. Public-opinion polls
reported that up to 70 percent of the electorate favored the initiative, and many commentators flatly predicted that the initiative would succeed. Nevertheless, the signature drive failed,

collecting only 130,000 of the 450,000 required signatures. Attributing the failure to organizational problems, the proponents vowed to introduce the legislation again in California and in other states in 1990.

Experience in the Netherlands has shown that a liberal democratic government can tolerate and defend the practice of euthanasia. Although euthanasia is technically illegal in the Netherlands, in fact it is part of Dutch public policy today.[1,12-16] There is agreement at all levels of the judicial system, including the Supreme Court, that if physicians follow the procedural guidelines issued by a state commission, they will not be prosecuted for performing euthanasia.[16] The Dutch guidelines emphasize five requirements: an explicit, repeated request by the patient that leaves no doubt about the patient's desire to die; very severe mental or physical suffering, with no prospect of relief; an informed, free, and consistent decision by the patient; the lack of other treatment options, those available having been exhausted or refused by the patient; and consultation by the doctor with another medical practitioner (and perhaps also with nurses, pastors, or others).[13] The usual method of performing euthanasia is to induce sleep with a barbiturate, followed by a lethal injection of curare.[1] An estimated 5,000 to 10,000 patients receive euthanasia each year in the Netherlands.[16]

In view of these developments, we urge physicians to consider some reasons for resisting the move toward euthanasia. This article criticizes the main arguments offered by proponents and presents opposing arguments. The case for euthanasia is described in detail elsewhere.[10,17]

Critique of the Case for Euthanasia

In the debate about euthanasia, imprecision of language abounds. For the purposes of this article, euthanasia is defined as the deliberate action by a physician to terminate the life of a patient. The clearest example is the act of lethal injection. We distinguish euthanasia from such other acts as the decision to forego life-sustaining treatment (including the use of ventilators, cardiopulmonary resuscitation, dialysis, or tube feeding—the issue raised in the Cruzan case[18]); the administration of analgesic agents to relieve pain; "assisted suicide," in which the doctor prescribes but does not administer a lethal dose of medication; and "mercy killing" performed by a patient's family or friends. The Dutch guidelines described above and the terms proposed in the California initiative represent two versions of euthanasia.

The case for euthanasia is based on two central claims.[10,17] First, proponents argue that patients whose illnesses cause them unbearable suffering should be permitted to end their distress by having a physician perform euthanasia. Second, proponents assert that the well-recognized right of patients to control their medical treatment includes the right to request and receive euthanasia.

Relief of Suffering

We agree that the relief of pain and suffering is a crucial goal of medicine.[19] We question, however, whether the care of dying patients cannot be improved without resorting to the drastic measure of euthanasia. Most physical pain can be relieved with the appropriate use of analgesic agents.[20] Unfortunately, despite widespread agreement that dying patients must be provided with necessary analgesia,[21] physicians continue to underuse analgesia in the care of dying patients because of concern about depressing respiratory drive or creating addiction. Such situations demand better management of pain, not euthanasia.

Another component of suffering is the frightening prospect of dying shackled to a modern-day Procrustean bed, surrounded by the latest forms of high technology. Proponents of euthanasia often cite horror stories of patients treated against their will. In the past, when modern forms of life-saving technology were new and physicians were just learning how to use them appropriately, such cases occurred often; we have begun to move beyond that era. The law, public policy, and medical ethics now acknowledge the right of patients to refuse life-sustaining medical treatment, and a large number of patients avail themselves of this new policy.[22-24] These days, competent patients may freely exercise their right to choose or refuse life sustaining treatment; to carry out their preferences, they do not require the option of euthanasia.

We acknowledge that some elements of human suffering and mental anguish—not necessarily related to physical pain—cannot be eliminated completely from the dying process. These include the anticipated loss of important human relationships and membership in the human community, the loss of personal independence, the feeling of helplessness, and the raw fear of death. Euthanasia can shorten the duration of these emotional and psychological hardships. It can also eliminate fears about how and when death will occur. Finally, euthanasia returns to the patient a measure of control over the process of dying. These are the benefits of euthanasia, against which its potential harms must be balanced.

Individual Rights

The second argument in favor of euthanasia is based on the rights of the individual. Proponents contend that the right of patients to forego life-sustaining medical treatment should include a right to euthanasia. This would extend the notion of the right to die to embrace the concept that patients have a right to be killed by physicians. But rights are not absolute. They must be balanced against the rights of other people and the values of society. The claim of a right to be killed by a physician must be balanced against the legal, political, and religious prohibitions against killing that have always existed in society generally and in medicine particularly. As the President's Commission for the Study of Ethical Problems in

Medicine and Biomedical and Behavioral Research has observed, "Policies prohibiting direct killing may also conflict with the important value of patient self-determination. . . . The Commission finds this limitation on individual self-determination to be an acceptable cost of securing the general protection of human life afforded by the prohibition of direct killing."[22] We agree. In our view, the public good served by the prohibition of euthanasia outweighs the private interests of the persons requesting it.

The Case Against Euthanasia

The arguments against euthanasia are made from two perspectives: public policy and the ethical norms of medicine.

Euthanasia Is Perilous Public Policy

Proponents of euthanasia use the concept of individual rights to support their claim, but this same concept can be used for the opposite purpose. The argument against euthanasia on grounds of civil rights involves a consideration of the rights not just of those who would want euthanasia themselves but of all citizens. As public policy, euthanasia is unacceptable because of the likelihood, or even the inevitability, of involuntary euthanasia—persons being euthanized without their consent or against their wishes.

There are four ways in which a policy of voluntary euthanasia could lead to involuntary euthanasia. The first is "crypthanasia" (literally, "secret euthanasia").[15] In the Netherlands, for instance, it is alleged that vulnerable patients are euthanized without their consent. Dutch proponents of euthanasia disavow these reports and claim that they are unrelated to the toleration of voluntary euthanasia. We suggest, however, that a political milieu in which voluntary euthanasia is tolerated may also foster involuntary euthanasia and lead to the killing of patients without consent. The second way in which involuntary euthanasia may occur is through "encouraged" euthanasia, whereby chronically ill or dying patients may be pressured to choose euthanasia to spare their families financial or emotional strain.[25] The third way is "surrogate" euthanasia. If voluntary euthanasia were permissible in the United States, the constitutional guarantees of due process, which tend to extend the same rights to incompetent as to competent patients, might permit euthanizing incompetent patients on the basis of "substituted judgment" or nebulous tests of "burdens and benefits." Finally, there is the risk of "discriminatory" euthanasia. Patients belonging to vulnerable groups in American society might be subtly coerced into "requesting" euthanasia. In the United States today, many groups are disempowered, disenfranchised, or otherwise vulnerable: the poor, the elderly, the disabled, members of racial minorities, the physically handicapped, the mentally impaired, alcoholics, drug addicts, and patients with the acquired immunodeficiency syndrome. In a society in which discrimination is common and many citizens do not have access even to basic health care, the legalization of euthanasia would create another powerful tool with which to discriminate against groups whose "consent" is already susceptible to coercion and whose rights are already in jeopardy.

The proponents of euthanasia contend that procedural safeguards, such as the five provisions of the Dutch guidelines noted above, will prevent involuntary euthanasia. They claim further that society permits many dangerous activities if adequate procedural safeguards are provided to reduce risk and protect the public. We agree that safeguards would reduce the risk of involuntary euthanasia, but they would not eliminate it entirely. In the case of euthanasia, safeguards have not been adequately tested and shown to be effective. Even in their presence, we are concerned that patients could be euthanized without their consent or even against their wishes. Even one case of involuntary euthanasia would represent a great harm. In the current era of cost containment, social injustice, and ethical relativism, this risk is one our society should not accept.

Euthanasia Violates the Norms of Medicine

In addition to being perilous as public policy, euthanasia violates three fundamental norms and standards of medicine. First, as noted above, it diverts attention from the real issues in the care of dying patients—among them, improved pain control, better communication between doctors and patients, heightened respect for the patient's right to choose whether to accept life-sustaining treatment, and improved management of the dying process, as in hospice care. The hospice movement has demonstrated that managing pain appropriately and allowing patients control over the use of life-sustaining treatments reduce the need for euthanasia.

Second, euthanasia subverts the social role of the physician as healer. Historically, physicians have scrupulously avoided participating in activities that might taint their healing role, such as capital punishment or torture. Physicians should distance themselves from euthanasia to maintain public confidence and trust in medicine as a healing profession.

Third, euthanasia strikes at the heart of what it means to be a physician.[26] Since the time of Hippocrates, the prohibition against it has been fundamental to the medical profession and has served as a moral absolute for both patients and physicians. This prohibition has freed physicians from a potential conflict of interest between healing and killing and in turn has enabled patients to entrust physicians with their lives. It has enabled physicians to devote themselves singlemindedly to helping patients achieve their own medical goals. This prohibition may even have encouraged medical research and scientific progress, because physicians, with the consent of patients, are motivated to perform risky, innovative procedures that are aggressive and sometimes painful, with a total commitment to benefit the patient.

Conclusions

Pressure to legalize euthanasia will surely increase in an era of spiraling health care costs, but it must be resisted. Euthanasia represents a development that is dangerous for many vulnerable patients and that threatens the moral integrity of the medical profession. Physicians must become more responsive to the concerns of patients that underlie the movement for euthanasia and must provide better pain management, more compassionate terminal care, and more appropriate use of life-sustaining treatments. But physicians need to draw the line at euthanasia. They and their professional associations should defend the integrity of medicine by speaking out against the practice.

Finally, even if euthanasia is legalized in some jurisdictions, physicians should refuse to participate in it, and professional organizations should censure any of their members who perform euthanasia.

For Reflection and Discussion

1. The authors state that "imprecision of language abounds." Give some examples from your own experience—regarding euthanasia and other topics. How does this impact society's discussion of these issues?

2. Is the authors' presentation of the case for euthanasia—elimination of fear, control over the process of dying, right to be killed by a physician—fair and sufficient? Based on your reading and experience, can you add other reasons?

3. Is the authors' presentation of the case against euthanasia—better management of pain, public good and the problem of involuntary euthanasia, fundamental norms and meaning of medicine—fair and convincing? Can you add other reasons?

4. Do you agree with their balancing of benefits and potential harms of euthanasia? Why/why not?

Notes

1. M. Angell, "Euthanasia," *New England Journal of Medicine* 319 (1988) 1348-50.
2. P.A. Singer, "Should Doctors Kill Patients?" *Canadian Medical Association Journal* 138 (1988) 1000-1.
3. T.D. Kinsella, P.A. Singer, M. Siegler, "Legalized Active Euthanasia: an Aesculapian Tragedy," *Bulletin of the American College of Surgeons* 74(12) (1989) 6-9.
4. S.H. Wanzer, D.D. Federman, S.J. Adelstein, et al., "The Physician's Responsibility Toward Hopelessly Ill Patients: A Second Look," *New England Journal of Medicine* 320 (1989) 844-9.
5. "It's over, Debbie," *JAMA* 259 (1988) 272.
6. K.L. Vaux, "Debbie's Dying: Mercy Killing and the Good Death," *JAMA* 259 (1988) 2140-1.
7. W. Gaylin, L.R.. Kass, E.D. Pellegrino, M. Siegler, "Doctors Must Not Kill," *JAMA* 259 (1988) 2139-40.
8. G.D. Lundberg, "'It's over, Debbie' and the Euthanasia Debate," *JAMA* 259 (1988) 2142.
9. The Council on Ethical and Judicial Affairs of the American Medical Association. *Euthanasia*, Report: C (A-88). AMA council report. (Chicago: American Medical Association, 1988:1).
10. R.L. Risley, "A Humane and Dignified Death: A New Law Permitting Physician Aid-in-Dying," (Glendale, CA: Americans Against Human Suffering, 1987).
11. A. Parachini, "Mercy, Murder & Morality: Perspectives on Euthanasia: The California Humane and Dignified Death Initiative," *Hastings Center Report* 19, no. 1 (1989) 10-2.
12. G.E. Pence, "Do Not Go Slowly Into that Dark Night: Mercy Killing in Holland," *American Journal of Medicine* 84 (1988) 139-41.
13. H. Rigter, E. Borst-Eilers, H.J.J. Leenen, "Euthanasia across the North Sea," *BMJ* 297 (1988) 1593-5.
14. H. Rigter, "Mercy, Murder & Morality; Euthanasia in the Netherlands: Distinguishing Facts from Fiction," *Hastings Center Report* 19, no. 1 (1989) 31-2.
15. R. Fenigsen, "Mercy, Murder, & Morality: Perspectives on Euthanasia: A Case Against Dutch Euthanasia," *Hastings Center Report* 19, no. 1 (1989) 22-30.
16. M.A.M. de Wachter, "Active Euthanasia in the Netherlands," *JAMA* 262 (1989) 3316-9.
17. D. Humphry, A. Wickett, *The Right to Die: Understanding Euthanasia* (New York: Harper & Row, 1986).
18. M. Angell, "Prisoners of Technology: The Case of Nancy Cruzan," *New England Journal of Medicine* 322 (1990) 1226-8.
19. E.J. Cassell, "The Nature of Suffering and the Goals of Medicine," *New England Journal of Medicine* 306 (1982) 639-45.
20. K.M. Foley, "The Treatment of Cancer Pain," *New England Journal of Medicine* 313 (1985) 84-95.
21. M. Angell, "The Quality of Mercy," *New England Journal of Medicine* 306 (1982) 98-9.
22. President's Commission for the Study of Ethical Problems in Medicine and Biomedical and Behavioral Research, *Deciding to Forego Life-sustaining Treatment: A Report on the Ethical, Medical, and Legal Issues in Treatment Decisions* (Washington, DC: Government Printing Office, 1983).

23. The Hastings Center, *Guidelines on the Termination of Life-sustaining Treatment and the Care of the Dying: A Report* (Briarcliff Manor, NY: Hastings Center, 1987).
24. E.J. Emanuel, "A Review of the Ethical and Legal Aspects of Terminating Medical Care," *American Journal of Medicine* 84 (1988) 291-301.
25. Y. Kamisar, "Some Non-religious Views Against Proposed 'Mercy-Killing' Legislation," *Minnesota Law Review* 42 (1958) 969-1042.
26. L.R. Kass, "Neither for Love nor Money: Why Doctors Must Not Kill," *Public Interest* 94, Winter (1989) 25-46.

10

Declaration on Euthanasia

*Sacred Congregation
for the Doctrine of the Faith*

THE RIGHTS AND VALUES PERTAINING TO THE HUMAN PER-
son occupy an important place among the questions discussed
today. In this regard, the Second Vatican Ecumenical Council
solemnly reaffirmed the lofty dignity of the human person, and
in a special way his or her right to life. The council therefore
condemned crimes against life "such as any type of murder,
genocide, abortion, euthanasia, or willful suicide" (pastoral
constitution "Gaudium et Spes" no. 27).

More recently, the Sacred Congregation for the Doctrine
of the Faith has reminded all the faithful of Catholic teaching
on procured abortion.[1] The congregation now considers it opportune to set forth the church's teaching on euthanasia.

It is indeed true that, in this sphere of teaching, the recent
popes have explained the principles, and these retain their full
force;[2] but the progress of medical science in recent years has
brought to the fore new aspects of the question of euthanasia,
and these aspects call for further elucidation on the ethical
level.

In modern society, in which even the fundamental values
of human life are often called into question, cultural change ex-
ercises an influence on the way of looking at suffering and
death; moreover, medicine has increased its capacity to cure

and to prolong life in particular circumstances, which sometimes give rise to moral problems.

Thus, people living in this situation experience no little anxiety about the meaning of advanced old age and death. They also begin to wonder whether they have the right to obtain for themselves or their fellowmen an "easy death," which would shorten suffering and which seems to them more in harmony with human dignity.

A number of episcopal conferences have raised questions on this subject with the Sacred Congregation for the Doctrine of the Faith. The congregation, having sought the opinion of experts on the various aspects of euthanasia, now wishes to respond to the bishops' questions with the present declaration in order to help them to give correct teaching to the faithful entrusted to their care, and to offer them elements for reflection that they can present to the civil authorities with regard to this very serious matter.

The considerations set forth in the present document concern in the first place all those who place their faith and hope in Christ, who, through his life, death and resurrection, has given a new meaning to existence and especially to the death of the Christian, as St. Paul says: "If we live, we live to the Lord, and if we die, we die to the Lord" (Romans 14:8; cf. Philippians 1:20).

As for those who profess other religions, many will agree with us that faith in God the creator, provider and lord of life—if they share this belief—confers a lofty dignity upon every human person and guarantees respect for him or her.

It is hoped that this declaration will meet with the approval of many people of good will, who, philosophical or ideological differences notwithstanding, have nevertheless a lively awareness of the rights of the human person. These rights have often in fact been proclaimed in recent years through declarations issued by international conferences;[3] and since it is a question here of fundamental rights inherent in every human person, it is obviously wrong to have recourse to arguments from political pluralism or religious freedom in order to deny the universal value of those rights.

I. The Value of Human Life

Human life is the basis of all goods, and is the necessary source and condition of every human activity and of all society. Most people regard life as something sacred and hold that no one may dispose of it at will; but believers see in life something greater, namely a gift of God's love, which they are called upon to preserve and make fruitful. And it is this latter consideration that gives rise to the following consequences:

1. No one can make an attempt on the life of an innocent person without opposing God's love for that person, without violating a fundamental right, and therefore without committing a crime of the utmost gravity.[4]

2. Everyone has the duty to lead his or her life in accordance with God's plan. That life is entrusted to the individual as a good that must bear fruit already here on earth, but that finds its full perfection only in eternal life.

3. Intentionally causing one's own death, or suicide, is therefore equally as wrong as murder; such an action on the part of a person is to be considered as a rejection of God's sovereignty and loving plan. Furthermore, suicide is also often a refusal of love for self, the denial of the natural instinct to live, a flight from the duties of justice and charity owed to one's neighbor, to various communities or to the whole of society—although, as is generally recognized, at times there are psychological factors present that can diminish responsibility or even completely remove it.

However, one must clearly distinguish suicide from that sacrifice of one's life whereby for a higher cause, such as God's glory, the salvation of souls or the service of one's brethren, a person offers his or her own life or puts it in danger (cf. John 15:14).

II. Euthanasia

In order that the question of euthanasia can be properly dealt with, it is first necessary to define the words used.

Etymologically speaking, in ancient times euthanasia meant an easy death without severe suffering. Today one no longer thinks of this original meaning of the word, but rather of some intervention of medicine whereby the sufferings of sickness or of the final agony are reduced, sometimes also with the danger of suppressing life prematurely. Ultimately, the word euthanasia is used in a more particular sense to mean "mercy killing," for the purpose of putting an end to extreme suffering, or saving abnormal babies, the mentally ill or the incurably sick from the prolongation, perhaps for many years, of a miserable life, which could impose too heavy a burden on their families or on society.

It is therefore necessary to state clearly in what sense the word is used in the present document.

By euthanasia is understood an action or an omission which of itself or by intention causes death, in order that all suffering may in this way be eliminated. Euthanasia's terms of reference, therefore, are to be found in the intention of the will and in the methods used.

It is necessary to state firmly once more that nothing and no one can in any way permit the killing of an innocent human being, whether a fetus or an embryo, an infant or an adult, an old person, or one suffering from an incurable disease, or a person who is dying. Furthermore, no one is permitted to ask for this act of killing, either for himself or herself or for another person entrusted to his or her care, nor can he or she consent to it, either explicitly or implicitly. Nor can any authority legitimately recommend or permit such an action. For it is a question of the violation of the divine, an offense against the dignity of the human person, a crime against life, and an attack on humanity.

It may happen that, by reason of prolonged and barely tolerable pain, for deeply personal or other reasons, people may be led to believe that they can legitimately ask for death or obtain it for others. Although in these cases the guilt of the individual may be reduced or completely absent, nevertheless the error of judgment into which the conscience falls, perhaps in good faith, does not change the nature of this act of killing, which will always be in itself something to be rejected.

The pleas of gravely ill people who sometimes ask for death are not to be understood as implying a true desire for euthanasia; in fact it is almost always a case of an anguished plea for help and love. What a sick person needs, besides medical care, is love, the human and supernatural warmth with which the sick person can and ought to be surrounded by all those close to him or her, parents and children, doctors and nurses.

III. The Meaning of Suffering for Christians and the Use of Painkillers

Death does not always come in drastic circumstances after barely tolerable sufferings. Nor do we have to think only of extreme cases. Numerous testimonies which confirm one another lead one to the conclusion that nature itself has made provision to render more bearable at the moment of death separations that would be terribly painful to a person in full health. Hence it is that a prolonged illness, advanced old age, or a state of loneliness or neglect can bring about psychological conditions that facilitate the acceptance of death.

Nevertheless the fact remains that death, often preceded or accompanied by severe and prolonged suffering, is something which naturally causes people anguish.

Physical suffering is certainly an unavoidable element of the human condition; on the biological level, it constitutes a warning of which no one denies the usefulness; but, since it affects the human psychological makeup, it often exceeds its own biological usefulness and so can become so severe as to cause the desire to remove it at any cost.

According to Christian teaching, however, suffering, especially suffering during the last moments of life, has a special place in God's saving plan; it is, in fact, a sharing in Christ's Passion and a union with the redeeming sacrifice which he offered in obedience to the father's will. Therefore, one must not be surprised if some Christians prefer to moderate their use of painkillers, in order to accept voluntarily at least a part of their sufferings and, thus, associate themselves in a conscious way with the sufferings of Christ crucified. (cf. Matthew 27:34).

Nevertheless, it would be imprudent to impose a heroic way of acting as a general rule. On the contrary, both human and Christian prudence suggest for the majority of sick people the use of medicines capable of alleviating or suppressing pain, even though these may cause as a secondary effect semi-consciousness and reduced lucidity. As for those who are not in a state to express themselves, one can reasonably presume that they wish to take these painkillers, and have them administered according to the doctor's advice.

But the intensive use of painkillers is not without difficulties, because the phenomenon of habituation generally makes it necessary to increase their dosage in order to maintain their efficacy. At this point it is fitting to recall a declaration by Pius XII, which retains its full force; in answer to a group of doctors who had put the question: "Is the suppression of pain and consciousness by the use of narcotics permitted by religion and morality to the doctor and the patient (even at the approach of death and if one foresees that the use of narcotics will shorten life)?

The pope said: "If no other means exist, and if, in the given circumstances, this does not prevent the carrying out of other religious and moral duties: Yes."[5] In this case, of course, death is in no way intended or sought, even if the risk of it is reasonably taken; the intention is simply to relieve pain effectively, using for this purpose painkillers available to medicine.

However, painkillers that cause unconsciousness need special consideration. For a person not only has to be able to satisfy his or her moral duties and family obligations, he or she also has to prepare himself or herself with full consciousness for meeting Christ. Thus Pius XII warns: "It is not right to deprive the dying person of consciousness without a serious reason."[6]

IV. Due Proportion in the Use of Remedies

Today it is very important to protect, at the moment of death, both the dignity of the human person and the Christian concept of life against a technological attitude that threatens to become an abuse. Thus, some people speak of a "right to die," which is an expression that does not mean the right to procure death either by one's own hand or by means of someone else, as one pleases, but rather the right to die peacefully with human and Christian dignity. From this point of view, the use of therapeutic means can sometimes pose problems.

In numerous cases, the complexity of the situation can be such as to cause doubts about the way ethical principles should be applied. In the final analysis, it pertains to the conscience either of the sick person or of the doctors to decide, in the light of moral obligations and of the various aspects of the case.

Everyone has the duty to care for his or her own health or to seek such care from others. Those whose task it is to care for the sick must do so conscientiously and administer the remedies that seem necessary or useful.

However, is it necessary in all circumstances to have recourse to all possible remedies?

In the past, moralists replied that one is never obliged to use "extraordinary" means. This reply, which as a principle still holds good, is perhaps less clear today, by reason of the imprecision of the term and the rapid progress made in the treatment of sickness. Thus, some people prefer to speak of "proportionate" and "disproportionate" means.

In any case, it will be possible to make a correct judgment as to the means by studying the type of treatment to be used, its degree of complexity or risk, its cost and the possibilities of using it, and comparing these elements with the result that can be expected, taking into account the state of the sick person and his or her physical and moral resources.

In order to facilitate the application of these general principles, the following clarifications can be added:

- If there are no other sufficient remedies, it is permitted, with the patient's consent, to have recourse to the means provided by the most advanced medical techniques, even if these means are still at the experimental stage and are not without risk. By accepting them, the patient can even show generosity in the service of humanity.

- It is also permitted, with the patient's consent, to interrupt these means, where the results fall short of expectations. But for such a decision to be made, account will have to be taken of the reasonable wishes of the patient's family, as also of the advice of the doctors who are specially competent in the matter. The latter may in particular judge that the investment in instruments and personnel is disproportionate to the results foreseen; they may also judge that the techniques applied impose on the patient strain or suffering out of proportion with the benefits which he or she may gain from such techniques.

It is also permissible to make do with the normal means that medicine can offer. Therefore one cannot impose on anyone the obligation to have recourse to a technique which is already in use but which carries a risk or is burdensome. Such a refusal is not the equivalent of suicide; on the contrary, it should be considered as an acceptance of the human condition, or a wish to avoid the application of a medical procedure disproportionate to the results that can be expected, or a desire not to impose excessive expense on the family or the community.

• When inevitable death is imminent in spite of the means used, it is permitted in conscience to take the decision to refuse forms of treatment that would only secure a precarious and burdensome prolongation of life, so long as the normal care due to the sick person in similar cases is not interrupted. In such circumstances the doctor has no reason to reproach himself with failing to help the person in danger.

Conclusion

The norms contained in the present declaration are inspired by a profound desire to serve people in accordance with the plan of the creator. Life is a gift of God, and on the other hand death is unavoidable; it is necessary therefore that we, without in any way hastening the hour of death, should be able to accept it with full responsibility and dignity. It is true that death marks the end of out earthly existence, but at the same time it opens the door to immortal life. Therefore all must prepare themselves for this event in the light of human values, and Christians even more so in the light of faith.

As for those who work in the medical profession, they ought to neglect no means of making all their skill available to the sick and the dying; but they should also remember how much more necessary it is to provide them with the comfort of boundless kindness and heartfelt charity. Such service to people is also service to Christ the Lord, who said: "As you did it to one of the least of these my brethren, you did it to me." (Matthew 25:40)

At the audience granted to the undersigned prefect, His Holiness John Paul II approved this declaration, adopted at the ordinary meeting of the Sacred Congregation for the Doctrine of the Faith, and ordered its publication.

Rome, the Sacred Congregation for the Doctrine of the Faith, 5 May 1980.

Franjo Cardinal Seper, Prefect
Jerome Hamer, O.P., Secretary Titular Archbishop of Lorium

For Reflection and Discussion

1. Discuss the foundational meaning and significance of human dignity. What, according to this statement, is the source of this dignity? What are other possible sources? Describe an event in your life in which you experienced the importance of human dignity (whether it was affirmed or denied).

2. What is meant by "God's sovereignty and loving plan"? Can you show what this means in the ordinary events of your life? Do suicide and euthanasia contradict this sovereignty?

3. Discuss the statement's very precise definition of euthanasia. How does this compare and contrast with other definitions presented in this text? Does the statement accept the distinction between active and passive euthanasia?

4. The human family has always faced suffering. How do you "make sense" of suffering? How do you react to the statement's understanding of the role of suffering?

Notes

1. Declaration on Procured Abortion, November 18, 1974. AAS 66 (1974) 730-47.
2. Pius XII, address to those attending the Congress of the International Union of Catholic Women's Leagues, September 11, 1947, AAS 39 (1947) 2483; address to Midwives, October 29, 1951, AAS 43 (1951) 835-54; speech to the Members of the International Office for Documentation, October 19, 1953, AAS 45 (1953) 744-54; address to those taking part in the Ninth Congress of the Italian Anaethesiological Society, February 24, 1957, AAS 49 (1957) 146. Cf. also Paul VI, address to the Members of the United Nations Special Committee on Apartheid, May 22, 1974: AAS 66 (1974) 346; John Paul II, address to the Bishops of the United States of America, October 5, 1979, AAS 71 (1979) 1225.

3. One thinks especially of recommendation 779 (1976) on the rights of the sick and dying, of the Parliamentary Assembly of the Council of Europe at its 25th ordinary session; cf. *Sipeca*, no. 1 (March 1977) 14-15.

4. We leave aside completely the problems of the death penalty and of war, which involve specific considerations that do not concern the present subject.

5. Pius XII, address of February 24, 1957, AAS 49 (1957) 147.

6. *Ibid.*, 145. Cf. address of September 9, 1958, AAS 50 (1958) 694.

11

Initiative 119:
What Is At Stake?

Albert R. Jonsen, Ph.D.

THE STATE OF WASHINGTON IS A PLACE OF SERENE AND MA-
jestic beauty. Wide expanses of water, towering forests, broad
plains, and splendid mountains surround its five million inhabitants in the northwest corner of the "lower forty-eight," as our
Alaska neighbors say. In the midst of this beauty lies peril.
One of its peaks, Mt. St. Helens, erupted ten years ago, dev-
astating the landscape and, only a few weeks ago, geologists
announced that our risk of major earthquake was much greater
than had previously been assumed. The Pacific Plate could
slip beneath our lovely landscape and busy cities and tear our
state to pieces.

The State of Washington is also on the edge of a moral
cataclysm. On November 5, 1991, the citizens of this state will
vote on Initiative 119. This ballot provision would allow a
competent, terminally-ill patient to request of his or her physician "aid-in-dying." These innocuous, indeed benign words,
refer to what its proponents describe as "a new medical service." This service consists in the administration or provision
of a lethal drug to effect the immediate death of the patient.
The benign phrase, "aid-in-dying," like the deceptively beauti-
ful slopes of Mt. St. Helens, conceals the potential for cataclysm. If our citizens approve Initiative 119, we will make our

state the first American jurisdiction, indeed, the first jurisdiction in the world, to legalize active euthanasia.

Some persons, particularly its proponents, would see this not as a moral cataclysm, but as moral enlightenment. At last, they say, a government has listened to the voices of those philosophers who construct rational arguments justifying euthanasia and to the pleas of suffering patients requesting a humane and dignified death. Obviously, I take a different view. I am opposed to Initiative 119 and to any policy permitting active euthanasia. However, I rely on others in this issue to put forth extended arguments against the proposition. I will explain what Initiative 119 is and how Washington came to be the site for this historic public decision.

The State of Washington has a history of reasonable public policy about death and dying. California passed the first Natural Death Act in 1976; Washington was the second state to do so, enacting a bill substantially similar to California's in 1979. Its Natural Death Act permits persons to prepare an advance directive authorizing their physician to withhold or withdraw life-sustaining procedures when death is imminent. The legislature subsequently passed a Durable Power of Attorney for Health Care law and amended the state statutes to include a list of authorized surrogate decision makers for incompetent patients. Several Supreme Court decisions in the early 1980s endorsed the concepts of total brain death, of forgoing life support of the patient in a persistent vegetative state, and of the right to refuse life-sustaining care. Only on the issue of withdrawal of nutrition and hydration has Washington's Supreme Court maintained a conservative position, at least for mentally incapacitated persons. That decision, *In the Matter of Grant*, is a legal chimera: the majority opinion presents an eloquent argument justifying withdrawal, while the majority vote rejects withdrawal, a judicial oddity resulting from one justice who changed her vote on reconsideration after the opinion was published!

The state, then, has a legal climate open to liberal opinions about issues of death and dying. Its judicial and legislative policies reflect the wide agreement among bioethics scholars and national advisory groups on most issues. This climate might be a favorable one in which to introduce the next question: Should the law tolerate active euthanasia? The Hemlock Society has been seeking an opportunity to put this question before the public. California, Oregon, and Washington are among the few states that have an initiative and referendum process; Washington's dates back to 1911. This process is the heritage of the strong populism that reigned in the Western states at the turn of the century. Citizens can circulate a petition for signatures and, if enough are obtained, place their proposition on the ballot at a general election. A legislative system such as this is ideal for the debate and resolution of broad issues of public concern, although it can place severe restraints on policymakers on such issues as taxation and education.

The Hemlock Society chose to bring the issue of the legality of active euthanasia before the people of California in 1988. The Society had its first chapter in Southern California and had developed an organizational base in the state. The group began to gather signatures on an initiative that would exempt from prosecution under the homicide statutes any physician who caused the death of a patient voluntarily requesting such assistance. Because only 137,000 of the requisite 378,000 signatures had been obtained by the deadline, the initiative failed to reach the ballot. Hemlock officials believe that the failure to obtain sufficient signatures was due not so much to opposition to their proposal as to the large number of signatures needed. Given the size of California's electorate, paid signature-gatherers are necessary and Hemlock did not have the funds to organize such an extensive activity. Next, an attempt to mount an initiative in Oregon failed to qualify for signature gathering because of a successful challenge to the ballot title.

Washington was the next target of opportunity. In many ways it was more ideal than California. Its population is much smaller and thus only 150,000 signatures were needed. In addition to the progressive legislation and judicial climate about death, Washington has a liberal ethos. The state has a heritage of progressive, even radical, politics. (In the 1930s, one of Roosevelt's cabinet officers raised a toast to "the forty-seven states and the Soviet of Washington!") Perhaps most significant, the attitude of Washington inhabitants is strongly live-and-let-live (or, in this case, let die). Respect for autonomy and privacy is a cherished social value in the Great Northwest. Also, religious opposition, which could be expected to be strong, would not be as powerful in Washington as elsewhere. A recent survey showed Washington as one of the most unchurched states in the nation: at 14 percent, it is surpassed only by its neighbor Oregon (17 percent) in the number of persons who claim no religious affiliation (the national average is 8 percent). Thus, Hemlock's message would be received with tolerance in such a political and moral climate. Initiative 119 was circulated with the official ballot title, "Shall adult patients who are in a medically terminal condition be permitted to request and receive from a physician aid-in-dying?" The official summary of the initiative read:

> This initiative expands the right of adult persons with terminal conditions to have their wishes, expressed in a written directive, regarding life respected. It amends current law to: Expand the definition of terminal condition to include irreversible coma and persistent vegetative state or condition which will result in death within six months; specify which life-sustaining procedures may be withdrawn; permit adult persons with terminal conditions to request and receive aid-in-dying from their physicians, facilitating death.

The current law which these provisions will expand is the 1979 Natural Death Act. This legislation, following the California model, has been criticized for its overly cautious definition of "terminal condition" and for its omission of explicit reference to nutrition and hydration as life-sustaining measures that may be forgone. The initiative amends the act to correct these deficiencies. This aspect of the initiative has generally been welcomed (although defining persistent vegetative state as a "terminal condition" seems a semantic sleight of hand). The final provision, permitting "aid-in-dying," is the radical departure from prevailing law and medical ethics.

The Natural Death Act would be amended to define "aid-in-dying" as "aid in the form of a medical service, provided in person by a physician, that will end the life of a conscious and mentally competent qualified patient in a dignified, painless, and humane manner, when requested voluntarily by the patient through a written directive . . . at the time the medical service is to be provided." The directive is to be witnessed by two unrelated and impartial persons, and the patient must be declared "in a terminal condition" by two physicians. While it is odd to find this mention of an active, voluntary request in a document otherwise devoted to advance directives to be carried out on behalf of incompetent patients, the idea of amending the extant Natural Death Act was politically and psychologically astute. It makes this radical change seem less radical by incorporating it into accepted legislation. It associates it with useful and broadly approved amendments. It fits the radical provision within the relatively conservative safeguards of the extant act.

These safeguards are, however, only relatively conservative. Like most Natural Death legislation, they require witnesses unrelated by family or financial interest and the written declaration by two physicians that the patient is in a terminal condition, that is, the reasonable medical judgment that death will result within six months. However, there is no mention of presence or evaluation of pain and suffering, no reference to stability of the patient's request over time, no requirement for psychological evaluation (safeguards that are mentioned in reports of the Dutch tolerance of active euthanasia). The patient must simply be diagnosed as being in a terminal condition and make an uncoerced request for aid-in-dying. Most important (and most different from the Dutch practice), Initiative 119 appears to remove the aid-in-dying decision and execution from all legal oversight. The failure of the California initiative, which directly called for exemption from the homicide statutes, was instructive. Initiative 119 buries this feature in the text, mingling it with the previous exemption from criminal liability for physicians who forego life-sustaining treatments in accord with a Directive to Physicians (a very different issue, legally and ethically!).

The public response to the initiative was quite positive. Washington Citizens for Death with Dignity, supported by the Hemlock Society, was able to gather 223,000 signatures. Fortuitously, two cases that received media exposure occurred during the signature gathering: the U.S. Supreme Court's decision in the matter of Nancy Cruzan, which stimulated interest in advance directives, and the "mercy killing" of Janet Adkins by means of Dr. Jack Kevorkian's "suicide machine." Ironically, neither case would fit under the provisions of the amended act, since Ms. Cruzan was incapable of making a voluntary request and Mrs. Adkins was not suffering from a "terminal condition." Still, the exposure in the media must have stimulated interest and spurred the signature campaign. The evidence of public acceptance is not out of line with the results of recent national opinion polls that show slight majorities in favor, when asked clear questions about the permissibility of active euthanasia.

Washington's initiative and referendum law allows an approved initiative to go before the state legislature for action. If the legislature fails to enact the initiative, it is to go on the ballot at the next general election. The legislature decided not to consider the initiative. Astute politicians judged that a ballot measure would split the vote in such a way that Initiative 119 would be assured of victory.

Reaction within the medical community has been hard to interpret. The Washington State Medical Association (WSMA) found itself in a quandary. It had previously endorsed the AMA Ethics and Judicial Council statement that forbids physicians to participate in active euthanasia. At the annual meeting in 1990, the WSMA House of Delegates voted by an overwhelming majority to oppose Initiative 119. However, by March 1991, WSMA members seemed nearly evenly split over the issue. An informal poll of 2,000 members (50 percent responding) indicated a shift in attitude: 49 percent favored WSMA support of Initiative 119, while 51 percent opposed it. The same poll, however, showed that only 28 percent of respondents thought that it should be legal for a physician to give a lethal injection to knowingly hasten death, and 30 percent stated that they would personally be willing to aid in a patient's death. In April, the WSMA board of trustees, without rescinding the earlier House of Delegates vote, decided not to recognize officially the private group, Washington Physicians Against 119, which was formed to mount a campaign against passage of the initiative. The WSMA spokesperson stated that since the membership was divided, "there were other ways to oppose it without getting directly involved." The Washington State Hospital Association takes an opposed position and, while it will not actively campaign, will assist its member institutions to do so. The Washington State Nurses Association at first opposed the initiative and then, after intense lobbying, withdrew its statement of opposition in favor of "no position."

As of this writing [August, 1991], opposition efforts have been modest. Most media coverage has tended to present the initiative in a favorable light, since the appealing stories relate tragic instances of terminal care. It appears to many observers that the public continues to confuse the problem of foregoing life-support with the problem of active euthanasia. The ambiguity of the phrase "aid-in-dying" contributes to that confusion. Most of the anecdotes tell of overuse of life-sustaining technologies rather than of unrelieved pain and suffering. An informal and unpublished survey taken by some opponents suggests that public approval of Initiative 119 diminishes somewhat when people are informed of the difference and when terms such as lethal injection are used rather than aid-in-dying. Still, a recent poll showed that if the vote were held today, 119 would pass. Whether opposition can effect a change in public understanding and sympathy between now and November remains to be seen.

This article began with the dire prediction of a moral cataclysm. This may seem an extreme judgment. Yet, to become the first jurisdiction in the world to authorize by formal legal enactment active euthanasia has, in my view, cataclysmic implications. The term literally means a deluge. There will be a flood of persons seeking aid-in-dying, coming from all over the United States and Canada, since only in Washington will their desire to end their lives be honored without fear of prosecution. Hospitals will have to decide not only what stance they will take, but how to inform patients of their position (in accord with the new patient self-determination provisions of Medicare) and even how the new law will affect their admissions and credentialing policies. Physicians will have to form their consciences and, if they choose to provide aid-in-dying, learn how to do it (as a new "medical service" it will, like all others, require standards and training: it is not so easy to effect a "dignified and humane" death). Professional groups will be faced with the task of establishing appropriate self-discipline and surveillance, since, like other medical services, aid-in-dying falls within professional self-regulation. Third-party payers will have to decide whether aid-in-dying is a covered and reimbursable medical service. Legal authorities, since they seem to have no jurisdiction, will have to determine how they deal with suspicious cases and allegations of abuse. Above all—and this is the properly "moral" aspect of the cataclysm—all persons will be presented with the opportunity to relieve themselves and their families and the society of the burdens of their own final illnesses. This is not, I think, an unambiguous opportunity: its implications go far beyond the beneficent promotion of autonomy and the relief of pain and suffering. The considerations, private and public, that must surround it will constitute a social order that, as the dictionary defines cataclysm, sweeps away the old order of things.

For Reflection and Discussion

1. Clarify what is meant by a Natural Death Act and by Durable Power of Attorney for Health Care. How are these related to euthanasia and Initiative 119?

2. Discuss the social and political context of Washington. How is this related to euthanasia? What is the context of your state?

3. According to Jonsen, several crucial and controversial issues are buried in the text of Initiative 119. What are they? Does this "burying" raise questions about the whole process of legalizing euthanasia? About the public's ability to distinguish carefully and to be properly informed?

4. Do you agree or disagree with Jonsen's judgment that Initiative 119 is a radical change? A moral cataclysm? Why?

12

Euthanasia:
Consider the Dutch

Carlos F. Gomez, M.D.

HOW OUGHT WE DIE? SHOULD WE DECIDE WHEN AND HOW
to die? Should we seek death before it finds us, even as a
release from our pains, physical and otherwise? Should physicians be the agents who help us commit suicide?

What was once a small, if insistent, chorus of voices lobbying for legalization of euthanasia has grown in both number
and volume. It is a chorus of voices that has newly found le-
gitimacy, and has captured the attention of a serious audience
in medical circles. This reawakened interest in euthanasia has
also generated political activity, the most prominent of which is
Initiative 119, which the voters of Washington state will face
this November [1991]. The referendum, if passed, would in essence overturn existing laws that prohibit physicians from intentionally killing patients.

The focus of concern in this debate over the permissibility
of euthanasia has been those patients afflicted with a terminal
disease who are dying a slow, disfiguring death. Exhausted
from their struggle, dispirited over their prospects, and facing
weeks or months of pain, these patients, it is argued, should be
offered something that does no more than hasten the inevitable.
If they are competent to make decisions—and if they are so in-
clined—these patients should be allowed to seek assistance

with suicide. More specifically, physicians should be permitted (in the words of the Washington Initiative) to "render a medical service" to consenting patients, namely, the proffering of drugs with the sole intent of killing.

Those who make this argument in favor of euthanasia—especially those now engaged in crafting new legislation in Washington state and elsewhere—proceed from two premises, neither of which is easily refuted. The first is that to end a patient's suffering through euthanasia is a humane and charitable enterprise, that it fits well (or should fit well) with the traditionally accepted role of physician as alleviator of pain. When all else fails—when medicine's curatives and analgesics neither heal nor palliate—the physician should be able to end a consenting patient's suffering by killing the patient. The second premise, which complements the first, exalts the widely accepted principle of autonomy and suggests that freely consenting individuals—physicians and patients—should be relatively unfettered in this matter. If a patient so chooses to end his or her life, and if a physician is a willing participant, then euthanasia is permissible. This argument from autonomy finds bold expression in the words of H. Tristram Englehardt ("Death by Free Choice: Variations on an Antique Theme," in *Suicide and Euthanasia*, edited by Baruch Brody, Kluwer Academic Publishers, 1989). An apologist for the practice, Englehardt suggests that:

> . . . against any claims regarding the sanctity of life, counterclaims can be advanced regarding the sanctity of free choice. Another way of putting this is that killing cannot be shown to be a *malum in se* . . . What is wrong with murder is taking another person's life without permission. *Consent cures. The competent suicide consents* [emphasis added].

Laws, taboos, and professional canons of conduct that impinge on this freedom, that prohibit what is seen as a charitable act, should be modified or repealed. Moreover, so the argument goes, well-crafted legislation in this area has the added advantage of regulating a practice that occurs with greater frequency and regularity than we care to admit.

I am skeptical of these arguments (even in their most elegant form), and in particular, I am opposed to the end that they serve. There is a suasive power in these images of patients disfigured physically and emotionally by pain and illness, yet I am unconvinced that the proper response—either from the profession of medicine or from society as a whole—should be to assist in suicide. My objections have several sources. Some derive from a basic disagreement with apologists for physician-assisted suicide over what constitutes a fitting role for physicians in society, and what part physicians may and may not play in their patients' lives. Other objections follow from a profound mistrust that what is portrayed as an act of charity is, in fact, beneficent and good: to acquiesce in a demand, however sincere, is not necessarily the same as to act lovingly.

Were I to develop these objections more fully, this would be a rather different article, focusing on matters more philosophical and theological. I leave that important task to my other colleagues writing in this issue of *Commonweal*, and instead concentrate here on more specific worries: What would this newly codified practice of euthanasia look like? Will it be, as its defenders insist, an exercise of last resort, used only under the most rigidly controlled and tightly circumscribed of circumstances? What kinds of patients will ask for euthanasia, and how will we evaluate their requests? Finally, and most importantly, how will we regulate this practice? How will we assure ourselves that the weak, the demented, the vulnerable, the stigmatized—those incapable of consent or dissent—will not become the unwilling objects of such a practice?

It is this latter concern which makes me most uneasy, and even if I were won over by other arguments, prudence would still bid me to oppose giving public sanction to the practice. The vulnerable among us are already more exposed than the rest to injustice in various forms; some forms of injustice are more onerous and dangerous than others. No injustice, I would contend, would be greater than being put to death, innocent of crime and unable to articulate one's interests. It is the possibility—or, in my estimation, the likelihood—of such injustice occurring that most hardens my resistance to calls for giving public sanction to euthanasia.

Those who are now proposing the decriminalization of euthanasia, however, argue that it is a practice that can, and should, be well controlled. To argue as I do, it is said, is to deny dying patients a needed and welcome option because of misplaced and unfounded fears. There are certainly dangers here, the argument continues, but a mature and democratic society should be willing and able to construct a public policy that enhances the autonomy of these dying patients, while protecting the rights of others. And that, say the proponents of Initiative 119, is precisely what the proposed law in Washington would do.

Of late, it has been at this point in the argument that proponents of euthanasia have pointed to the Netherlands as a model for this sort of practice. Some segments of the Dutch medical profession have practiced euthanasia, more or less openly, for almost two decades. Proponents of euthanasia in the United States look to the Netherlands as evidence that this practice can be well managed, and that it can be restricted to only those patients who are competent to make such decisions. The experience of the Dutch—who form a humane, tolerant, democratic society—should give at least *some* assurance that this practice does not necessarily degenerate into indiscriminate killing.

The comparison to the Dutch in this matter is an apt one in many ways. The reasoning of those in the United States who defend the permissibility of euthanasia on the grounds that patients should be able to choose the manner and time of their death, for example, is almost perfectly realized in the Dutch acceptance of euthanasia. The Dutch give such weight to the principle of patient autonomy, for instance, that political and legal institutions—such as the courts—have found other competing interests insufficient to override a request for euthanasia. Thus, claims that euthanasia lies outside the ethic of medical practice, or that it creates unjustifiable dangers for vulnerable patients, have been almost completely subordinated to what apologists for the practice cast as the right of patients to seek their end through physician-assisted suicide.

There is, moreover, a well-established sentiment in the Netherlands that parallels another argument of those in this country who would decriminalize euthanasia: that there is no distinction between withdrawing life-sustaining medical intervention during the agonal stages of a patient's illness and killing the patient outright. Thus, the Dutch have dispensed with the terms "active" and "passive" euthanasia, and use the term "euthanasia" simply and exclusively to denote the physician's intentional administration of a lethal drug at the express request of the patient.

The notion that the practice of euthanasia is one which the medical profession can safely incorporate into accepted standards of care, furthermore, receives support from organized medicine in the Netherlands. The K.N.M.G. (the Royal Dutch Society for the Promotion of Medicine) has advanced euthanasia as a permissible medical practice. The K.N.M.G. has not only drawn up guidelines for acceptable use of euthanasia, it has actively pursued legalization of the practice through the legislative and judicial branches of Dutch government. The K.N.M.G. was instrumental, for example, in lending support early on in the euthanasia movement by intervening on behalf of physicians accused of homicide for practicing euthanasia, and by testifying before government commissions on the desirability of the practice from a medical standpoint.

Thus, proponents of euthanasia in the U.S. are, in one sense, correct in drawing parallels between the aims of their movement and the experience of the Dutch with euthanasia. There is a sort of rough truth to the analogy, and defenders of the practice in this country can rightly point to public opinion surveys in the Netherlands that validate the overwhelming endorsement euthanasia receives from at least two-thirds of the lay public, and perhaps an even higher percentage of the medical profession. They can, moreover, point to repeated assurances from officials in both the government and in private professional organizations that the practice is not being abused. It is argued that the Dutch experiment with euthanasia, which is now several years old, demonstrates that the practice is essentially benign, or at the very least, that it has not degenerated into indiscriminate killing.

My own reading of the situation in the Netherlands, however, is more disturbing, and illuminates a side to this practice that rarely finds its way into public debate. I base my opinions on fieldwork I conducted there in 1989, which involved documenting case histories of euthanasia gathered from those most familiar with the practice: Dutch physicians themselves. The reality of euthanasia in the Netherlands is, I believe, miscast and misunderstood in this country. Were it better appreciated, it would, I believe, give pause to those now seeking public sanction for physician-assisted suicide in this country.

To begin with, euthanasia is still technically illegal in the Netherlands. Through a series of complicated landmark cases which began in 1973, however, the Dutch have created a *de facto* opening to the practice of euthanasia, which rests on the notion that physicians will report their acts of euthanasia to public prosecutors. As the practice now stands, tolerance of euthanasia presupposes that the killing of patients by their physicians will receive some sort of airing, that is, that physicians who practice euthanasia will have to give a public accounting of their actions. The intentional killing of a patient is formally a crime, and in reporting such a case to the district prosecutor (as mandated by court-established guidelines), physicians must claim not *innocence*, but mitigating circumstances—that they acted, in the words of the K.N.M.G., with their "backs against the wall." Thus, regulation of physician-assisted suicide, to the extent that euthanasia is regulated at all in the Netherlands, rests on the assumption that physicians will incriminate themselves in what is essentially an act of homicide.

It stretches the imagination, however, to believe that a stipulation of this sort provides any sort of regulatory force. Most acts of euthanasia in the Netherlands go unreported and uninvestigated by public authorities. What is more, this is widely known to be the case. There is wide agreement among both defenders and critics of the practice that the nearly two hundred cases of euthanasia reported in 1987 to the Ministry of Justice, for example, represent but a tiny fraction of the actual number of cases. In my own small sample of clinical histories, public prosecutors were notified less than 15 percent of the time. Thus, those in this country who look to the Netherlands for evidence of a well-regulated system of physician-assisted suicide are blithely accepting the assurances of Dutch apologists for the practice, who themselves would be hard-pressed to provide evidence of any sort of formal regulatory oversight.

Nevertheless, those in this country who defend the current euthanasia initiative counter that the Washington state proposal *is codified*, that unlike the Dutch situation, euthanasia in this country would have the added benefit of formal legal sanction. What is implied here is that formal rules, unlike the *de facto* legal situation in the Netherlands, somehow have more regulatory muscle to them. Yet one should note that the Washington proposition is *very* like the current Dutch arrangement. There is, in fact, no regulatory oversight in Initiative 119. Like the Dutch situation, the Washington proposal gives permission to physicians to perform what was heretofore an illegal act, stipulates punishment should physicians exceed the boundaries of permissible euthanasia, yet does not provide any mechanism of oversight. Like their counterparts in the Netherlands, the citizens of Washington would be subject to a law that is not *constraining*, but *expansive*. Euthanasia would be one more among the options available in a physician's armamentarium.

Some might argue here that the Washington proposal does nothing more than give physicians the same latitude they have with other therapies. But there is a slightly deceptive twist to the Washington proposal. A careful reading of the bill reveals that, remarkably enough, in a case of euthanasia, one could not, under the proposed law, impute that the physician's actions were the proximate cause of death. One suspects that this clause was inserted to avoid *any* possibility of criminal proceeding against a physician who followed the guidelines of Initiative 119. What it in effect does, however, is place the actions of a euthanist in a sort of regulatory limbo. It makes it difficult (if not impossible) to discern which deaths in a given time period were due to euthanasia. If "respiratory arrest"— and not the massive overdose of narcotics that led to the respiratory arrest—is the official cause of death in an instance of euthanasia, the most basic of epidemiologic studies would be almost impossible to undertake. Cases of euthanasia would blend imperceptibly into the larger background of deaths resulting from natural causes. Unlike *other* iatrogenic deaths— poorly tied surgical knots, inadequate or inappropriately administered medicines—euthanasia would escape the sort of rigorous analysis to which the medical profession routinely subjects, for example, its uncomplicated appendectomies.

The significance of this point is not to be minimized, and here again, the example of the Dutch is instructive. If euthanasia is to become, as its defenders suggest, an option of last resort, then a sense of the *numbers* of patients and *types* of patients being killed by their physicians is important. Yet in Holland, this most basic of information is impossible to ascertain with any assurance of accuracy, precisely because physicians misrepresent themselves on the death certificates. Moreover, absent this sort of essential information, more complicated epidemiologic information becomes a matter of guesswork and speculation.

Proponents of euthanasia here and in the Netherlands use this inaccuracy to their advantage in at least two ways. First, the numbers of patients killed by euthanasia each year are—at least to my mind—consistently underrepresented, because they are based not on mortality statistics but on estimates from surveys. In various articles and forums, for example, Dutch apologists for the practice suggest that euthanasia accounts for, at most, 2 to 3 percent of all deaths in the Netherlands. In a country with a published mortality rate of 120,000, this would mean that anywhere from 2,400 to 3,600 people die in the Netherlands from euthanasia each year. This number is used by defenders of the practice—both here and abroad—to demonstrate that euthanasia would be little more than a statistical blip essentially undetectable—on a country's already established mortality rate. But to give the Dutch estimates of the prevalence of euthanasia some perspective, one should note that if this rate of euthanasia were to take hold in the United States (with an annual mortality rate of approximately 2 million deaths per year), a "small" number of deaths from euthanasia would represent 40,000 to 60,000 people killed each year by their physicians.

Secondly, it is important to keep these numbers in mind even if they are, as I suggest, underestimates—because apologists for the practice suggest that not only are the numbers of people who die, or would die, from euthanasia small, evidence of abuse of the practice is even smaller. That is to say, most of this "small" number of people killed by euthanasia ardently requested to be put to death, were of sound mind, had no other options available, and so on. And to be fair, in my own sample of cases of euthanasia from the Netherlands, most cases did fit the criteria established by the courts and the Dutch medical profession. Yet there were enough cases—4 out of 26, to be exact—in which it was clear that the patient was incapable of giving consent, or in which it was doubtful that consent could have been obtained properly. In none of these cases, by the way, was the public prosecutor notified.

This raises, finally, the question of how well this practice can genuinely be regulated, and what this society would accept as a tolerable degree of assurance that its most vulnerable people—the weak, the unconscious, the demented, the socially stigmatized and marginalized—would be well protected from an unwanted death. If one were to assume that the accepted prevalence rates of euthanasia in the Netherlands would take hold in the U.S., then how many of the projected 40,000 to 60,000 deaths from euthanasia per year would we be willing to accept as "mistakes"? Even a relatively small percentage—say 1 percent—would mean that 400 to 600 people would die, innocent and unwilling, at the hands of physicians. And even that number, I suggest, would underestimate the proportions of the crime.

Those who now face the choice of the legalization of euthanasia in the State of Washington should, I submit, look at the issue with greater care. Moreover, if they use the Netherlands as a model, they might do well to take a second look, and see if the experience of the Dutch might better serve as a cautionary tale. To construct this matter of euthanasia as merely a question of patient autonomy is, I believe, to give short shrift to those who cannot be truly autonomous. The fact that these people are voiceless—that they do not vote, do not write or read articles, cannot advance their own interests—makes them particularly worthy of our concern. The practice of euthanasia—at least as currently envisaged for the State of Washington—would place these patients at intolerable risk. And if, as I have suggested, the Dutch—with their generous social services and universal health-care coverage—have a difficult time controlling the practice, it takes little imagination to see what might easily happen here, with a medical system groaning under the strain of too many demands on too few resources.

Those who would suggest that I am an alarmist—that I am raising the specter of "mercy-killing," with all its ugly and painful historical baggage—should stop to consider the *current* condition of vulnerable patients in this country. One needs only to walk some afternoon through the back wards of the larger municipal hospitals in this country to get an idea of how tenuous these patients' existence already is. To suggest that euthanasia would be anything but an unjustifiable danger to these patients is to close one's eyes to reality. The cries of those who die in pain and despair, amid the studied indifference of professionals whose duty it is to attend to their needs, should be heard. That their cries are gaining in intensity—that some segments of society feel that they should have the option of being helped in their suicide—stands as a reproach to us. What I ask, however, is that those desperate cries for release from pain be balanced against the needs of the voiceless, who even in their silence, still have a right to live.

For Reflection and Discussion

1. Discuss the two premises that ground the argument in favor of euthanasia. How do these fit with your experience? Do you agree or disagree with the objections raised by Gomez?

2. Why is there so much concern about the regulation of legalized euthanasia? How do the proponents of Initiative 119 respond to these concerns?

3. In what ways does the Dutch experience support the proponents of euthanasia in the United States?

4. What aspects of the Dutch experience lead Gomez to his stance of opposition? Do you have any direct experience of those he describes as "vulnerable patients"? How has this influenced you?

13

"Aid-In-Dying": The Social Dimensions

Daniel Callahan, Ph.D.

THE FEAR OF DYING IS POWERFUL. EVEN MORE POWERFUL sometimes is the fear of not dying, of being forced to endure destructive pain, or to live out a life of unrelieved, pointless suffering. The movement to legalize euthanasia and assisted suicide is a strong and, seemingly, historically inevitable response to that fear. It draws part of its strength from the failure of modern medicine to reassure us that it can manage our dying with dignity and comfort. It draws another part from the desire to be masters of our fate. Why must we endure that which need not be endured? If medicine cannot always bring us the kind of death we might like through its technical skills, why can it not use them to give us a quick and merciful release? Why can we not have "aid-in-dying," as Washington state's Initiative 119 phrases it?

Yet perhaps the most compelling attraction is that euthanasia appears as simply one more logical, long overdue extension of a right long recognized in this country. Exactly a century ago, in the 1891 *Union Pacific v. Botsford* case, the Supreme Court held that "No right is more sacred, or is more carefully guarded, by the common law, than the right of the individual to the possession and control of his own person." That right has been reaffirmed time and again, and especially underscored in those rulings—most recently the *Cruzan* case—that declare our right to terminate medical treatment and thus to die.

But if it should happen to be impossible for us to so easily bring about our own death, would it not be reasonable to ask someone else, specifically a doctor, to help us to die? Would it not, moreover, be an act of mercy for a doctor to give us that kind of a release? Is not the relief of suffering a high moral good?

To say "no" in response to questions of that kind seems both repressive and cruel. They invoke our cherished political values of liberty and self-determination. They draw upon our deep and long-standing moral commitment to the relief of suffering. They bespeak our ancient efforts to triumph over death, to find a way to bring it to heel.

Nonetheless, we should as a society say "no," and decisively so, to euthanasia and assisted suicide. Initiative 119 should be defeated. If a death marked by pain or suffering is a nasty death, a natural biological evil of a supreme kind, euthanasia and assisted suicide are wrong and harmful responses to that evil. To directly kill another person in the name of mercy (as I will define "euthanasia" here), or to assist another to commit suicide (which seems to me logically little different from euthanasia) would add to a society already burdened with man-made evils still another.

Euthanasia is mistakenly understood as only a personal matter of self-determination, the control of our own bodies, just a small step beyond the removal of legal prohibitions against suicide. Unlike suicide, euthanasia should be understood as of its nature a social act. It is social because, by definition, it requires the assistance of someone else, as the expression "aid-in-dying" itself makes clear.

Legalization would also provide an important social sanction for euthanasia, affecting many aspects of our society beyond the immediate relief of suffering individuals. The implications of that sanction are profound. It would change the traditional role of the physician. It would require the regulation and oversight of government. It would add to the acceptable range of permissible killing in our society still another occasion for one person to take the life of another.

We might decide that we are as a people prepared to live with those implications. But we should not deceive ourselves into thinking of euthanasia or assisted suicide as merely personal acts, just a slight extension of the already-established right to control our bodies and to have medical treatment terminated. It is a radical move into an entirely different realm of morality: that of the killing of one person by another.

All civilized societies have developed laws to reduce the occasions on which one person is allowed to kill another person. All have resisted the notion that private agreements can be reached allowing one person to take the life of another to serve the interests of one or both parties. Traditionally, only three circumstances have been acceptable for the taking of life: killing in self-defense or to protect another life, killing in the course of a just war, and, in the case of capital punishment, killing by agents of the state. Killing in both war and capital punishment has been opposed by some, and most successfully in the case of capital punishment, now banned in many countries, particularly those of Western Europe.

Apart from those long-standing debates, what is most notable about the historically licit conditions of killing is: (1) the requirement that killing is permissible only when relatively objective standards have been met (in war or self-defense, a genuine threat to life or vital goods, and the absence of an alternative means of meeting those threats), and (2) when the public good is thereby served. (Even in self-defense, the permission to kill has some element of fostering a sense of public security in the face of personal threats.)

The proposal for "aid-in-dying" is nothing less than a proposal to add a new category of acceptable killing to those already socially accepted. To do so would be to reverse the long-developing trend to limit the occasions of legally sanctioned killing (most notable in the campaigns to abolish capital punishment and to limit access to firearms). Civilized societies have slowly come to understand how virtually impossible it is to control even legally sanctioned killing. It seems of its nature to invite abuse. Most notably, the proposal would reinstate private killings. By a "private" killing, I mean one in which the agreement of one person to kill another is ratified in private by the persons themselves, not by public authorities (even if it were made legal and safeguards were put into effect). Do we want to give one person the right to kill another for the sake of the relief of pain and suffering? That is the question before us.

The law does not now allow, in the United States or elsewhere, the right of one person to kill another even if the latter requests, or consents, that it be done. All civilized societies have also outlawed private killings, either in the name of honor (dueling, for instance), or to right private wrongs (to revenge adulterous relationships, for instance).

Yet if we generally accept in our society a right to control our own life and body, why has the extension of that right to private killing been denied? The most obvious reason is a reluctance to give one person absolute and irrevocable power over the life of another, whether there is consent or not. That prohibition is a way of saying that the social stakes in the legitimization of killing are extraordinarily high. It is to recognize that a society should—for the mutual protection of all—be exceedingly parsimonious about conferring a right to kill on anyone, for whatever reason.

John Stuart Mill, in his classic essay *On Liberty*, noted that civilized societies do not grant individuals a legal right to sell themselves into slavery, even though that denial is a limitation on self-determination. "The principle of freedom," he wrote, "cannot require that he should be free not to be free. It is not freedom to be allowed to alienate his freedom."

Yet it is not just the ceding of freedom that is problematic. The absolute power that is put into the hands of another, I would add—the right to be a slaveholder—is not compatible with respect for our human dignity. Both the slaveholder and the enslaved are corrupted by the relationship, even if both have the good of the other as their motive. The one gives up too much, and the other has too much given him.

A similar consideration applies in the case of killings authorized in the name of mercy: they give one person an absolute power over another. Our right to self-determination can be likened, as Joel Feinberg has put it, to an absolute sovereignty (*Notre Dame Law Review*, February 1983). Our life is our own, not someone else's: "There is no such thing as 'trivial interference' with personal sovereignty; nor is it simply another value to be weighed in cost-benefit comparison. In this respect, if not others, a trivial interference with sovereignty is like a minor invasion of virginity: the logic of each concept is such that a value is respected in its entirety or not at all."

Understood one way, this is exactly the kind of argument that might conventionally be taken to justify euthanasia: my life is my own, to do with as I please. I draw exactly the opposite conclusion (though Feinberg may not). We cannot, I believe, transfer our sovereignty to another without contradicting it. A sovereignty that can legally and morally be given away is fragile and contingent—not sovereignty at all. To allow another person to kill us is the most radical relinquishment of sovereignty imaginable, not just one more way of exercising it. Our life belongs no longer to us, but to the person into whose power we give it. No person should have that kind of power over another, freely gained or not. No defender of civil liberties and the right of self-determination should want to see that possibility made available.

Does it not make a difference that the absolute power is given, not to subjugate another (as in slavery), but as an act of mercy, to bring relief from suffering? This might matter but for one crucial consideration. The suffering of the person to be killed is subjective, unmeasurable by and intangible to an outside observer. However real and intense to the person himself or herself, it cannot be gauged from the outside by any objective standard. We know that pain and suffering can vary enormously from one person to another, even those with identical medical conditions. To legalize euthanasia would thus be to authorize one person to kill another based on indeterminable, variable, and subjective expressions of suffering. I can think of no other area of medical practice where equally drastic, irreversible actions are taken on the basis of unmeasurable symptoms. There is no way for the doctor to distinguish between the reasonableness of one person who suffers greatly, but wants to continue living, and that of another person with similar suffering who wants to be dead. It is not the suffering as such that makes the difference, I believe, but the attitude taken toward it. In saying this, I do not deny the reality of suffering. I am only underscoring how inaccessible the intensity of suffering can be to the external observer, and also, how it must express the meaning given to it, not merely its brute psychological intensity.

We must, then, determine whether, with that inaccessibility in mind, it would be wise to sanction the absolute power of one individual to terminate the life of another. It is not sufficient to say that, in the case of some dying patients, they cannot otherwise exercise their own right to end their suffering (assuming suicide not to be possible), and that, therefore, they may, because they must, give over that right to another. The difference is that, by giving one person the right to kill another, we are creating a new social institution—private killing to relieve private suffering—and an institution that will rest upon the most insecure foundation, the transfer of our sovereign right of self-determination to another.

There is another problem. If the person who is to kill is to do so in a responsible fashion, then he or she must have some independent standards for determining when to honor such requests. This becomes all the more important when it is argued, as it sometimes is, that a doctor has not just a right to respond to a request for euthanasia but that, in the name of a duty to relieve suffering, there can be a positive obligation to do so.

We come here to a striking pitfall of the common argument for euthanasia and assisted suicide. Once the key premises of that argument are accepted, there will remain no logical way in the future to: (1) deny euthanasia to anyone who requests it for whatever reason, terminal illness or not; or (2) deny it to the suffering incompetent, even if they do not request it. We can erect legal safeguards and specify required procedures to keep that from happening. But over time they will provide poor protection if the logic of the moral premises upon which they are based are fatally flawed.

Where are the flaws here? Recall that there are two classical arguments in favor of euthanasia and assisted suicide: our right of self-determination, and our claim upon the mercy of others, especially doctors, to relieve our suffering if they can do so. These two arguments are typically spliced together and presented as a single contention. Yet, if they are considered independently—and there is no inherent reason why they must be linked—they display serious problems. Consider, first, the argument for our right of self-determination. It is said that a competent, adult person should have a right to euthanasia for the relief of suffering. But why must the person be suffering? Does not that stipulation already compromise the right of self-determination? How can self-determination have any limits? Why are not the person's desires or motives, whatever they may be, sufficient? How can we justify this arbitrary limitation of self-determination? The standard arguments for euthanasia offer no answers to those questions.

Consider next the person who is suffering but not competent, who is perhaps demented or mentally retarded. The standard argument (and the proposed Washington state law) would deny euthanasia to that person. But why? If a person is suffering but not competent, then it would seem grossly unfair to deny relief simply because that person lacks competence. Are the incompetent less entitled to relief from suffering than the competent? Will it only be affluent middle-class people, mentally fit and able, who can qualify? Will those who are incompetent but suffering be denied that which those who are intellectually and emotionally better off can have? Would that be fair? Do they suffer less for being incompetent? The standard argument about our duty to relieve suffering offers no response to those questions either.

Is it, however, fair to euthanasia advocates to do what I have done, to separate, and treat individually, the two customary arguments in favor of a legal right to euthanasia? The implicit reason for so joining them is no doubt the desire to avoid abuse. By requiring a showing of suffering and terminal illness, the aim is to exclude perfectly healthy people from demanding that, in the name of self-determination and for their own private reasons, another person can be called upon to kill them. By requiring a show of mental competence to effect self-determination, the aim is to exclude the nonvoluntary killing of the depressed, the retarded, and the demented.

My contention is that the joining of those two requirements is perfectly arbitrary, a jerry-rigged combination if ever there was one. Each has its own logic, and each could be used to justify euthanasia. But in the nature of the case that logic, it seems evident, offers little resistance to denying any competent person the right to be killed, sick or not; and little resistance to killing the incompetent, so long as there is good reason to believe they are suffering. There is no principled reason to reject that logic, and no reason to think it could long remain suppressed by the expedient of arbitrary legal stipulations.

There is a related problem worth considering. If the act of euthanasia, conventionally understood, requires the request and consent of the patient, it no less requires that the person to do the killing have his or her own independent moral standards for acceding to the request. The doctor must act with integrity. How can a doctor who voluntarily brings about, or is instrumental in, the death of another legitimately justify that to himself or herself? Would the mere claim of self-determination on the part of someone be sufficient—"it is my body, Doctor, and I request that you kill me"? There is a widespread resistance to that kind of claim, and doctors quite rightly have never been willing to do what patients want just because they want it. There is surely a legitimate fear that, if such a claim were sanctioned, there would be no reason to forbid any two competent persons from entering into an agreement for one to kill the other. Perhaps it arises out of a reluctance to put doctors in the role of taking life simply as a means of advancing patient self-determination, quite apart from any medical reasons for doing so.

The most likely reason for resistance to a pure self-determination standard is that we have, traditionally, defined the appropriate role of the physician as someone whose duty it is to relieve suffering. It has thus been customary, even among those pressing for euthanasia, to hang on to some part of the physician's traditional role. That is why a mere claim of self-determination is not enough. A doctor will not cut off my healthy arm simply because I decide my autonomy and well-being would thereby be enhanced. But the additional requirement that the physician also be relieving suffering carries with it the problem mentioned above. How can a physician determine, much less diagnose in any traditional medical sense, genuine and unrelievable suffering?

The doctor will not be able to use a medical standard. He or she will only be able to use a moral standard. Faced with a patient reporting great suffering, a doctor cannot, therefore, justify euthanasia on purely medical grounds (because suffering is unmeasurable and scientifically undiagnosable). To maintain professional and personal integrity, the doctor will have to justify it on his or her own moral grounds. The doctor must believe that a life of subjectively experienced intense suffering is not worth living. He must believe that himself if he is to be justified in taking the decisive and ultimate step of killing the patient; it must be his moral reason to act, not the patient's reason (even though they may coincide). But if he believes that a life of some forms of suffering is not worth living, then how can he deny the same relief to a person who cannot request it, or who requests it but whose competence is in doubt? This is simply a different way of making the point that there is no self-evident reason why the supposed duty to relieve suffering must be limited to competent patients claiming self-determination. Or why patients who claim death as their right under self-determination must be either suffering or dying.

There is, moreover, the possibility that what begins as a right of doctors to kill under specified conditions will soon become a duty to kill. On what grounds could a doctor deny a request by a competent person for euthanasia? It will not do, I think, just to specify that no doctor should be required to do that which violates his or her conscience. As commonly articulated, the argument about why a doctor has a right to perform euthanasia—the dual duty to respect patient self-determination and to relieve suffering—is said to be central to the vocation of being a doctor. Why should duties as weighty as those be set aside on the grounds of "conscience" or "personal values"?

These puzzles make clear that the moral situation is radically changed once our self-determination requires the participation and assistance of a doctor. It is then that doctor's moral life, that doctor's integrity, that is also and no less encompassed in the act of euthanasia. What, we might then ask, should be the appropriate moral standards for a person asked to kill another? What are the appropriate virtues and sensitivities of such a person? How should that person think of his or her own life and find, within that life, a place for the killing of another person? The language of a presumed right of someone to kill another to relieve suffering obscures questions of that kind.

I can imagine counter-arguments. Is not our duty to relieve suffering sufficiently strong to justify running some risks? Why should we be intimidated by the dangers in a decisive relief of suffering? Is not the present situation, where death can be slow, painful, and full of suffering, already a clear and present danger?

Our duty to relieve suffering cannot justify the introduction of new evils into society. The risk of doing just that in the legalization of "aid-in-dying" is too great, particularly since the number of people whose pain and suffering could not be relieved would never be a large one (so even most euthanasia advocates recognize). It is too great because it would take a disproportionate social change to bring it about, one whose implications extend far beyond the sick and dying. It is too great because, as the history of the twentieth century should demonstrate, killing is a contagious disease, not easy to stop once unleashed in society. It is too great a risk because it would offer medicine too convenient a way out of its hardest cases, those where there is ample room for further, more benign reforms. We are far from exhausting the known remedies for the relief of pain (frequently, even routinely, underused), and a long way from providing decent psychological support for those who suffer from despair and a sense of futility in continuing life.

Pain and suffering in the critically ill and dying are great evils. The attempt to relieve them by the introduction of euthanasia and assisted suicide is even greater. Those practices threaten the future security of the living. They no less threaten the dying themselves. Once a society allows one person to take the life of another based on their mutual private standards of a life worth living, there can be no safe or sure way to contain the deadly virus thus introduced. It will go where it will thereafter.

For Reflection and Discussion

1. How is euthanasia "a social act"? Discuss some of the tensions, found especially in the U.S. culture, between "individual" and "social" dimensions of human beings. Give some examples from your own life.

2. Discuss the key social implications of the legalization of euthanasia.

3. How do you understand and react to Callahan's discussion of sovereignty and suffering?

4. What flaws does Callahan find in the arguments in favor of euthanasia? How might a right become a duty to kill?

14

Living and Dying Well

Oregon and Washington Bishops

LAST YEAR THERE WERE NEARLY FOUR MILLION BIRTHS IN the United States. More than two million persons died. Most of these events happened without media comment. They were part of the rhythm of life. The children, for the most part, were healthy and their parents happy. The decisions made by the dying and their families were sometimes painful, but those too were part of the process of life. These families are part of the still large segment of the American population that think of the Lord as the giver and the taker of life. One such family gathered at the hospital.

> The atmosphere in the emergency room was charged. Even before the physicians diagnosed Mary's infection, her daughter extracted a promise from her. "You have to live, Mother," the daughter said. "Promise me you will hang on." And Mary promised.

> Only 48 hours later, the doctor told the family that death was inevitable. Her children gathered at her bedside. They prayed, and one by one they told her they loved her. One by one they gave her "permission" to die. "It's all right to let go," her daughter said, releasing her mother from her promise. And then, Joann—Mary's granddaughter—spoke. "It's okay, Granny," she said, "you can let go." Quickly, she added, "But hang on if you want to." Mary died within the hour. She died as

she lived, making her own decisions with the support of her family. She lived each moment fully, even the dying moments."

Yet some lives and some deaths are media events. There was, for instance, the death of Janet Adkins of Oregon, who took her own life last year with the aid of a suicide machine.

When Janet Adkins heard the diagnosis of Alzheimer's, she had some idea of what was before her. This vibrant and active woman—a talented woman who played the piano and tennis, spoke French and even climbed mountains—could not face the hardship of memory loss and possible dementia. Janet gave herself permission to be killed. It seems she was unwilling to allow herself to live.

Janet Adkins is only one of an increasing number of persons who fear the lessening of their physical abilities and the diminution of their intellectual capacities. They are persons who fear the possibility of being kept alive beyond the time they consider acceptable.

We have been told that Janet was a competent woman—a "caregiver" for her family, a woman who bore the burdens of others with love. There is no way for us to know the pressures that led her to make a decision for death. We do, though, have some idea of the social context within which such a decision is made and the implications that arise from it.

Making End-of-Life Decisions

One of the privileged ministries of physicians and nurses and other caregivers has always been to help people die well, but never to kill them or to assist them in euthanasia or suicide. The family, the priest, pastor or rabbi and the closest circle of friends and caregivers should support and assist the patient as decision-maker. Yet life-and-death decisions in our society are increasingly influenced by the secularization of society, economic pressures, the fear of malpractice suits, and the rapid and complex development of medical technology. Surrounded by machines and techniques, we often think that if we have them, we must use them. But we must ask why, for what benefit?

Decisions about birth and death are also increasingly becoming legal issues. By determining individual cases in our courts and by writing public policy in our legislative bodies, we affirm that the proper role of law is to protect life and to preserve the right to medical treatment by assuring universal access to it, respecting the treasured beliefs and values of the patient and society itself.

The Christian Perspective

"Where were you when I laid the foundations of the earth?" the Lord asks (Job 38:4). "The earth is the Lord's and the fullness thereof; the world and they that dwell therein" (Psalm 24:1).

In our Judaeo-Christian heritage, we view the beginning and end of life as confrontations with mystery and transcendence. We see ourselves as part of this mystery, and we wonder at the God who loves us into being. It is God who shapes the rhythm of our lives as surely as his law determines the flow of the rivers and the tides of the seas. Respect for this perspective ought to guide the development of public policy decisions with ethical or moral implications. It is appropriate, then, for persons with a religious or philosophical perspective to participate in discussions regarding the formation of such policies. Believers, even as citizens, are called to model attitudes and behaviors formed by gospel values and church teaching.

Throughout the ages, the Christian position has helped form and illumine the moral perspective of society. As representatives of the church, we are challenged to listen with compassion and to support those in pain, to educate the community and to provide moral vision. For these reasons, we write this pastoral letter, and direct it to all persons of good will.

> Most people regard life as something sacred and hold that no one may dispose of it at will, but believers see in life something greater, namely a gift of God's love, which they are called upon to preserve and make fruitful.[1]

The guiding principle for life, according to Catholic faith, is the value God places on human life. This principle is frequently in tension with society's or the individual's estimation of the worth of a particular human being. Catholics are convinced that life does not belong to them as a private possession. Their commitment to protect life is a statement about life and a statement about God, the giver of life.

Human life is a fundamental value. It is more basic than values such as freedom or equality and is the basis for the possession and exercise of any human right. It is therefore necessary for society to recognize, support and protect the most fundamental human right, the right to life itself. Society does this by laws which penalize and denounce as criminal any killing of innocent human beings. Such killing destroys human solidarity and places every other life in jeopardy.

Respect for human life as a fundamental value convinced us that suicide is as wrong as murder. At a time when media often denigrate life's value, society should clearly discourage both its young and its old from giving in to the despair that leads to suicide.

From a religious perspective, suicide must be considered

> as a rejection of God's sovereignty and loving plan. Furthermore, suicide is also often a refusal of love for self, the denial of the natural instinct to live, a flight from the duties of justice and charity owed to one's neighbor, to various communities or to the whole of so-

ciety—although, as is generally recognized, at times there are psychological factors present that can diminish responsibility or even completely remove it.[2]

Suffering and Pain in Human Life

Suffering, pain and even weakness are an inescapable part of the full unfolding of human life. They are burdens we bear and challenges we accept. Our human frailty gives us the opportunity to affirm our trust, our faith in God and God's providence. Being part of the suffering of others enables us to return to the community some of the sympathetic care we have ourselves received. Our efforts to remove unnecessary suffering in the lives of others are born of compassion and, as a human community, we are dedicated to relieving suffering insofar as that is possible. Still, the loss of all hope is a worse evil than physical suffering.

The development of new technologies throughout the last decades has surfaced new capabilities for extending life. New health-care options have helped us to avoid unnecessary death and to prolong and enhance life. But these new technologies also present profound challenges. The new problem in medical technology is that even when it cannot cure or relieve, it is sometimes able to delay the final experience of death beyond the point where the patient may value life or is capable of valuing anything at all. This kind of technological advance creates situations where the rights of the patient, including the right to accept or reject treatment, become public issues.

Despite its achievements, technological advance is frequently ambiguous. It has positive and negative aspects. When technology becomes an end in itself, the humane use of technology becomes problematic. Growing numbers of persons have fears about the end of life, e.g., being kept alive in a persistent vegetative (or permanently unconscious) state unable to make their own decisions, and so forth.

"Physician-assisted" suicide or direct killing through lethal injection is becoming a national issue with a local focus for those of us in the Pacific Northwest. This particular issue assumes greater importance with the actual filing of the "death with dignity" initiative in Washington (Initiative 119) and the introduction of euthanasia legislation (S.B. 1141) in Oregon in 1991. We in the Pacific Northwest are particularly vulnerable because of our initiative and referendum process, liberal beliefs and the large number of unchurched. Autonomy is a strong social value for us. In this regard, it is important to recognize that giving someone else power over one's own life denies autonomy in the most basic way. As ethicist Daniel Callahan, director of the Hastings Center, has said: "To allow another person to kill us is the most radical relinquishment of sovereignty imaginable, not just one more way of exercising it."[3]

In our judgment on the morality of euthanasia and in our discussions about why introducing euthanasia would be bad public policy, we need to be clear about what we are discussing. Many people today do not carefully distinguish between directly causing another person's or one's own death and refusing inappropriate medical treatment at a time of grave illness or approaching death.

Euthanasia

The 1980 Declaration on Euthanasia gives the best working definition:

By euthanasia is understood an action or an omission which of itself or by intention causes death, in order that all suffering may in this way be eliminated. Euthanasia's terms of reference, therefore, are to be found in the intention of the will and in the methods used.[4]

Phrases such as "mercy killing," "rational suicide," "physician-assisted suicide" and the like should not be allowed to obscure the fact that euthanasia is killing an innocent human being and, as such, is morally wrong and should not be condoned by any civilized society.

Suicide by vulnerable members of society is a sign that the community has failed to embody the trust that sustains life and to live out its commitment to protect and comfort the dying, the sick and the elderly.

Any suicide is a reminder of our failure to respond to an anguished plea for help and love, to embody as a community the commitment not to forsake one another. By condoning suicide and euthanasia, society would be abandoning its responsibility to care for the hopelessly ill and elderly.

Neither should we lightly dismiss efforts that could erode the trust persons have traditionally placed in their physicians. Those who have been considered the guardians of life should not be forced to become the agents of death.

Just as we rightly reject suicide and euthanasia, we can also receive clarity and guidance from the Catholic moral tradition about the extent of our obligation to sustain life.

> Everyone has the duty to care for his or her own health or to seek such care from others. Those whose task it is to care for the sick must do so conscientiously and administer the remedies that seem necessary or useful. But is it necessary in all circumstances to have recourse to all possible remedies?[5]

Here the Catholic tradition has consistently replied: No, it is not.

The Extent of Our Obligation to Sustain Life

We are obliged to use all reasonable and proportionate means to sustain life, and we may not participate in actions directly intended to hasten someone's death. But Catholic moral teaching does not view withholding or withdrawing useless or futile treatment as an act of euthanasia. Withholding or withdrawing treatment from a dying patient when nothing more can be done to reverse significantly the progressive deterioration is different from intervening to put the patient to death.

In 1957, Pope Pius XII taught, "Normally one is held only to use ordinary means according to the circumstances of persons, places, times and cultures, that is to say, means that do not involve any great burden for one's self or another."[6] As medical technology has developed, the terms "ordinary" and "extraordinary" have seemed less easy to define. As the 1980 declaration indicated:

> In the past, moralists held that one is never obliged to use "extraordinary" means. This reply, which as a principle still holds good, is perhaps less clear today, by reason of the imprecision of the term and the rapid progress made in the treatment of sickness. Thus some people prefer to speak of "proportionate" and "disproportionate" means. In any case, it will be possible to make a correct judgment as to the means by studying the type of treatment to be used, its degree of complexity or risk, its cost and the possibilities of using it, and comparing these elements with the result that can be expected, taking into account the state of the sick person and his or her physical and moral resources.[7]

Thus, it is appropriate to weigh the anticipated benefit of a medical treatment (e.g., a drug, an operation, a ventilator) and the burden it would impose on the patient (e.g., added pain, loss of limb or bodily function, high risk, serious financial burden) in assessing whether to provide, withhold or remove such medical treatment.

In applying these principles, every consideration should be given to the reasonable wishes of the patient and the patient's family, and to the advice of competent physicians.

The fear of overtreatment some people have is increased when they have a general sense that it is time to die, to "let go," and this sense is not respected, but instead is violated through the application of painful and expensive technologies to maintain life "at any cost." It is helpful to recall Catholic moral teaching on this point:

> It is permissible to make do with the normal means that medicine can offer. Therefore, one cannot impose on anyone the obligation to have recourse to a technique which is already in use but which carries a risk or is burdensome. Such a refusal is not the equivalent of suicide; on the contrary, it should be considered as an acceptance of the human condition, or a wish to avoid the application of a medical procedure disproportionate to the results that can be expected, or a desire not to impose excessive expense on the family or the community.

> When inevitable death is imminent in spite of the means used, it is permitted in conscience to take the decision to refuse forms of treatment that would only secure a precarious and burdensome prolongation of life, so long as the normal care due to the sick person in similar cases is not interrupted. In such circumstances the doctor has no reason to reproach himself with failing to help the person in danger.[8]

The context for judgments about what treatment should be provided or may be refused for a family member, friend or patient is respect for the law of God and loving care for the person who is ill or dying. It is important to ensure the comfort and normal care due to a dying person, even when the conscientious decision is made to refuse forms of treatment that would only secure a precarious and burdensome prolongation of life.[9]

Nutrition and Hydration

The question of withholding nutrition and hydration is more complex. As infants we were given food and drink before we could nourish ourselves. Similarly, many of us will need that assistance before we die. Instinctively, most people react against the possibility that this last link with life might be removed. Usual or normal eating and drinking must be continued as long as a person can tolerate it. It is generally not required to force persons to eat against their will.

Recognizing the delicacy of judgments in this area, the National Conference of Catholic Bishops recommended that our laws recognize the social significance of providing adequate nourishment even for those who are terminally ill.

> Because human life has inherent value and dignity regardless of its condition, every patient should be provided with measures which can effectively preserve life without involving too grave a burden. Since food and water are necessities of life for all human beings and can generally be provided without the risks and burdens of more aggressive means for sustaining life, the law should establish a strong presumption in favor of their use.[10]

When nutrition and hydration are supplied by medical intervention through artificial means in the case of a person who has been diagnosed as permanently unconscious, the ethical issues are not always easy to decide in a way that everyone finds satisfactory. The general principles of weighing the benefit to the person against the burdens imposed on him or her would seem to apply in such cases. Conscientious Catholic moral theologians and many others in our society have not achieved consensus about this point.

On the one hand, there are those who maintain that a permanently unconscious person who is sustained by artificially administered nutrition and hydration and is not dying from some other disease or trauma should continue to be nourished. Such nourishment is seen as part of the normal care given to any human being. Furthermore, these people would say that withdrawing artificial nutrition and hydration causes the person's death by omission and can be equivalent to euthanasia.

Persons who seek to sustain the life of a permanently unconscious family member or friend by artificially administered nutrition and hydration can give a powerful testimony to the value of life as God's precious gift and can be witnesses to a hope born out of true love for the unconscious person's recovery. Their convictions should be recognized and honored by medical caregivers and the law.

On the other hand, there are those who insist that provision of artificial nutrition and hydration is not obligatory when the burdens clearly outweigh the benefits, and they believe this to be the case when a person has been medically diagnosed as permanently unconscious. They contend that it is an acceptable moral position to view artificially administered hydration and nutrition as a life-sustaining treatment like a respirator or dialysis machine. The use of burden/benefit proportionality would indicate if it is futile or burdensome or beneficial.

Since the potential for abusing patients' interests or the sanctity of all human life is great when we consider withholding nutrition and fluids, there should be a presumption in favor of providing patients with these necessities of survival by whatever means are most easily tolerated. But decisions regarding artificially administered nutrition and hydration must also be made on a case-by-case basis, in light of the benefits and burdens they entail for the individual patient. In appropriate circumstances, the decision to withhold these means of life support can be in accord with Catholic moral reasoning and ought to be respected by medical caregivers and the laws of the land.

Because the wishes of the individual and the family are so important in this delicate area, it has proved difficult for legislators to formulate adequate legislation and for judges to give decisions which take into account the complex moral dimensions involved. People who argue for more restrictive legislation are legitimately concerned about a "slippery slope" mentality, in which the legally sanctioned option to withdraw lifesustaining treatment such as nutrition and hydration might encourage those in our society who are determined to promote euthanasia.

At the same time, were our laws not to permit the morally justified withdrawal of artificial nutrition and hydration from any permanently unconscious patients, many are convinced that public sympathy for the unnuanced position of the pro-euthanasia movement would be encouraged.

Living Wills/Durable Power of Attorney

With increasing frequency, people are being asked to state their medical treatment preferences in legally recognized documents. We agree that the old and infirm—indeed all citizens—have a continuing right to bear primary responsibility for decisions that must be made regarding their own care. Living wills (called "Directive to Physician" in Oregon and Washington) and the Durable Power of Attorney for Health Care are documents which enable a once-competent person to continue to direct his or her own health care either through a statement of general intent or through the intervention of another person. These documents have a well-recognized but limited role in the treatment of dying patients, and care must be taken to ensure that the directives given are in accord with correct moral principles.[11]

Those who choose to complete a Durable Power of Attorney for Health Care must be vigilant about authorizing the removal of all lifesustaining treatment, since in some states the law may construe this request to include withdrawal of artificially administered nutrition and hydration.

People can assure peace for their families by talking to them about dying and indicating their wishes clearly before life and death decisions are necessary.

Giving Hope to the Dying

We accept the gift of life—from conception to natural death—with its natural limitations. Too easily, persons can be led to believe that the value or quality of an elderly person's life is less than that of a young person, that the mentally or physically disabled have less right to life than others. We cannot judge the value of a human person by his or her usefulness or by whether he or she is "wanted."

Mortality patterns have changed throughout the years. Improved medicines and technology have resulted in longer lives for many. Many people die in institutional settings instead of at home or in a hospice.[12] These changing patterns affect the ways in which we perceive life and death. More and more, individuals think of both birth and death as isolated events rather than as part of life. Too often, the fragmentation of family life isolates individuals from the experiences of birth and death. As a consequence, family members, particularly children, are not exposed to the death of a person they know and love.

At the same time we are exposed to "megadeath" through the media. We see the results of natural tragedy, e.g., the death of 50,000 in an Iranian earthquake. Television, movies and even computer games expose us to fictional death. Violent death enters our living room with the evening news. Death thereby becomes an object which fascinates us, one which we can toy with and deny. Consequently, we are often not prepared to make decisions that are filled with emotional and deeply personal implications.

For all these reasons, the aged, the poor, minorities, those who are severely retarded or physically handicapped, and the terminally ill are inherently vulnerable to attacks on human life. The multiplication of public entities involved in health-care delivery does not come without risk or dangers—the greatest of which is that society might lose sight of the dignity of the individual in its desire to serve the greatest number. Depersonalization of health care threatens to come just when the elderly and infirm most need time, touch and tenderness.

Pain Control

When we recognize the futility of fighting to save a life that cannot be saved, the emphasis must be placed on symptom control, pain management and pastoral care so that those who are dying will not feel abandoned or isolated. Those who support assisted suicide would have us believe there are only two options available to those in this situation: take the lethal dose or be subjected to every possible form of high-tech medicine no matter how painful, futile or demeaning. This is simply not so.

We urge the medical community, which is publicly pledged to do no harm, and society as a whole to provide appropriate and humane treatment and care settings such as hospices that can help people live and die well. We cannot condone an atmosphere that would make it more appealing to have people dead than to provide what is necessary for them to live the last part of their lives with dignity and relieved from their pain.

A wide range of treatment and therapy is available for the treatment of pain. It is important to remember that the pain of terminal illness is rooted in many causes. Consequently, there is more than one way to manage pain. There are the traditional pain-killing medicines (from aspirin to morphine), antibiotics, radiotherapy and nerve-blocking procedures. Medications and other therapies to alleviate pain may be given as needed, with the consent of the patient, even if a foreseen and unintended side effect is the possible shortening of life.[13] The intent, in this instance, is to alleviate pain and not to hasten death or shorten the patient's life. Furthermore, the question of possible addiction ought not be a consideration in the final stages of dying. In all cases, pain relief should be as much as possible under the control of the patients. They should decide the level of pain they are willing to accept. Especially praiseworthy is the practice of Christians who use the discomfort of illness as a prayerful work in which they respond, like St. Paul, to the invitation to "fill up what is lacking in the sufferings of Christ for the sake of his body, the church" (Colossians 1:24).

The Challenge to the Community

Euthanasia is a lethal, violent and unacceptable way of terminating care for the infirm. The challenge and task for the community is to show the sick and the dying that they are not abandoned by the human community or by God. The demand for euthanasia will increase if structures of support and skills to care for the sick and dying do not keep pace with the demand.

At this time, we call for increased public support for hospice and home-care programs based on a philosophy that rejects the active taking of life. We implore the medical community to educate caregivers to provide better pain management to ease the suffering of the dying. We ask parishes to develop support groups for terminally ill patients and their families, to help persons find meaning in suffering, and to educate the faithful about the issues surrounding death. We commend Catholic and other hospitals for their innovative programs of community outreach and training of pastoral and other caregivers. At this time, it is important that persons of faith reach out to others of good will to resist public policy initiatives that will change fundamental law in this area.

As a community, we are challenged to remember the call to "choose life." Christ, through his life, death and resurrection to new life, has given a new meaning to existence. Death is not the ultimate evil. Jesus' exercise of power is one of healing, liberation and restoration to wholeness. The church is the continuation of Christ's presence and must express the healing and redemptive love that was characteristic of his ministry. Christians are called to be faithful stewards in caring for that gift.

Prayerful and reverent dialogue about life is part of the Christian tradition. In our religious conversation, we discover God's presence in the activities of life. Death is an integral part of our life experience, and our discussions should consider it thoroughly. We need to share our hopes and fears, our faith and our feelings with one another in the prayerful atmosphere that enables us to be educated in faith as well as in fact.

As Christians, we are called to express our belief that human life is of God. We are called and redeemed by God, and our faith in the resurrection is stronger than our fear of death. As human persons, we share in the actions of all humankind. The offenses of others are as much a shame to us as their achievements are a matter of pride. Resisting those who would dismiss the value of human life and kill their brothers and sisters is a matter of conscience. For death to have true dignity, life must have full integrity.

For Reflection and Discussion

1. "Yet life-and-death decisions in our society are increasingly influenced by the secularization of society, economic pressures, the fear of malpractice suits, and the rapid and complex development of medical technology." Discuss each of these factors and, if possible, give examples from your own experience.

2. Do you think the "fear of overtreatment" is contributing to the growing acceptance of euthanasia in society? How? Does the statement's discussion of life-support procedures adequately respond to this fear?

3. Why is the question of nutrition and hydration an especially complex part of the life-support debate? What are your own reactions and judgments about this issue? (Other articles will continue this discussion.)

4. What role can public policy play regarding euthanasia? What role can religion play? What role can hospice play?

Notes

1. Vatican Congregation for the Doctrine of the Faith, *Declaration on Euthanasia*, §9, 1980.
2. *Ibid.*, §12.
3. Daniel Callahan, "'Aid in Dying': The Social Dimensions," *Commonweal* (August 9, 1991).
4. Vatican Congregation for the Doctrine of the Faith, *Declaration on Euthanasia*, §17 1980.
5. *Ibid.*, §28 and 29.
6. Pope Pius XII, *The Prolongation of Life*, November 24, 1957; English translation, *The Pope Speaks*, Vol. 4, 1958, pp. 393-398.
7. *Declaration on Euthanasia*, §30, 1980.
8. *Ibid.*, §34 and 35.
9. *Cf. Ibid.*, §36.
10. National Conference of Catholic Bishops Committee for Pro-Life Activities, "Statement on Uniform Rights of the Terminally Ill Act," 1986, No. 2.
11. The Florida Catholic Conference issued the following cautions: ". . . document should clearly distinguish between a terminal condition in which death is imminent and other conditions in which one could live a long time with easily provided medical care. Second, one should never ask for or demand euthanasia, mercy killing or the withholding of 'ordinary means' of sustaining life. This is not only wrong for the signer of the document, but it also does a serious injustice to physicians, family and medical personnel to whom such immoral demands are made. Third, if there is any possibility that the signer may become pregnant, then certainly every measure should be called for to preserve the life of the unborn child." *Life, Death and the Treatment of Dying Patients*, Florida Catholic Conference, April 27, 1989.
12. We enthusiastically support those hospice programs which are guided by a philosophy that rejects the active taking of life.
13. Cf. Pope Pius XII, *The Prolongation of Life*, November 24, 1957; English translation *The Pope Speaks*, Vol. 4, 1958, pp. 393-398.

Part III:
Patient Self-Determination Act (PSDA)

15

Sources of Concern About the Patient Self-Determination Act

Susan M. Wolf, J.D., Philip Boyle, Ph.D., Daniel Callahan, Ph.D., Joseph J. Fins, M.D., Bruce Jennings, M.A., James Lindemann Nelson, Ph.D., Jeremiah A. Barondess, M.D., Dan W. Brock, Ph.D., Rebecca Dresser, J.D., Linda Emanuel, M.D., Ph.D., Sandra Johnson, J.D., John Lantos, M.D., Dacosta R. Mason, J.D., Mathy Mezey, Ed.D., R.N., David Orentlicher, M.D., J.D., Fennella Rouse, J.D.

ON DECEMBER 1, 1991, THE PATIENT SELF-DETERMINATION act of 1990 (PSDA)[1] went into effect. This is the first federal statute to focus on advance directives and the right of adults to refuse life-sustaining treatment. The law applies to all health-care institutions receiving Medicare or Medicaid funds, including hospitals, skilled-nursing facilities, hospices, home health and personal care agencies, and health maintenance organizations (HMOs).

The statute requires that the institution provide written information to each adult patient on admission (in the case of hospitals or skilled-nursing facilities), enrollment (HMOs), first receipt of care (hospices), or before the patient comes under an agency's care (home health or personal care agencies). The information provided must describe the person's legal rights in that state to make decisions concerning medical care, to refuse treatment, and to formulate advance directives, plus the relevant written policies of the institution. In addition, the institution must document advance directives in the person's medical record, ensure compliance with state law regarding advance directives, and avoid making care conditional on whether or not patients have directives or otherwise discriminating against them on that basis. Finally, institutions must maintain pertinent written policies and procedures and must provide staff and community education on advance directives. The states must help by preparing descriptions of the relevant law, and the Secretary of Health and Human Services must assist with the development of materials and conduct a public-education campaign. The Health Care Financing Administration has authority to issue regulations.

A goal of the statute is to encourage but not require adults to fill out advance directives—treatment directives (documents such as a living will stating the person's treatment preferences in the event of future incompetence), proxy appointments (document such as a durable power of attorney appointing a proxy decision-maker), or both. There is widespread agreement that directives can have many benefits.[2-5] These include improved communication between doctor and patient, increased clarity about the patient's wishes, and ultimately greater assurance that treatment accords with the patient's values and preferences. Yet few Americans have executed advance directives. Estimates range from 4 to 24 percent[6-8] (and Knox RA: personal communication).

A second goal of the PSDA is to prompt health professionals and institutions to honor advance directives. The U.S. Supreme Court's *Cruzan* decision suggests that advance directives are protected by the federal Constitution.[9] The great majority of states and the District of Columbia also have specific statutes or judicial decisions recognizing treatment directives.[10] In addition, all states have general durable-power-of-attorney statutes, and most states further specify how this or another format can be used to appoint a proxy for health-care decisions.[10] Patients, thus, have a right to use directives that is based in constitutional, statutory, and common law, and others must honor the recorded choices.[11] There is evidence, however, that advance directives are ignored or overridden one-fourth of the time.[12]

Efforts to educate patients about directives and to educate health-care professionals about their obligation to honor them thus seem warranted. But the PSDA has caused concern.[6,13,14] Implementation may result in drowning patients in written materials on admission, insensitive and ill-timed inquiry into patients' preferences, and untrained bureaucrats attempting a job that should be performed by physicians. Indeed, one can favor directives yet oppose the PSDA because of these dangers. The question is how to accomplish the statute's positive underlying goals while minimizing the potential adverse effects.

The key to avoiding an insensitive and bureaucratic process is to ensure that physicians integrate discussion of directives into their ongoing dialogue with patients about current health status and future care. Many have urged that doctors do this.[4,6,15] Yet the literature shows that physicians still have reservations about advance directives,[6,12,13,16-19] and some remain reluctant to initiate discussion.[7,15,20,21] Only by forthrightly addressing these reservations can we successfully make directives part of practice, realize the potential benefits for all involved, and avoid implementing the PSDA in a destructive way.

Our multidisciplinary group—including physicians, a nurse, philosophers, and lawyers—convened to address those reservations in order to dispel doubts when appropriate and delineate continuing controversy where it exists.

Reservations About Treatment Directives

Patients do not really want to discuss future incompetence and death, and so would rather not discuss advance directives. Future incompetence, serious illness, and death are not easy topics to discuss for either patients or physicians. Yet studies indicate that most patients want to discuss their preferences for future treatment[4,7,18,22] and that such discussion usually evokes positive reactions and an enhanced sense of control.[18,23]

Misconceptions nonetheless remain and may produce anxiety in some patients. Some people wrongly assume that treatment directives are used only to refuse treatments and thus shorten life.[24] But people use directives to request treatments as well.[4,25] Such a demand for treatment can raise important ethical problems later if the physician becomes concerned that the treatment may be medically inappropriate or futile for that patient. These problems are currently being debated.[26,29] Yet they are not peculiar to advance directives; they can arise whenever a patient or surrogate demands arguably inappropriate treatment. The point is that treatment directives are a way to express the patient's preferences for treatment, whatever they may be.

There are substantial advantages to both patients and doctors in discussing and formulating treatment directives. A discussion of future medical scenarios can reduce the uncertainty of patients and physicians, strengthen rapport, and facilitate decision-making in the future.[16,23,30] Beyond their clinical advantages, directives are one way to fulfill the legal requirement in some states that there be "clear and convincing evidence" of the patient's wishes before life-sustaining treatment is withdrawn.[31,32] The state statutes on treatment directives also generally give physicians a guarantee of civil and criminal immunity when they withhold or withdraw life-sustaining treatment relying in good faith on a patient's directive.

Some debate remains, however, about when directives should first be discussed and with which patients.[4,21,33] The

PSDA requires giving information to all adults when they first enter a relevant institution or receive care. This will involve some healthy patients and patients who are expected to return to good health after treatment for a reversible problem. Yet even healthy persons and young people wish to engage in advance planning with their physicians.[4]

Concern nonetheless persists about whether the time of admission or initial receipt of treatment is an appropriate moment to broach the topic of directives. Ideally, initial discussion should take place in the outpatient setting, before the patient experiences the dislocation that often attends inpatient admission. Many patients, however, will reach admission without the benefit of such discussion. If the discussion on admission is handled sensitively and as the first of many opportunities to discuss these matters with the physician and other care givers, admission is an acceptable time to begin the process. For patients who already have directives, admission is a logical time to check the directives in the light of their changed medical circumstances.

Discussion of advance directives takes too much time and requires special training and competence. The discussion of advance directives is an important part of the dialogue between doctor and patient about the patient's condition, prognosis, and future options. But the physician need not discharge this function alone. Others in the health-care institution may play an important part in answering questions, providing information, or assisting with documents. The PSDA helpfully makes health-care institutions and organizations responsible for the necessary staff education. However, because patients considering treatment directives need to understand their health status and treatment options, physicians have a central role.

Physicians may nonetheless harbor understandable concern about the amount of time that will be required to counsel each patient. An initial discussion of directives structured by a document describing alternative medical scenarios can be accomplished in 15 minutes,[4] but some will undoubtedly find that the initial discussion takes longer, and further discussion is also necessary in any case. Institutions may want to acquire brochures, videotapes, and other materials to help educate patients, and may enlist other personnel in coordinated efforts to assist patients. In addition, the PSDA requires institutions and organizations to engage in community education, which may reach patients before they are admitted. All these efforts promise to facilitate the discussion between doctor and patient.

Treatment directives are not useful, because patients cannot really anticipate what their preferences will be in a future medical situation and because patients know too little about life-support systems and other treatment options. The first part of this objection challenges the very idea of making decisions about medical situations that have not yet developed. Patients who make such decisions will indeed often be making decisions that are less fully informed than those of patients facing a current health problem.[6] Yet the decisions recorded in directives, even if imperfect, give at least an indication of what the patient would want. If the goal is to guide later treatment decisions by the patient's preferences, some indication is better than none.

The question, then, is not whether the decisions embodied in directives are just as informed as those made contemporaneously by a competent patient. It is, instead, whether the recorded decisions accurately indicate the patient's preferences as best he or she could know them when competent. The answer to that question depends largely on how skillful physicians are in explaining possible medical scenarios and the attendant treatment options. There are many spheres in which we ask people to anticipate the future and state their wishes—wills governing property and most contracts are examples. But in each case the quality of their decisions depends a good deal on the quality of the counseling they receive. It is incumbent on physicians to develop their skills in this regard. Several instruments have been described in the literature to help them communicate successfully with patients.[19,34,35] In addition, the patient's designation of a proxy can provide a person to work with the physician as the medical situation unfolds.

Good counseling by physicians is the best remedy for patients' ignorance about life-support systems, too. Patients need to understand these treatments in order to judge whether the expected burdens will outweigh the benefits in future medical circumstances. Yet a patient choosing in advance will usually have a less detailed understanding than a patient facing an immediate and specific decision, who may even try the treatment for a time to gain more information.[3] This too supports the wisdom of designating a proxy to work with the medical team.

Treatment-directive forms are too vague and open to divergent interpretations to be useful guides to treatment decisions later. Some forms do contain outmoded language. Terms such as "extraordinary" treatment and "heroic" care have been widely discredited as being overly vague[3,36] (even though "extraordinary" is used in some state laws),[37] and patients should be discouraged from using such generalities. Instead, patients who wish to use treatment directives should be encouraged to specify which treatments they wish to request or refuse, and the medical circumstances under which they want those wishes to go into effect. Although such specification has been challenged,[17] it is a more effective way for patients to communicate their wishes than a general refusal of life-sustaining treatment. The desire for a particular treatment may well vary according to diagnosis and prognosis[4,38]—for instance, artificial nutrition may be desired if the patient is conscious and has a reversible condition, but unwanted if the patient is in a persistent vegetative state. Another way to communicate wishes is for patients to state their preferred goals of treatment, depending on diagnosis[39]—for example, in case of terminal illness, provide comfort care only.

It is nonetheless almost impossible to write a directive that leaves no room for interpretation. Whatever language the patient uses, the goal is to try to determine the patient's intent. Often family members or other intimates can help. Even a vague directive will usually provide some guidance. Some patients will choose to avoid problems of interpretation and application by appointing a proxy and writing no treatment directive. The proxy can then work with the physician as circumstances unfold. Yet the proxy must still strive to choose as the patient would. If the patient has left a treatment directive or other statement of preferences, it will fall to the proxy to determine what the patient intended.

The incompetent patient's best interests should take precedence over even the most thoughtful choices of a patient while competent. Some people argue that the choices stated in a directive are sometimes less relevant than the current experience of the now incompetent patient.[40,41] In the vast majority of cases, this problem does not arise, because the patient's earlier decisions do not conflict with his or her best interests when incompetent. Yet some demented patients, in particular, may seem to derive continued enjoyment from life, although they have a directive refusing life-sustaining treatment. The argument for discounting the directive is that these patients are now such different people that they should not be bound by the choices of their earlier selves, they may no longer hold the values embodied in the directive, and they may appear to accept a quality of life they formerly deemed unacceptable.

Our group did not reach agreement on this argument for overriding some directives. Members who rejected it argued that it is essential that competent patients who record their wishes know those wishes will be followed later, a person's values and choices should govern even after loss of competence because he or she remains essentially the same person, and to recognize the proposed exception would invite widespread disregard of treatment directives. Although we did not resolve this controversy, we did agree on certain procedural safeguards. A treatment directive should not be overridden lightly. In cases in which this controversy arises, only the patient's appointed proxy, a court, or a court-appointed decision-maker should be able to consider overriding the directive. Finally, physicians should specifically discuss with patients what the patients' preferences are in the event of dementia.

Even if a directive is valid in all other respects, it is not a reliable guide to treatment because patients may change their minds. Patients may indeed change their minds as their circumstances change. Physicians should therefore reexamine directives periodically with their patients. Data suggest, however, that there is considerable stability in patients' preferences concerning life-sustaining treatment.[16,42-44] In one study of hospitalized patients, 65 to 85 percent of choices did not change during a one-month period, the percentage depending on the illness scenario presented (kappa = 0.35 to 0.70, where 0 represents random and 1 perfect agreement).[42] In another study there was 58 and 81 percent stability in patients' decisions over a six-month period when they were presented with two scenarios (kappa = 0.23 and 0.31).[43] Further research is necessary, but in any case, patients are always free to change or revoke earlier directives. Once a patient has lost competence and the physician can no longer check with the patient about treatment preferences, a directive becomes the most reliable guide to what the patient would want. Physicians cannot justifiably disregard directives because the patient might hypothetically have changed his or her mind.

Reservations About Proxy Appointments

Patients may appoint a proxy to make treatment decisions in the event of incompetence, using a durable power of attorney or other document. Some patients both appoint a proxy and execute a treatment directive. Proxy appointments raise some different sources of concern than treatment directives.

The appointed proxy may later seem to be the wrong surrogate decision maker. This concern may arise for one of several reasons. The proxy may have had no involvement in the patient's health planning, and may not even realize that the patient has chosen him or her as proxy. To avoid this problem the physician should encourage the patient both to secure the proxy's acceptance of the appointment and to consider involving the proxy in the process of making decisions about future care. The proxy will then be prepared to discharge the function and will have some knowledge of the patient's wishes. The physician should also encourage the patient to tell family members and other intimates who the chosen proxy is, especially since some patients will prefer to designate a proxy from outside their families. This will reduce the chance of surprise and disagreement later.

Physicians may nonetheless encounter appointed proxies with little previous involvement in the patient's planning process and daily life. Yet a patient's designation of a proxy is an exercise in self-determination. The physician is bound to contact that person if the patient loses competence and the appointment goes into effect, rather than ignore the appointment and simply turn to someone else. There may be no further problems, because everyone may agree anyway on what course of treatment the patient would wish. But uncertainty or disagreement about the right choice of treatment may force the resolution of questions about who the most appropriate proxy is. If the medical team or the patient's relatives or other intimates have serious doubts about whether the designated proxy can fulfill the required functions, it is their responsibility to address these doubts through discussion. If the problem cannot be resolved in this way, they may need to seek judicial resolution and the appointment of an alternate.

Sometimes the designated proxy seems inappropriate not because the person is too remote but because the person is so involved that his or her own wishes and interests seem to govern, rather than the patient's. Family members and other intimates almost always have to deal with their own emotional and financial issues in serving as a proxy decision-maker, and the mere existence of such issues does not disqualify them. Physicians and other members of the medical team have a responsibility to work with proxies, helping them to identify their own matters of concern, to separate those from the patient's, and to focus on the patient's wishes and interests in making decisions about treatment. Occasionally, the medical team will encounter a proxy who simply cannot do this. If efforts among the involved parties to remedy the problem fail, then caregivers may have to seek judicial scrutiny and the appointment of another proxy.

Even a diligent proxy cannot tell what the patient wanted without an explicit treatment directive, so a proxy's choice should carry no particular weight. Family members, other intimates, and physicians often fail to select the same treatment the patient chooses when asked.[45-49] In one study there was 59 to 88 percent agreement, depending on the illness scenario the researchers posed (kappa < 0.3 in all cases)[45]; in another study, agreement was 52 to 90 percent (kappa < 0.4 in all cases).[49] Advising the proxy to choose as the patient would, rather than simply asking for a recommendation, seems to act as a partial corrective.[46]

These data should come as no surprise. Even a person's relatives and other intimates are not clairvoyant and may not share identical values. Moreover, proxies are not always adequately informed that their choices for the patient must be based on the patient's wishes and interests, even when those do not accord with the proxy's. Yet there is often no one better informed about the patient's past values and preferences than the proxy, and the patient in any case has manifested trust by appointing that person. Physicians should encourage patients not only to appoint a proxy, but also to provide instructions to guide the proxy. Physicians should also explicitly clarify for the proxy the primacy of the patient's wishes and interests.

The proxy may make a treatment choice contrary to the patient's treatment directive, claiming that the proxy appointment takes precedence over the directive. Some patients will appoint a proxy and leave no treatment directive or other instructions to limit the proxy's authority. Others will guide their proxy by writing a treatment directive or other record of preferences.[5] Problems may then arise if the proxy tries to override the preferences. The law in individual states often directly addresses the relation between proxy appointments and treatment directives.[50-53] In general, the proxy is ethically and legally bound to effectuate the patient's treatment choices. When the patient has failed to make explicit treatment choices, either in a treatment directive or orally, the proxy is bound to extrapolate from what is known of the patient's values and preferences to determine as best he or she can what the patient would want; this is typically labeled an exercise in "substituted judgment." If not enough is known of the patient's values and preferences to ground such a judgment, the proxy is bound to decide in the patient's best interests. A proxy's authority is thus governed by certain decision-making standards, and the proxy is obligated to honor the patient's wishes, whether stated in a treatment directive or elsewhere. One caveat has been noted: there is some disagreement over whether a proxy can override a treatment directive that seriously threatens an incompetent but conscious patient's best interests.

The proxy may make a decision with which the physician or institution disagrees. This is not a problem peculiar to appointed proxies or advance directives. Disagreement surfaces with some frequency between physicians and patients, families, other intimates, and proxies. As always, it is crucial for the physician to discuss the disagreement with the relevant decision maker, attempting to understand the source and resolve the matter. If resolution is elusive, others within the institution can sometimes assist. Judicial resolution is available if all else fails.

One source of disagreement deserves special mention. The proxy (or for that matter, the treatment directive itself) may state a treatment choice that an individual physician believes he or she cannot carry out as a matter of conscience or that violates the commitments and mission of the institution. There has been scholarly discussion[54,55] and some adjudication[56] of the circumstances under which institutions and physicians or other caregivers can exempt themselves from carrying out treatment choices. Caregivers and institutions are not free to impose unwanted treatment. The PSDA recognizes, however, that a number of states (such as New York) allow providers to assert objections of conscience.[57] Before a patient is admitted, institutions should give notice of any limitation on their willingness to implement treatment choices. Similarly, an individual physician should give as much notice as possible and should assist in the orderly transfer of the patient to a physician who can carry out those choices.

Conclusion

Advance directives have provoked a number of reservations. As the PSDA goes into effect, requiring discussion and implementation of directives, it will be essential to address physicians' further reservations as they arise.

Yet that necessary step will not be sufficient to ensure that the PSDA produces more benefit than harm. There is a risk that written advance directives may wrongly come to be viewed as the only way to make treatment decisions for the future. Physicians and other caregivers may improperly begin to require an advance directive before treatment may be forgone for incompetent patients. To avoid this, staff education must include discussion of the various ways to decide about life-sustaining treatment and plan future care. Even under the PSDA, not all patients will use advance directives.

There is a further risk of confusion about the procedures and materials to use in implementing the PSDA. All personnel in the relevant institutions will need clarification of the step-by-step process to be followed with patients, the written materials to use, and how to resolve specific questions. The information conveyed to patients must be understandable, accurate in summarizing the patients' rights, and sensitively communicated. All staff members who are involved must be trained. Institutions must design appropriate protocols.

Finally, there is a risk that the PSDA will reduce the discussion of treatment options and directives to a bureaucratic process dominated by brochures and forms. To avoid this, the discussion of advance directives must be part of an ongoing dialogue between physician and patient about the patient's health status and future. Doctors must accept responsibility for initiating these discussions and conducting them skillfully. Such discussions should begin early in the patient's relationship with the doctor, and the content of directives should be reviewed periodically. Institutions and organizations should set up complementary systems to support this effort. The PSDA's requirements must become not a ceiling but a floor—a catalyst for broader innovation to integrate directives into good patient care.

For Reflection and Discussion

1. Have you been admitted to a hospital and asked about advance directives? What were your reactions, fears, questions? The authors emphasize physicians' responsibility to integrate discussion of advance directives into their overall health care. Have you discussed advance directives with your doctor?

2. What is the difference between a living will and a durable power of attorney for health care? Do you see any need for one of these in your life? Why/why not?

3. What are some of the usual objections to advance directives? How do the authors respond to these? Do you agree with the authors? Where might conflicts of conscience occur?

4. Are you aware of the specific legislation concerning advance directives in your state? How can you find out more information?

Notes

1. Omnibus Budget Reconciliation Act of 1990. Pub.L. No. 101-508 §§4206, 4751 (codified in scattered sections of 42 U.S.C., especially §§1395cc, 1396a (West Supp. 1991).

2. President's Commission for the Study of Ethical Problems in Medicine and Biomedical and Behavioral Research, *Making Health-Care Decisions: the Ethical and Legal Implications of Informed Consent in the Patient-Practitioner Relationship*, Vol. I. Report (Washington, DC: Government Printing Office, 1982).

3. *Guidelines on the Termination of Life-Sustaining Treatment and the Care of the Dying* (Bloomington IN: Indiana University Press and the Hastings Center, 1987).

4. L.L. Emanuel, M.J. Barry, J.D. Stoeckle, L.M. Ettelson, E.J. Emanuel, "Advance Directives for Medical Care—a Case for Greater Use," *New England Journal of Medicine* 324 (1991) 889-95.

5. G.J. Annas, "The Health Care Proxy and the Living Will," *New England Journal of Medicine* 324 (1991) 1210-3.

6. J. La Puma, D. Orentlicher, R.J. Moss, "Advance Directives on Admission: Clinical Implications and Analysis of the Patient Self-Determination Act of 1990," *JAMA* 266 (1991) 402-5.

7. E.R. Gamble, P.J. McDonald, P.R. Lichstein, "Knowledge, Attitudes, and Behavior of Elderly Persons Regarding Living Wills," *Archives of Internal Medicine* 151 (1991) 277-80.

8. R.A. Knox, "Poll: Americans Favor Mercy Killing," *Boston Globe*, November 3, 1991:1, 22.

9. *Cruzan v. Director*, Missouri Department of Health, 110 S. Ct. 2841 (1990).

10. Society for the Right to Die, *Refusal of Treatment Legislation: A State by State Compilation of Enacted and Model Statutes* (New York: John Wiley, 1991).

11. A. Meisel, *The Right to Die* (New York: John Wiley, 1989).

12. M. Danis, L.I. Southerland, J.M. Garrett, et al. "A Prospective Study of Advance Directives for Life-sustaining Care," *New England Journal of Medicine* 324 (1991) 882-8.

13. M.L. White, J.C. Fletcher, "The Patient Self-Determination Act: On Balance, More Help than Hindrance," *JAMA* 266 (1991) 410-2.

14. P.J. Greco, K.A. Schulman, R. Lavizzo-Mourey, J. Hansen-Flaschen, "The Patient Self-Determination Act and the Future of Advance Directives," *Annals of Internal Medicine* 115 (1991) 639-43.
15. J. Teno, J. Fleishman, D.W. Brock, V. Mor, "The Use of Formal Prior Directives Among Patients with HIV-related Diseases," *Journal of General Internal Medicine* 5 (1990) 490-4.
16. K.W. Davidson, C. Hackler, D.R. Caradine, R.S. McCord, "Physicians' Attitudes on Advance Directives," JAMA 262 (1989) 2415-9.
17. A.S. Brett, "Limitations of Listing Specific Medical Interventions in Advance Directives," *JAMA* 266 (1991) 825-8.
18. B. Lo, G.A. McLeod, G. Saika, "Patient Attitudes to Discussing Life-sustaining Treatment," *Archives of Internal Medicine* 146 (1986) 1613-5.
19. L.L. Emanuel, E.J. Emanuel, "The Medical Directive: A New Comprehensive Advance Care Document," *JAMA* 261 (1989) 3288-93.
20. M. Kohn, G. Menon, "Life Prolongation: Views of Elderly Outpatients and Health Care Professionals," *Journal of American Geriatric Society* 36 (1988) 840-4.
21. S.V. McCrary, J.R. Botkin, "Hospital Policy on Advance Directives: Do Institutions Ask Patients About Living Wills?" *JAMA* 262 (1989) 2411-4.
22. R.H. Shmerling, S.E. Bedell, A. Lilienfeld, T.L. Delbanco, "Discussing Cardiopulmonary Resuscitation: A Study of Elderly Outpatients," *Journal of General Internal Medicine* 3 (1988) 317-21.
23. T.E. Finucane, J.M. Shumway, R.L. Powers, R.M. D'Alessandri, "Planning with Elderly Outpatients for Contingencies of Severe Illness: A Survey and Clinical Trial," *Journal of General Internal Medicine* 3 (1988) 322-5.
24. F. Ackerman, "Not Everybody Wants to Sign a Living Will," *New York Times*, October 13, 1989:A32.
25. D.W. Molloy, G.H. Guyatt, "A Comprehensive Health Care Directive in a Home for the Aged," *Canadian Medical Association Journal* 145 (1991) 307-11.
26. D. Callahan, "Medical Futility, Medical Necessity: The Problem Without a Name," *Hastings Center Report* 21(4) (1991) 30-5.
27. S.J. Youngner, "Futility In Context," *JAMA* 264 (1990) 1295-6.
28. *Idem.*, "Who Defines Futility?" *JAMA* 260 (1988) 2094-5.
29. J.D. Lantos, P.A. Singer, R.M. Walker, et al. "The Illusion of Futility in Clinical Practice," *American Journal of Medicine* 87 (1989) 81-4.
30. L.L. Emanuel, "Does the DNR Order Need Life-sustaining Intervention? Time for Comprehensive Advance Directives," *American Journal of Medicine* 86 (1989) 87-90.
31. D. Orentlicher, "The Right to Die after *Cruzan*," *JAMA* 264 (1990) 2444-6.
32. R.F. Weir, L. Gostin, "Decisions to Abate Life-sustaining Treatment for Non-autonomous Patients: Ethical Standards and Legal Liability for Physicians After *Cruzan*," *JAMA* 264 (1990) 1846-53
33. S.B. Hardin, H.G. Welch, E.S. Fisher, "Should Advance Directives Be Obtained in the Hospital? A Review of Patient Competence During Hospitalizations Prior to Death," *Clinical Research* 39 (1991) 626A.
34. D.J. Doukas, L.B. McCullough, "The Values History: The Evaluation of the Patient's Values and Advance Directives," *Journal of Family Practice* 32 (1991) 145-53.
35. J.M. Gibson, "National Values History Project," *Generations* 14 (1990) 51-64.

36. S.J. Eisendrath, A.R. Jonsen, "The Living Will: Help or Hindrance?" *JAMA* 249 (1983) 2054-8.
37. North Carolina Gen Stat. §90-321(a)(2) (1991).
38. L. Forrow, E. Gogel, E. Thomas, "Advance Directives for Medical Care," *New England Journal of Medicine* 325 (1991) 1255.
39. L. Emanuel, "The Health Care Directive: Learning How to Draft Advance Care Documents," *Journal of American Geriatric Society* 39 (1991) 1221-8.
40. R.S. Dresser, "Advance Directives, Self-determination, and Personal Identity," in: C. Hackler, R. Moseley, D.E. Vawter, eds. *Advance Directives in Medicine*, (New York: Praeger Publishers, 1989) 155-70.
41. A.E. Buchanan, D.W. Brock, Deciding for Others: The Ethics of Surrogate Decision-making," (New York: Cambridge University Press, 1989) 152-89.
42. M.A. Everhart, R.A. Pearlman, "Stability of Patient Preferences Regarding Life-sustaining Treatments," *Chest* 97 (1990) 159-64.
43. M.D. Silverstein, C.B. Stocking, J.P. Antel, J. Beckwith, R.P. Roos, M. Siegler, "Amyotrophic Lateral Sclerosis and Life-sustaining Therapy: Patients' Desires for Information, Participation in Decision-making, and Life-sustaining Therapy," *Mayo Clinical Proceedings* 66 (1991) 906-13.
44. L.L. Emanuel, M.J. Barry, J.D. Stoeckle, E.J. Emanuel, "A Detailed Advance Care Directive: Practicality and Durability," *Clinical Research* 38 (1990) 738A.
45. A.B. Seckler, D.E. Meier, M. Mulvihill, B.E.C. Paris, "Substituted Judgement: How Accurate Are Proxy Predictions?" *Annals of Internal Medicine* 115 (1991) 92-8.
46. T. Tomlinson, K. Howe, M. Notman, D. Rossmiller, "An Empirical Study of Proxy Consent for Elderly Persons," *Gerontologist* 30 (1990) 54-64.
47. N.R. Zweibel, C..K. Cassel, "Treatment Choices at the End of Life: A Comparison of Decisions by Older Patients and Their Physician-selected Proxies," *Gerontologist* 29 (1989) 615-21.
48. J.G. Ouslander, A.J. Tymchuk, B. Rahbar, "Health Care Decisions Among Elderly Long-term Care Residents and Their Potential Proxies," *Archives of Internal Medicine* 149 (1989) 1367-72.
49. R.F. Uhlmann, R.A. Pearlman, K.C. Cain, "Physicians' and Spouses' Predictions of Elderly Patients' Resuscitation Preferences," *Journal of Gerontology* 43 (1988) M115-M121.
50. Kansas State Annals §58-629 (Supp. 1990).
51. Vermont State Annals 14, §3453, 3463 (Supp. 1991).
52. West Virginia Code §16-30A-4 (Supp. 1991).
53. Wisconsin State Annals §155.20 (1989-90).
54. G.J. Annas, "Transferring the Ethical Hot Potato," *Hastings Center Report* 1987; 17(1):20-1.
55. S.H. Miles, P.A. Singer, M. Siegler, "Conflicts Between Patients' Wishes to Forgo Treatment and the Policies of Health Care Facilities," *New England Journal of Medicine* 321 (1989) 48-50.
56. In re Jobes, 529 A.2d 434 (N.J. 1987).
57. New York Public Health Law §2984 (McKinney Supp. 1991).

16

The Patient Self-Determination Act of 1990

John J. Paris, S.J., Ph.D.
Kevin J. O'Connell, J.D.

IN HIS INFLUENTIAL TEXT ON THE PATIENT-PHYSICIAN RELA-tionship, *The Silent World of Doctor and Patient,*[1] Jay Katz exposes the reality of that relationship as one of silence rather than open communication. In the encounter with silence, truths are left unspoken; significant realities left unexplored. Proof of Katz's insight is found in repeated surveys and polls that reveal that the overwhelming majority of both the general population and practitioners believe that in cases of terminal illness or permanent unconsciousness, previously expressed wishes about life-support should be honored. Yet, despite this belief, relatively few people—less than 15% of the popula-tion—have completed advanced directives, and fewer still have made their wishes regarding life-sustaining treatment known to their primary care physician.

What would lead to such a breakdown in communication in an area as vital as life-death decisions? The limited empiri-cal studies of the topic indicate a widespread belief on the part of both patients and physicians that the other party has the responsibility to initiate the conversation. A study by La Puma shows that physicians and providers view advanced directives as an opportunity to initiate the conversation. La Puma's study also shows that physicians and providers view advanced directives as a patient rather than a professional or institutional responsibility.[2] Further support for that finding comes from a national study of hospitals with policies on advanced directives that show only 4% asked their patients whether they had advanced directives; 96% of the institutions assumed that those who had such directives would inform the hospital.[3]

Patients have just the opposite expectation. Emanuel's study of advanced directives reveals that the most frequently cited barrier to their use was patients' expectation that the physician should take the initiative in raising the topic.[4] That study found that while 93% of the outpatients and 89% of the general public who were surveyed wanted a document specifying future care, only 7% had one and only 5% had ever had a discussion on the topic with their physicians.

The Patient Self-Determination Act of 1990 (PSDA),[5] which Congress passed as part of the Omnibus Budget Reconciliation Act, is designed, in part, to break that stalemate. The law, which takes effect on December 1, 1991, requires all hospitals, nursing facilities, hospices, home health-care services and health maintenance organizations that receive Medicare or Medicaid to inform their adult patients on admission or enrollment of their right to make decisions regarding their medical care and of their right under applicable state law to write a living will or durable power of attorney.

The Act also requires as a condition for Medicare or Medicaid funding that these institutions do the following:

1. document in the patient's medical record whether the individual has executed an advanced directive;

2. follow the directives in compliance with state laws;

3. educate both their own staffs and the general community concerning advanced directives.

Critics of the Act, such as Alexander Capron, believe that the moment of a patient's admission is not the time to address the issue of living wills and proxy decision-makers.[6] The Act's critics fear that the process will amount to nothing more than admitting clerks putting a bureaucratic check in the appropriate box to indicate that patients have been duly apprised of their rights under the law. This "Miranda warning" approach to the statute, critics protest, would give physicians the wrong message—hospitals and other health-care institutions, not physicians, have the duty to sound out patients about living wills and durable powers of attorney.

While it is true that hospital admission is not the optimal time to raise the issue of advanced directives, two responses seem on point. First, physicians have consistently defaulted on their obligation to learn their patients' concerns and values regarding potentially life-prolonging measures. They have also failed to learn in timely fashion who is to speak for the patient should he or she become incapacitated. The PSDA nudges the issue into the open and legitimates the otherwise hushed over topic.

Second, the PSDA's requirement that institutions implement educational and training programs on advanced directives for their staffs and general public will not only place these topics in the public forum, but will also, it is hoped, make what has until now been spoken of only obliquely—the fact that patients are mortal, that they die, and that the interventions provided for them at the end of life are often unwanted, intrusive, and abusive—a necessary subject for discussion between patient and physician.

Historical Background

The PSDA does not create any new rights or privileges for patients. It grants no new rights to citizens. The PSDA merely requires health-care providers to inform patients of their existing rights to refuse unwanted medical treatment. As the United States Supreme Court noted in its recent *Cruzan* opinion, that common law right is constitutionally protected as part of our basic fundamental "liberty interests."[7] As an earlier Supreme Court had put it: "No right is held more sacred, or is more carefully guarded by the common law, than the right of every individual to the possession and control of his person, free from all restraint or interference of others, unless by clear and unquestionable authority of law."[8]

The medical implications of a person's right of autonomy were first articulated in 1914 by Justice Benjamin Cardozo, then of the New York Court of Appeals, when he wrote in his now landmark *Schloendorff v. Society of New York Hospitals* opinion: "Every human being of adult years and sound mind has a right to determine what shall be done with his own body; and a surgeon who performs an operation without his patient's consent commits an assault, for which he is liable in damages."[9] *Schloendorff*, which forms the basis for the doctrine of informed consent, made clear, as *Cruzan* was to reiterate 75 years later, that the competent patient has a right to decline any and all medical interventions including those that might be potentially life-prolonging.

Difficulties arise when the question of patient autonomy is applied to noncompetent patients. How do we determine what medical treatment, if any, the unconscious Karen Ann Quinlan or Nancy Cruzan would want? The problem in answering this question is exacerbated by technological advances which have greatly increased medicine's ability to preserve and prolong life. Procedures that once were only dreams have become reality—artificial means to replace failed lungs, hearts, and kidneys are now commonplace. Like all human artifacts, however, sophisticated techniques can be abused: the very means used to preserve life may transform it into a sublethal extension of monitoring machines and sustaining apparatus. Life can become a hellish nightmare from which there is seemingly no exit.

That possibility was realized in the case of Karen Ann Quinlan. Her well-known plight led to demands by individuals and families alike for some manner of protection from such a fate, short of the costly and cumbersome judicial process. Traditionally, physicians understood that decisionally incapable patients such as Ms. Quinlan retain the right to decline unwanted treatment, and that the proxy exercise of that right belonged to the patient's family or guardian. However, as the older world of private physicians who knew and cared for the patient and family gave way to tertiary care facilities and "stranger medicine," the knowledge and trust between family and physician was lost. Today, the treating physician often does not know the patient or her values. In large medical centers, patients are frequently seen by a horde of subspecialists and teams of residents. Consequently, decisions that were once commonly agreed upon and easily effected directly by the physician became diffused amidst a large, diverse cadre of unknown caregivers. The gain was scientific advance; the loss was concern for the integrity and values of the patient.

Living Wills

A way around the problem of protecting the rights and dignity of the incompetent patient was proposed in 1969 by Louis Kutner, who described a document, which he termed a "living will," in which a now competent adult could put in writing directions for future medical care to be used by his health-care provider should he become incapacitated and unable to communicate his wishes.[10] The need for such an instrument became clear in 1976 with the now famous *Quinlan* case.[11] That case focused attention on the problem of decision-making for the noncompetent patient and on the fact that physicians' fear of potential legal liability is a factor in the refusals to honor families' requests to disconnect life-prolonging procedures in many instances.

The plight of Karen Ann Quinlan led the California legislature to enact the nation's first living will statute, the California Natural Death Act, in 1976. That statute was so narrowly drawn that, though inspired by her story, it ironically would not have helped Ms. Quinlan. The California statute, which remains the law of that state, requires that a declaration be executed only 14 days or more after the patient is diagnosed as having a terminal illness, which is defined as an illness that will cause the patient's "imminent" death. Ms. Quinlan was not terminally ill, and, furthermore, had lapsed into unconsciousness before any prognosis could have been determined.

By 1990, some 41 states and the District of Columbia had enacted living will statutes. Though differing widely in detail, all of those statutes grant immunity to physicians and healthcare providers who follow the patient's expressed wishes. George Annas has noted that most of those statutes suffer from four major shortcomings: (1) they are applicable only to those who are "terminally ill"; (2) they limit the types of treatment that can be refused to "artificial" or "extraordinary" therapies; (3) they make no provisions for the person to designate another person to make the decision on his or her behalf or set criteria for such decisions; and (4) they do not provide for a penalty in the event that health care providers fail to honor these documents.[12]

The American Medical Association's Committee on Medico-Legal Problems has also evaluated these statements and has found significant drawbacks.[13] First and most important, no matter how carefully crafted, no legislation can provide guidance for unanticipated circumstances. If drafted in general language to cover a broad range of circumstances, the law may be too vague, abstract or ambiguous to apply to specific situations.

Moreover, many living will statutes are drawn so narrowly that they are applicable only in very limited circumstances. For example, some statutes state that they are to be effective only in cases of "terminal condition." Such language excludes from their provisions such persons as Karen Ann Quinlan, Paul Brophy and Nancy Jobes who were not terminally ill but in a persistent vegetative state.

Some nine states, including Florida, Connecticut and Missouri, have statutes that exclude feeding tubes and artificial nutrition and fluids from "medical treatments" that can be withdrawn even from terminally ill patients. Legal challenges to those states' statutes have resulted in authorization by courts of final jurisdiction of the withdrawal of artificial feeding systems from irreversibly comatose patients on common law or constitutional grounds. [*Corbett* (FL),[14] *McConnell* (CT),[15] and *Cruzan* (MO)[16]]. The statutory language, however, might influence patients' stated preferences when they compose their own living wills. State courts, as was true of the Missouri Supreme Court, may be influenced by the language of the living will statute in deciding the scope of a patient's right to refuse artificial supports.

The ambiguity and vagueness of language and the need for physicians to make decisions based on an interpretation of a document, rather than on a discussion with someone acting on behalf of the patient, can result in decisions contrary to what a patient would want. This can be seen in New York's Wirth case.[17] Tom Wirth, a New York City man with AIDS, had signed a living will stating that should he become incapable of making his own decisions and should his condition be "irreversible," he would not want "extraordinary" measures taken to extend his life. When Mr. Wirth developed a brain infection from toxoplasmosis, his physician, over the companion's strenuous objections, continued to treat Mr. Wirth because, in the physician's judgment, "toxoplasmosis is potentially reversible." The court upheld the physician's position.

Mr. Wirth, despite intensive treatment, eventually succumbed to the infection. The appointment of the companion as health care proxy would have obviated the difficulties found in Mr. Wirth's blunt, unnuanced written statement. The appointment of an identifiable person, especially one who knows the person and his values, assures that the decision will be clinically situated, attuned to changing conditions, and in the hands of someone who the patient knows and whose judgment the patient trusts.

Durable Powers of Attorney

The static nature of a living will has led to proposals to replace what one commentator labels "a bloodless document" with a flesh and blood person who could speak for the patient.[18] This can be done effectively by assigning a "durable power of attorney" to a designated person who would speak for the individual should that individual become incapacitated. The terminology used for the document which identifies the surrogate, proxy or agent (the terms are used interchangeably in the literature)—the "durable power of attorney"—is confusing and misleading. The instrument, though developed from probate law, has nothing to do with lawyers. One does not need a lawyer to draft a durable power of attorney, nor does the proxy or agent named therein need to be a lawyer.

Any competent adult can write a statement naming any other competent adult—spouse, parent, child, sibling, companion or friend—as his or her proxy for health-care decisions. To prevent potential abuses or conflicts of interest, it is best that, except for relatives, direct health-care providers not be named as agents. (Many statutes, in fact, exclude such providers from being named as health-care proxies.) Once designated in a written witnessed document, the proxy has the same health-care decision-making power the patient would have had were he or she able to make decisions.

Justice Sandra Day O'Connor, in her concurring opinion in the *Cruzan* case, strongly advocated the use of durable power of attorney as an efficient and effective way of guaranteeing that patients' wishes with regard to health decisions will be respected. She went so far as to suggest that while the question of their authority was not before the Court, that "does not preclude a further determination that the Constitution requires the States to implement the decisions of a duly appointed surrogate."[19]

In making medical decisions for the now incompetent patient, the proxy is bound by the expressed wishes of the patient to the extent that such wishes are known. Otherwise, the agent is to act in ways consistent with the values or the best interests of the patient. As Annas correctly notes, "the goal of appointing a proxy is to simplify the process of making decisions and to make it more likely that the patient's wishes will be followed—not to complicate existing problems." (12, p. 1211). The Nebraska Supreme Court's recent *Bergstedt* opinion emphasizes that perspective: "If the process involved in validating a patient's election to refuse or terminate medical treatment is unduly protracted, the patient's rights become hollow and meaningless, if not entirely ineffectual."[20]

If hospitals concentrate on paperwork rather than on the way decisions should be made, the process of open and full communication between physician and patient will be impeded. If, as Annas reports, that process disintegrates into hospital attorneys drafting 13-page, single-spaced proxy forms that are utterly unintelligible to nonlawyers, or if hospital lawyers probe requests to find reasons why physicians or hospitals might want to seek judicial review before honoring the decision of the health-care agent, then the process will be counterproductive and self-destruct.

To eliminate uncertainty and to minimize the potential for dispute and disruption, the durable power of attorney should be a simple document written in plain language and intelligible to anyone with a basic grammar school education. It should not, as one study observes, "require reading skills at the advanced college level and have an average ease of readability comparable to that of the *New England Journal of Medicine.*"[21]

Annas himself falls short of his own admonition to provide "a simple one-page document that sets forth all necessary information in easily comprehensible language" when he endorses a form prepared by the Massachusetts Medical Society and the Massachusetts Hospital Association:

> My agent shall have the authority to make all health care decisions, subject to any limitations I state below, if I am unable to make decisions myself. My agent's authority becomes effective if my attending physician determines in writing that I lack the capacity to make or to communicate health care decision . . .
>
> I direct my agent to make decisions on the basis of my agent's assessment of my personal wishes.

Witness Statement

> We, the undersigned, each witnessed the signing of this Health Care Proxy by the principal or at the direction of the principal and state that the principal appears to be at least 18 years of age, of sound mind, and under no constraint or undue influence. (12, p. 1213).

What non-lawyer speaks like that? To most people, a "principal" is the person who runs a grammar or high school. Except for an attorney, who would use the term to describe the person who wrote the document? As one physician who reviewed a similar document wrote: "They are so complicated that I have trouble understanding by whom and by what authority I am being directed, let alone how to translate the directive into appropriate action in any one of hundreds of different clinical situations." (18, p. 15).

A form able to be read by the average person might look like the following:

Sample Health-Care Proxy Form

I, _____, appoint _____ to make health-care decisions for me if I am unable to do so for myself (my proxy).

If the person I named as my proxy is unable, unwilling or unavailable to make decisions for me, I appoint _____ to act for me.

I want the person I named as my proxy to know what I would and would not want for medical treatments. (List them here):

_____

_____

_____

_____

_____

Signature _____

Address _____

Date _____

Name of proxy _____

Address of proxy _____

Telephone number of proxy _____

Name of substitute _____

Address of substitute _____

Telephone number of substitute _____

Witness _____ Date _____

Witness _____ Date _____

No matter the form or format, the focus of advanced directives, and more particularly of the appointment of a health-care proxy, should be on the substantive issues rather than on the process. The object is to assure patients that their wishes regarding medical treatment will be known and will be honored. If this assurance is given, families will be relieved of the anxiety and burden of trying to determine "what mother would want." Physicians and other caregivers will also be confident that they did "the right thing" for the patient.

What is Needed to Implement an Effective Use of PSDA: Physician-Patient Communication

Merely producing a living will or announcing that you are the legally appointed health-care proxy does not guarantee that the desired or even the appropriate medical care will occur.[22] Most physicians are uncomfortable discussing life-sustaining treatments and fail to raise the issue of the patient's terminal status until the patient's condition is obvious to everyone. Studies of DNR orders indicate that most such orders are written in the last days of the patient's life and generally after the patient is no longer able to articulate his or her preference with regard to resuscitation.[23] This avoidance of early and opportune discussion by physicians is frequently based on the misperception that patients will be discouraged and give up hope if told the truth. In a 1927 *Harper's Monthly* article, Dr. James Collins, a proponent of that theory, proposed that "every physician should cultivate the fine art of lying." They must do this, he writes, to protect their patients from becoming "poor shrunken things, full of melancholy and indisposition, unpleasant to themselves and those who love them."[24]

Empirical data shows that far from succumbing to unrelieved melancholy, when told their condition, most patients want to know the truth about their status.[25] The President's Commission report on *Making Health Care Decisions* indicates that information about medical status and risks and benefits of proposed procedures does not deter patients from undergoing recommended procedures.[26]

What is needed, as the Commission's report on *Deciding to Forgo Life-Sustaining Treatment* notes, is open, frank, and honest communication between patient and physician, communication that involves both parties and reveals what each believes is important and valued.[27] The physician's role is to provide a full and complete diagnosis of the patient's condition. Most physicians do extremely well at that aspect of practice. They are also quick to provide the good news if there is a ready solution to the patient's problem.

The more difficult and demanding task is to convey the prognosis when the prospects are bleaker or even grim. The patient relies on the physician's expertise to translate the test results and raw data into an intelligible prognosis. Franz Ingelfinger, the late editor of the *New England Journal of Medicine*, goes even further. He insists that it is the physician's duty to use his or her experience not only to make a prognosis, but to winnow down the various possibilities into a concrete recommendation. In his words, "A physician who merely spreads an array of vendibles in front of the patient [or the patient's proxy] and then says 'Go ahead and choose, it's your life,' is guilty of shirking his duty, if not malpractice."[28]

Once the recommendation has been made, the patient (or the proxy) is free to accept or reject it based on personal psycho-social values. If rejected, the discussion begins again with an assessment of other possible alternatives and continues until there is agreement on a treatment plan.

One caveat should be noted. While the patient or proxy may decline a treatment, that does not imply that a physician must follow whatever treatment demands that patient or proxy might make. If a requested treatment goes beyond the physician's professional assessment of appropriate care for the patient's condition, the physician may legitimately decline to provide it.[29] The patient or proxy, may, of course, seek another physician, but neither a proxy nor a competent patient may compel a physician to act in a manner contrary to the physician's professional judgment.[30] As George Annas forcefully puts it: "Physicians retain the right not to offer treatment that is counterindicated, useless, or futile." (12, p. 1212).

Potential Difficulties and Benefits of PSDA

It is not only important that an individual have clear and effective communication with his or her physician, it is essential that the patient's desires and values be known to those who will have decision-making responsibility if the individual becomes incapacitated. That possibility, as the *Quinlan* and *Cruzan* cases made clear, is not confined to the infirm or the elderly.

The PSDA, it is to be hoped, will be a mechanism that will encourage discussion within families and facilitate access to advanced directives. The educational component should also help overcome both patient and physician reluctance to broach the topic. If so, patient autonomy and self-determination will be enhanced and anxiety about the future reduced. If the educational and training programs are successful in reducing physician fear of liability, there should also be greater willingness to honor patient preferences.

The PSDA is not a panacea; it is not without its own problems. The clinical, ethical and legal barriers to a successful implementation of the Act have been catalogued by La Puma. Among the clinical issues is that a patient, besieged by admissions clerks and unintelligible forms, may have difficulty understanding what the fuss is all about. A checklist "medical directive" about what they would want should they become demented, comatose, in a persistent vegetative state or terminally ill, may so frighten patients that they avoid the topic altogether.[31] Even if completed, the form may be put aside, misplaced and never read by the physician. Worst of all, an acutely ill hospitalized patient who is too sick to benefit from a discussion of future choices may out of fear, discomfort or pain, make choices that reflect only a desire to get through the process and into a bed.

The legal barriers are even more perplexing. Hastily or poorly drafted statutes may seemingly exclude choices that are constitutionally protected (e.g., living will statutes that exclude

nutrition and fluids from those treatments that may be omitted).
Patients may be told that in the absence of a statutory authorization, living wills are illegal. Worse still is a legal "interpretation" of a statute that defies common sense. For example,
the Maryland Attorney General wrote an advisory report which
cautioned that those who wished to decline medical treatment if
in a persistent vegetative state should use only a durable power
of attorney since the living will statute in Maryland applied
only to imminently dying, terminally ill patients. This opinion
suggests that signing a directive on the specific types of treatment one does not want somehow serves as a waiver of the
common law and federal constitutional rights announced in
Cruzan to decline any form of medical treatment.[32]

White and Fletcher are on point when they note that lawyers whose areas of expertise do not include health care, or
hospital attorneys who have the institution and not the patient
as their client, may provide misleading or inaccurate information about state laws relating to the withdrawal of treatment.[33]
These authors wisely suggest that hospital attorneys and risk
managers should be included in the educational efforts undertaken in compliance with the Act. While there is a potential
for legally inspired mischief, the PSDA should prove con-
structive if those charged with implementing the statute keep
the focus on the goal of enhancing patient-proxy-physician
communication rather than on protecting the institution from
potential liability.

The cost containment implications of the Act present potential ethical concerns. Its passage within the Omnibus Reconciliation Act of 1990 gives rise to questions as to whether it
was designed to protect patients or contain costs. There are
dangers that providers may use the PSDA to minimize Medicare losses on DRG "outliers." Patients who are illiterate, indi-
gent or unaware of advanced directives' significance may be
manipulated into signing statements that they neither understand or want.

Such dangers are real, but it must be remembered that the impetus for living will legislation and for the more than 50 "right-to-die" cases that have occurred since *Quinlan* has not been provider concern for costs, but patient or family desire to end unwanted treatments. The protection of the vulnerable from callous attempts at cost containment must rest with the professional commitment to patient well-being and vigilant ethics committees; it cannot be guaranteed by limiting the choice of all to protect the few.

Goal of PSDA

These barriers and caveats ought not distract caregivers and patients from the practical goal of the Patient Self-Determination Act: to encourage productive patient-physician dialogue concerning the patient's medical treatment choices. Once informed of what the physician can provide, competent individuals can and should make their desires and values known. These should be recorded by the physician in the patient's medical record, and, if desired, put into writing by the patient and given to family members or others who might be called upon in the future to make decisions for the patient. Further, patients should designate someone to act on their behalf should they become incapacitated. Doing so will relieve physicians and families of ambiguity, anxiety and guilt and will help to assure individuals that their wishes will be known, respected and upheld.

The process by which this is achieved is precisely that—a process. It is not an end in itself. As with informed consent, the goal is a well-formulated discussion between physician and patient, one that results in a knowledgeable choice. It is not—and ought not be confused with—a hastily scrawled signature on a preprinted form. Forms provided by hospitals on advanced directives should be the starting point, not the closure, of the dialogue. Ideally this process, which studies show can be accomplished in less than 15 minutes (4, p. 892), is begun in a primary care setting as part of a routine history and physical.

Further, as La Puma observes: "Affirming the patient's decision-making capacity, determining the patient's treatment goals, informing the patient of what goals are possible, and asking whether and why the patient wishes to limit treatment are *clinical activities*" (emphasis added) (2, p. 405). As such, advanced directives must be part of the clinical process, part of the physician's involvement with treating his or her patient. It cannot and ought not be relegated to an admission clerk or hospital administrator.

The Patient Self-Determination Act is not a bureaucratic hurdle designed to complicate good patient care. It is not just another form to fill out; it is not merely a "Disclosure of Rights"; it is not a federal intrusion into the practice of medicine. The PSDA is an invitation and an opportunity for physicians and patients to undertake what both say they want: better communication and understanding of the patient's choices regarding medical treatment.

For Reflection and Discussion

1. Discuss the breakdown in communications between patient and physician. Can you give examples from your own experience of this lack of communication? How can the PSDA help?

2. What are the advantages and disadvantages of a living will and of a durable power of attorney?

3. Discuss some of the potential difficulties and benefits of PSDA. How might PSDA influence the debate about euthanasia?

Notes

1. J. Katz, *The Silent World of Doctor and Patient* (New York: Free Press, 1984).

2. J. La Puma, D. Orentlicher, R.J. Moss, "Advanced Directives on Admission: Clinical Implications and Analysis of the Patient Self-Determination Act of 1990." *JAMA* 66 (1991) 402-405.

3. T.E. Finucaue, J.M. Schumway, R.L. Powers, and R.M. Alessandri, "Planning With Elderly Patients for Contingencies of Severe Illness," *Journal of Internal Medicine* 3 (1988) 322-325.

4. L.L. Emanuel, M.J. Barry, J.D. Stockle, et al. "Advanced Directives for Medical Care—A Case for Greater Use," *The New England Journal of Medicine* 324 (1991) 889-895.

5. 42 U.S.C. 1395 cc(a)(1) et seq. (as amended Nov. 1990).

6. Capron A.M., "The Patient Self-Determination Act: Not Now," *The Hastings Center Report,* 20, no. 5 (1990) 35-36.

7. *Cruzan v. Director Missouri Dept. of Health,* 110 S.Ct. 2841 (1990).

8. *Union Pacific Railway Company v. Bostford,* 141 U.S. 250 (1891).

9. *Schloendorff v. Society of New York Hospitals,* 211 N.Y. 125, 105 N.E. 92 (1914).

10. L. Kutner, "Due Process of Euthanasia: The Living Will a Proposal," *Indiana Law Journal* 44 (1969) 539.

11. *In re Quinlan,* 70 N.J. 10, 355 A.2d 647 (1976).

12. G. Annas, "The Health Care Proxy and the Living Will," *New England Journal of Medicine* 324 (1991) 1210-1213.

13. Report of the Board of Trustees of the American Medical Association. *Living Wills, Durable Powers of Attorney, and Durable Powers of Attorney for Health Care,* Chicago: American Medical Association, 1989.

14. *Corbett v. D'Alessandro.* 487 So. 3d 368 (Fla. Dist. Ct. App., 1986).

15. *McConnell v. Beverly Enterprises, Inc.* 209 Conn. 692, 553 A.2d 596 (1989).

16. *Cruzan v. Harmon,* 760 S.W. 2d 408 (Mo. 1988)., see also, *Couture v. Couture,* 48 Ohio App. 3d 208 (Ohio Ct. App. 1989).

17. E. Rosenthal, "Filling the Gap Where a Living Will Won't Do," *New York Times,* January 17, 1991, cl.

18. P.R. Alper, "A Living Will is a Bloodless Document," *Wall Street Journal,* January 11, 1991, p. 15.

19. *Cruzan v. Director Missouri Dept. of Health,* 110 S.Ct. 2841 (1990). Concurring.

20. *McKay v. Bergstedt,* 106 Nevada Supreme Court Advance Opinion 142, November 30, 1990, 15.

21. K.J. Tarnowski, D.M. Allen, C. Mayhall, P.A. Kelly, "Readability of Pediatric Biomedical Research Informed Consent Forms," *Pediatrics* 85 (1990) 58-62.

22. Davis M., Southerland L.I., Garrett J.M., et al. "A Prospective Study of Advanced Directives for Life-Sustaining Care," *The New England Journal of Medicine,* 324 (1991) 882-88.

23. Bedell S.E., Delbanco T.L., Cook E.F., Epstein F.H., "Survival After Cardiopulmonary Resuscitation in the Hospital," *The New England Journal of Medicine,* 309 (1983) 569-75.

24. Collins J. "Should Doctors Tell the Truth?" in *Ethics in Medicine* eds. Resier, Dyck and Curran. (Cambridge: The MIT Press, 1977).

25. Ende J., Kazis L., Ash A., Moskowitz M.D. "Measuring Patients' Desires for Autonomy: Decision-Making and Information-Seeking Preferences Among Medical Patients," *Journal of General Internal Medicine,* 4 (1989) 23-30.

26. President's Commission for the Study of Ethical Problems in Medicine and Biomedical and Behavioral Research, *Making Health Care Decisions* (Washington D.C.: U.S. Government Printing Office, 1982).

27. President's Commission for the Study of Ethical Problems in Medicine and Biomedical and Behavioral Research. *Deciding to Forgo Life-sustaining Treatment* (Washington D.C.: U.S. Government Printing Office, 1982).

28. F. Ingelfinger, "Arrogance," *New England Journal of Medicine* 303 (1980) 1507-09.

29. J.J. Paris, R. Crone, F.F. Reardon, "Physician's Refusal of Requested Treatment: The Case of Baby L," *New England Journal of Medicine* 322 (1990) 1012-15.

30. T. Tomlinson H. and Brady "Futility and the Ethics of Resuscitation," *JAMA* 264 (1990) 1276-1280; J.C. Hackler. and F.C. Hiller, "Family Consent to Orders Not to Resuscitate: Reconsidering Hospital Policy," *JAMA* 264 (1990) 1281-1283.

31. L.L. Emanuel, and E.J. Emanuel, "The Medical Directive: A New Comprehensive Advanced Care Document," *JAMA,* 261 (1989) 3288-3293.

32. Opinion of the Attorney General of Maryland. Opinion No. 90-044 (September 24, 1990).

33. White M.L., and Fletcher J.C., "The Patient Self-Determination Act: On Balance, More Help than Hindrance," *JAMA* 266 (1991) 410-412.

Part IV:
Nutrition and Hydration

17

Deciding About Death

Kenneth R. Overberg, S.J.

YOUR FATHER IS IN A COMA AND HAS BEEN FOR MONTHS following a severe stroke. Although he is permanently unconscious, his bodily systems are functioning. But the doctors tell you his condition is "irreversible"—he will never regain consciousness. If it weren't for the feeding tube, he soon would die. With the feeding tube, the vegetative state could go on for years, and cost thousands of dollars. What is the right thing to do?

Many people have had to decide whether or not to withdraw life-support systems from a loved one who was dying. As our technology improves, the number of such situations will increase. Experience and reflection have helped us to discern when such things as respirators and even antibiotics do not need to be used. Questions still surround the use of medical nourishment and fluids, however.

Those questions evoke strong feelings—and demand careful moral analysis. What ought we to do in such situations? This article will provide some direction in answering this challenging question. Two cases which received national attention help focus the important issues concerning withdrawing life-support systems.

Two Court Cases

Paul Brophy was a 46-year-old Massachusetts firefighter when he underwent emergency brain surgery. He never recovered consciousness after the operation and entered a vegetative state, unable voluntarily to control his muscles or respond to verbal statements. Medical experts considered Brophy's condition irreversible.

Apart from severe brain damage, Brophy's health was good. He was not in danger of imminent death, and could have lived for years with continued feeding through a tube inserted into his stomach. On several occasions before the surgery, he had expressed his conviction that he did not want to be put on a life-support system. After Brophy persisted in this vegetative state for more than a year, Patricia Brophy, his wife, requested that tube feeding end because he had no quality of life remaining.

Claire Conroy was an 84-year-old nursing home resident. She suffered from irreversible mental and physical problems, including heart disease, diabetes and hypertension. She was unable to swallow, and was fed by a tube through her nose. Though she would smile or moan in response to some stimuli, she could not speak. Her movements were very limited: she was restricted to a semifetal position. Thomas Whittemore, Miss Conroy's nephew and guardian, requested that the feeding tube be removed from his awake but severely mentally incapacitated aunt.

Not surprisingly, both of these cases were taken to the courts. Each had decisions made and overturned. Legal experts are grappling with these issues, but that is not the focus of this article. Here we will concentrate on moral questions. But it is necessary to remember the distinction between legality and morality: What is legal is not necessarily moral and what is moral is not always legal.

The basic question which emerges in these cases is this: Is withholding or withdrawal of artificial nutrition and hydration (foods and fluids) killing the person or simply allowing the person to die (that is, not needlessly interfering with the dying process)? Is artificial nutrition and hydration a medical procedure? When nutrition and hydration are withdrawn, are we intending death for the patient?

Our Choice of Words Is Critical

To do careful moral analysis, we must consider some language and concepts used in the discussion about life support. In our talk may be built-in meanings, evaluations, even prejudices. Take, for example, the two words *killing* and *murder*. What is implied in each? *Killing* indicates that one person has ended the life of another. That is an unfortunate event, indeed an evil. But we do not know if it is a justified killing, for example, in self-defense. *Murder* describes the same physical act—one person has ended the life of another—but also includes a moral evaluation—this was an unjustified act, and so a moral evil.

Let's examine the language of our basic question: *Is the withdrawal of artificial nutrition and hydration killing the person or simply allowing the person to die?* Generally, "killing" implies an activity, and "allowing to die" implies a certain passivity. But there is more. "Allowing to die" can be either justified or unjustified. Justified allowing to die means one does not needlessly interfere with the dying process. This implies a certain passivity, yet may include withdrawing life-support systems. Unjustified allowing to die means one fails to take steps that ought to be taken. This unjustified allowing to die is killing—or more accurately, murder. Thus, the ethical dilemma we are analyzing can be expressed this way: When is the withdrawal of artificial nutrition and hydration justified and when is it not?

What about the use of the term "nutrition and hydration?" Would "food and water" give a very different feel to our question? Does one phrase suggest a medical procedure while the other a basic human need? One some kind of medical device, the other a bowl of soup? Does our choice of words subtly determine our position and color our ethical reasoning?

Two other words are extremely important and frequently used in evaluating life-support: *extraordinary* and *ordinary* means. Probably a combination of effective communication and common sense has led to the widespread appreciation of this distinction. One must make use of ordinary means of medical help; extraordinary means are optional. All kinds of folks—from the simple to the highly educated—find this distinction helpful in making moral decisions about medical issues.

There are two problems, though: First, ethicists are not referring to medical procedures alone when they speak of *ordinary* and *extraordinary*. They are speaking of the overall effort made to keep a person alive in relation to how those efforts will help the patient pursue life's purposes. Secondly, even if one equates the terms *ordinary* and *extraordinary* solely with medical procedures, as many people do, whether a procedure is ordinary or extraordinary depends upon what medical help is available in a given place. That distinction is continually changing as improved technology becomes available. What was extraordinary 10 years ago is now very ordinary. What is ordinary here in the United States is very extraordinary in a Third World country.

Why do people continue to rely upon such ambiguous terms? Perhaps the words *ordinary* and *extraordinary* are used not so much to help reach a conclusion as to express a conclusion already decided. Like the word *murder,* these words carry along an inbuilt evaluation: *ordinary* implies a judgment that these medical procedures ought to be done; *extraordinary* points to optional use.

If we return to our fundamental question and ask whether artificial nutrition and hydration are ordinary or extraordinary means, the answer must be: both! It depends on the total situation.

Ordinary vs. Extraordinary: A Closer Look

In their writings, moral theologians Richard McCormick, S.J., and John Paris, S.J., have traced the Catholic tradition regarding the duty to preserve life. They point out that the distinction between ordinary and extraordinary means of prolonging life was articulated several hundred years ago. From the very beginning *extraordinary* referred *not solely to the technique or the means employed, but also to treatment in relation to the condition of the patient.* Historically, if even the most simple and basic remedy offered no hope of benefit to the patient, it was deemed extraordinary and, therefore, morally optional. A regular example given in this type of case was food and water.

This tradition continued for centuries. It was expressed in this century by the Jesuit moral theologian Gerald Kelly. In the early 1950s he asked if there is a moral obligation to continue intravenous feeding of an irreversibly comatose, terminally ill patient. His answer was that no remedy is obligatory unless it offers a reasonable hope of checking or curing a disease. He focused attention on the traditional understanding that ordinary and extraordinary referred not to the quality of the technique employed but to the proportionate burden and benefit it provides the patient.

Also in this century, Pope Pius XII said simply that one must use only those means that do not involve any grave burdens for oneself or another. He added that life, health and all temporal activities are, in fact, subordinated to spiritual ends.

Where, then, did the confusion come from? Probably from two very different sources. The first is medical technology developing much more rapidly than medical-moral reflection and analysis. This, along with the increasing number of lawsuits, has led to defining techniques, rather than efforts in relation to a patient's condition, as ordinary or extraordinary. The second source is caution within the moral (particularly Roman Catholic) analysis itself. Thus, theologians such as

Kelly were concerned that to discontinue intravenous feeding might be misinterpreted as a form of Catholic euthanasia, and that insensitive people might all too readily stop nourishment for anyone whose life was considered "useless." For some, what started as caution has developed into nearly absolute opposition.

When Is Withdrawal Justified? Three Approaches

If the distinction between extraordinary and ordinary means has become too confused and subjective to be truly helpful, how then do we answer our basic question: When is the withdrawal of artificial nutrition and hydration morally justified? Let's look at three possible positions.

Position #1—'Euthanasia Is OK'. At one extreme are those who support euthanasia. Clearly they endorse not only the withdrawal of artificial life-support but also the active shortening of a patient's life, for example, by lethal injection. Their position comes from a strong emphasis on individual rights, with the concepts of "right to privacy," "self-determination" and "death with dignity" at the heart of their argument. This position has always been rejected by the Catholic Church.

Position #2—'Life Must Be Sustained at All Costs'. At the other extreme we have those who hold that the withdrawal of artificially provided food and fluids, even from people with severe disabilities, cannot be ethically justified, except in very rare situations. Central to this position is that remaining alive is never rightly regarded as a burden, because human bodily life is inherently good and not merely instrumental to other goods.

Therefore, it is never morally right to deliberately kill innocent human beings. Such killing can result from acts of omission such as the failure to provide adequate food and fluids. This second position prohibits the deliberate killing of the innocent, even if motivated by an anguished or merciful wish to end painful and burdened life.

This position acknowledges that means of preserving life may be withheld or withdrawn if those means are judged either useless or excessively burdensome. Traditionally, a treatment has been judged useless if it offers no reasonable hope of benefit. A treatment is excessively burdensome when whatever benefits it offers are not worth pursuing for some reason, such as it is too painful, too restrictive of the patient's liberty or too expensive.

Significantly, the "useless or excessive burden" criteria are not applied to those who are permanently unconscious (for example, Paul Brophy) or to those who require medical nourishment as a result of suffering from something like Lou Gehrig's or Alzheimer's diseases (for example, Claire Conroy). Feeding these patients and providing them with fluids by means of tubes is *not* useless because it does bring to these patients a great benefit, namely, the preservation of their lives. Artificial nourishment can only be considered useless or excessively burdensome in the case of imminent death from other causes.

Finally, although it recognizes the treatment's cost in time and energy, this position emphasizes the benefits to the nondying patient (life itself) and to the caregiver (an experience of mercy, compassion and appreciation for human dignity).

Position #3—'Life Is a Fundamental But Not Absolute Good'. This approach attempts to find a middle path between the above two extremes. On the one hand it rejects euthanasia, judging deliberate killing to be a violation of human dignity. On the other hand, while life is valued as a great and fundamental good, it is not seen as an absolute to be sustained in every situation. Accordingly, in some situations, artificial nutrition and hydration may be removed.

This position, which is supported by prominent theologians such as Kevin O'Rourke, O.P., and Richard McCormick, S.J., and by the American Medical Association, holds that to focus the debate only on cases of imminent death may be too narrow. Instead, we should ask if a disease or condition that will lead to death (a fatal pathology) is present. For example, a patient in an irreversible coma cannot eat and swallow and thus will die of the effects of the coma in a short time unless life-prolonging devices are used. Withholding artificial nutrition and hydration from a patient in an irreversible coma does not cause a new fatal disease or condition. It simply allows an already existing fatal pathology to take its natural course. Here, then, is a fundamental idea of this third position: If a fatal condition is present, the ethical question we must ask is whether we are morally obligated to intervene.

But how do we decide either to treat a fatal pathology or to let it take its natural course? To be alive is a great and fundamental good, a necessary condition for pursuing life's purposes: happiness, fulfillment, love of God and neighbor. Does the obligation to prolong life ever cease? Yes, this position holds, if prolonging life does not help the person in striving for the purposes of life. Pursuing life's purposes implies some ability to function at the level of reasoning, relating and communicating. If efforts to restore this cognitive-affective function can be judged useless or would result in profound frustration (that is, a severe burden) in pursuing the purposes of life, then the ethical obligation to prolong life is no longer present.

This third approach recognizes that making decisions for others is especially difficult. In such situations, we must realize that persons with limited bodily and spiritual functions can still pursue the purposes of life. Thus, simply because a person is seriously impaired does not imply automatically that this person can be allowed to die from an existing fatal pathology.

Finally, even the person who has physiological function but no hope of recovering cognitive-affective function is still a human being, and so deserves comfort and care.

A Moral Theologian's Advice

How are these three significantly different positions judged by the Roman Catholic Church? The Catholic position has consistently opposed euthanasia. But there is no definitive Catholic position regarding the other two approaches. Vatican commissions, state Catholic conferences and moral theologians have come down on both sides. Evidently, the dialogue must continue!

As part of that dialogue, I'd like to make a few comments about the three previous contrasting views and then state my position. First, euthanasia has always provided me with a challenge, a challenge for careful moral reasoning. In many cases, euthanasia does initially seem to be the merciful response. The highly respected moral theologian James Gustufson asks whether we have turned a decisive corner once we have decided to let a person die. Would it not then be more merciful to hasten that death?, he asks.

There is an emotional tug here. But however strong that tug, I continue to find a profound difference between allowing to die and causing death, a difference surely not for the patient but for us, the doers of the action. Taking life, even though for a good motive, is an action which will undermine our humanity. It is a line we ought not to cross.

Second, there are real differences in the language used in the second and third positions. The second, which generally opposes the withdrawal of nourishment, usually uses "food" and "fluids" and "feeding through tubes," rather than "artificial nutrition and hydration" and "medical nourishment," the language preferred by proponents of the third position. Does this usage slant the discussion in a particular direction? I think so.

Third, I agree with the caution expressed by both the second and third perspectives. Our society does evaluate people too easily in terms of productivity. We must be careful to proclaim the unique value of each person and to protect the rights of people with physical handicaps, mental illnesses and disabilities or other special needs.

Finally, I agree with the emphasis on human dignity expressed in the second and third positions. This dignity is philosophically rooted in an understanding of what it means to be human. More importantly, it is rooted theologically: From our Judeo-Christian heritage comes the conviction that we are created in God's image, and from our Christian experience that we have been redeemed by Jesus. God is the source and goal of our life.

Is the withdrawal of artificial nutrition and hydration killing the person or simply allowing the person to die? In my judgment the answer must be: It depends. If a fatal pathology is present and if life-prolonging efforts would be useless or a severe burden in pursuing the purpose of life—happiness, fulfillment, love of God and neighbor—then the answer to our question is that we are "allowing the person to die." Artificial nutrition and hydration are considered medical procedures. In this kind of situation we are not intending death by starving the person but merely allowing a pathology to take its normal course. This conclusion can be expressed in other words: Withdrawing artificial nutrition and hydration is justified when a fatal pathology is present and when life-prolonging efforts would be useless in pursuing the purpose of life.

We began this article with the difficult case of a permanently unconscious parent. In that situation, careful moral reasoning points to the withdrawal of the feeding tube as a responsible form of stewardship and a faithful caring for the gift of life. You desire to spare your father the burdens of prolonging his life when he can derive no benefit from such prolongation.

Your decision, made only after extensive consultation with the medical and pastoral-care staffs, fully respects and appreciates human dignity. It recognizes life as a fundamental but not absolute good. Death is not the ultimate evil; alienation from God is. Though not without sorrow, death marks the passage to new life. You can entrust your father to our gracious God, the source and goal of all life.

For Reflection and Discussion

1. Have you ever been involved in a decision to remove feeding tubes? How does your experience fit together with the descriptions in this article?

2. What is the main ethical question regarding the withdrawal of feeding tubes? What are the responses to this situation of three commonly-held positions? What is your position?

3. What is the full meaning of the distinction between ordinary and extraordinary means? How have you heard or made use of this distinction? Has it been helpful?

4. Review the article by James Rachels, "Active and Passive Euthanasia." Contrast that article with the third position presented in this article. Which do you find more convincing? Why?

18

'Moral Considerations' Ill Considered

Richard A. McCormick, S.J.

CONTROVERSIES ARE AT TIMES LIKE HOUSE PESTS: JUST when you think they have died out, they reappear. So it is with the ethical discussion of artificial nutrition and hydration for patients in a persistent vegetative state (P.V.S.).

The majority of philosophers and theologians—along with most courts—had concluded that the provision of such nutrition and hydration is not morally mandatory because it can no longer benefit the patient.

Now along comes the Dec. 12, 1991 statement of the bishops of Pennsylvania entitled "Nutrition and Hydration: Moral Considerations" (*Origins*, Jan. 30, 1992). What have the bishops said? First, they have stated that "in almost every instance there is an obligation to continue supplying nutrition and hydration to the unconscious patient." Second, the only exceptions to this conclusion are instances when death is imminent or the patient is "unable to assimilate what is being supplied." Third, outside of these two cases of "futility," withdrawal of nutrition and hydration from a P.V.S. patient is "euthanasia by omission," "killing by omission." As the bishops word it: "Sad to say, the intent is not to relieve suffering but, rather, to cause the patient to die. Nor can it be argued that it is merely the intention to 'allow' the patient to die, rather than to 'cause his death.' The patient in the persistent vegetative state is not thereby in a terminal condition, since nutrition and hydration and ordinary care will allow him to live for years. It is only if that care is taken away—and barring any other new disease or debilitation—that the patient will die. It is the removal of the nutrition and hydration that brings about the death. This is euthanasia by omission rather than by positive lethal action, but it is just as really euthanasia in its intent."

Finally, the bishops turn to advance directives such as the living will and durable power of attorney. "Neither the patient nor the surrogates of the patient have the moral right to withhold or withdraw treatment that is ordinary." But artificial nutrition and hydration for a P.V.S. patient is (except in the two instances noted above) ordinary care. Therefore, it may not be withheld or withdrawn. Briefly, the bishops state that it is immoral to specify in one's living will or to one's durable attorney "no artificial nutrition and hydration if I am in a P.V.S.," for this would be to refuse an ordinary means, one that is neither futile (in the bishops' sense) nor excessively burdensome.

Now, what have the bishops of Pennsylvania done? As I read their document, they have: (1) appealed to their teaching prerogatives and responsibilities (2) to impose a concrete application of more general principles (3) that represents one side of a disputed question (4) and used a questionable analysis (5) to arrive at extremely questionable conclusions. A word about each is in place if my criticism is to stand up.

A Teaching Statement.

"Nutrition and Hydration: Moral Considerations" is not a casual white paper floated to facilitate discussion groups. It is, as Cardinal Anthony Bevilacqua of Philadelphia states in the foreword, "an effort on our part to fulfill our responsibilities as bishops to give guidance to all the Catholic faithful of this state who are entrusted to our care." He concludes: "Our statement is intended to express, as well as we are currently able, the teaching of the Catholic Church as it affects these admittedly difficult cases." These statements are self-explanatory. The bishops view their reflections as a teaching statement.

A Concrete Application

Catholic moral teaching, at the level of general principle, maintains that life is a basic good but not an absolute one and that, therefore, not all means must be used to preserve it. As Pope Pius XII noted in 1957: "But normally one is held to use only ordinary means—according to the circumstances of persons, places, times and culture—that is to say, means that do not involve any grave burden for oneself or another. A more strict obligation would be too burdensome for most and would render the attainment of the higher, more important good too difficult. Life, health, all temporal activities are in fact subordinated to spiritual ends."

When these general statements are fitted to specific instances, we are dealing with applications.

The Florida bishops noted this in their statement on treatment of the dying: "The application of these principles to a patient who has been diagnosed with medical certainty to be permanently comatose, but whose death is not imminent, has aroused controversy" (*Origins*, June 1, 1991).

Why is it important to note that discussion surrounding treatment of P.V.S. patients is an *application*? For the simple reason that the bishops do not, indeed cannot, claim the same authority for applications as they do for their statement of general principles. They noted this in "The Challenge of Peace": "We stress here at the beginning that not every statement in this letter has the same moral authority. At times we reassert universally binding moral principles (e.g., noncombatant immunity and proportionality). At still other times we reaffirm statements of recent Popes and the teaching of Vatican II. Again, at other times we apply moral principles to specific cases." The bishops then note that, where applications are concerned, "prudential judgments are involved based on specific circumstances which can change or which can be interpreted differently by people of good will." They note that their judgments of application should be taken seriously but are "not binding in conscience." Notwithstanding its juridical ring, this last statement wisely withdraws from the type of magisteriolatry that would expect the Pope or bishops to dot every moral "i" and cross every moral "t" regardless of specificity.

Yet phrases used by Cardinal Bevilacqua such as "fulfill our responsibilities as bishops," "give guidance to all of the Catholic faithful of this state" and "express . . . the teaching of the Catholic Church" fairly droop with authoritative accents. That is why above I used the word "impose." Such weighted phrases could easily mislead people into thinking that what the bishops say is "the teaching of the Catholic Church." It is not. It is an application that involves us in circumstances that "can be interpreted differently by people of good will." Judgments of application should, as "The Challenge of Peace" notes, be "taken seriously." One of the ways to do that is to point out their weaknesses and inadequacies where they exist. And that brings us to the next point.

Artificial Nutrition and Hydration as a Controverted Subject

By saying that withdrawal of nutrition and hydration is controverted, I refer to philosophical-theological controversy. Most courts and several medical groups (e.g., The American Medical Association, The American Academy of Neurology) have approved such withdrawal, as did the President's Commission for the Study of Ethical Problems in Medicine and Biomedical and Behavioral Research.

Writing in *Issues in Law and Medicine* (1987) a group of ethicists (including William May, Germain Grisez, William Smith, Mark Siegler, Robert Barry, O.P., and Orville Griese) argued: "In our judgment, feeding such patients [who are permanently unconscious] and providing them with fluids by means of tubes is not useless in the strict sense, because it does bring to these patients a great benefit, namely, the preservation of their lives." They go on to note that the damaged or debilitated condition of the patient has been the key factor in recent court cases and conclude that decisions to withdraw food have been made "because sustaining life was judged to be of no benefit to a person in such poor condition. These decisions have been unjust."

On the other hand, bioethicists such as the Rev. Dennis Brodeur, Kevin O'Rourke, O.P., Albert S. Moraczewski, O.P., John Paris, S.J., James Walter, James Bresnahan, S.J., Daniel Callahan, Albert Jonsen, Thomas Shannon, George Annas and James Drane—to mention but a few—have come to a different conclusion.

Let Father Brodeur be a single example here. Artificial nutrition-hydration that "simply puts off death by maintaining physical existence with no hope of recovery . . . is useless and therefore not ethically obligatory" (*Health Progress,* June 1985). It is "vitalism" to think otherwise. Brodeur correctly rejects a notion of quality of life that states that a certain arbitrarily defined level of functioning is required before a person's life is to be valued. But if this notion refers to the relationship between a person's biological condition and the ability to pursue life's goals, it is critical to good decision-making. "In some circumstances" he concludes, "science's ability to respond helpfully to allow a person to pursue the goals of life is so limited that treatment may be useless."

This controversy is manifested even at the episcopal level. The Texas bishops (*Origins,* June 7, 1990) do not agree with the Pennsylvania bishops. Neither do the bishops of Washington and Oregon. After noting the two different approaches outlined above, these latter urge that there "should be a presumption in favor of providing patients with these necessities of survival." They finally conclude: "In appropriate circumstances, the decision to withhold these means of life support can be in accord with Catholic moral reasoning and ought to be respected by medical caregivers and the laws of the land" (*Origins*, Nov. 7, 1991). The same conclusion is drawn by Bishop John Leibrecht (Springfield-Cape Girardeau) in his comments on the Nancy Cruzan case. He discusses the two different approaches and says of the second that it is "a valid Catholic position which approves removal of Nancy Cruzan's tube." He concludes: "Unless there is an official and binding decision from church authorities, Catholics would be mistaken to hold that only one or the other line of Catholic moral reasoning is correct" (*Origins*, Jan. 11, 1990).

I recently discussed the Pennsylvania document with 19 physicians responsible for ethics committees around the country. They were in unanimous disagreement with the conclusions of the Pennsylvania bishops.

Why underline the controverted character of withdrawal of nutrition-hydration from P.V.S. patients? The answer can be found in the old (1948) "Ethical and Religious Directives for Catholic Hospitals," drawn up by the eminent Gerald Kelly, S.J. Directive No. 3 reads: "As now formulated, the directives prohibit only those procedures which, according to present knowledge of facts, seem certainly wrong. In questions legitimately debated by theologians, liberty is left to physicians to follow the opinions which seem to them more in conformity with the principles of sound medicine."

This directive may sound a little quaint to contemporary ears. But it embodies the centuries-old wisdom of probabilism. As Father Kelly explains in his commentary: "The provisions of directive three are but concrete applications of the sound general principle that obligations (i.e., precepts and prohibitions) are not to be imposed unless they are certain."

We must remember that the question of artificial nutrition-hydration is extremely practical. It affects physicians, nurses, families, hospitals, legislators, etc. It touches every individual who constructs advance directives. If it is, indeed, "legitimately debated"—as it is—it is beyond the competence of a group like the Pennsylvania bishops to settle the debate.

Questionable Moral Reasoning

The guidance provided by the Pennsylvania bishops is based on very questionable reasoning. They argue that withdrawal of artificial nutrition-hydration involves, in most cases, the intent to kill. It is "murder by omission." How do they arrive at that stark judgment? As follows. The P.V.S. patient is not in a terminal condition. It is only if nutrition-hydration is removed that the patient will die. "It is the removal of the nutrition and hydration that brings about the death." This is not merely "allowing to die." The bishops believe it involves the "clear intent to bring about death."

Is this the proper way the situation of P.V.S. should be analyzed? Not according to the Texas bishops. They note that life-sustaining means, including artificial nutrition and hydration, may be omitted "under conditions which render those means morally nonobligatory." Certainly, diagnosed P.V.S. is one of those conditions, in their view. They then add, interestingly: "In those appropriate cases the decision-maker is not guilty of murder, suicide, or assisted suicide, since there is no moral obligation under these circumstances to impede the normal consequences of the underlying pathology. The physical cause of death is ultimately the pathology which required the use of those means in the first place."

The Texas bishops, then, do not view the P.V.S. patient as nonterminal. They see such a person as "stricken with a lethal pathology which, without artificial nutrition and hydration, will lead to death." The moral question is: When should we intervene to prevent the "normal consequences of a disease or injury?" When it is decided that the patient can no longer benefit from the intervention, the underlying pathology is allowed to take its natural course. This does not involve the intent to bring about death.

This is the analysis proposed by Kevin O'Rourke, O.P (*America*, Nov. 22, 1986). Father O'Rourke, in an analysis almost identical to that of the Texas bishops, observes that "withholding artificial hydration and nutrition from a patient in an irreversible coma does not induce a new fatal pathology; rather it allows an already existing fatal pathology to take its natural course." Therefore, Father O'Rourke argues that we should not be discussing whether death is imminent, but "whether a fatal pathology is present." If it is, the key moral question is "whether there is a moral obligation to seek to remove the fatal pathology or at least to circumvent its effects."

This is also the approach of Daniel Callahan in his book *What Kind of Life.* Dealing with exactly these cases, Callahan asks: "On the level of physical causality, have we killed the patient or allowed him to die? In one sense, it is our action that shortens his life, and yet in another sense it is his underlying disease that brings his life to an end. I believe it reasonable to say that, since his life was being sustained by artificial means (respirator or tube), and that was necessary because of the fact that he had an incapacitating disease, his disease is the ultimate reality behind his death" (p. 234).

Because of this decisive causal role played by the underlying disease, Callahan states: "To allow someone to die from a disease we cannot cure (and that we did not cause) is to *permit the disease to act as the cause of death*" (my emphasis). In brief, those who argue that by withdrawing nutrition-hydration we introduce a new cause of death and therefore kill the patient have overlooked the lethal causal character of the underlying pathology. This is precisely the point urged by Sidney Callahan. Persons who believe we must sustain a body in an endless limbo "confuse withdrawing the feeding tube with active killing partly because they refuse to take into account that it is an injury or disease that has ended the person's human future" (*Health Progress,* April 1991).

The origin of the analysis adopted by the Pennsylvania bishops must remain somewhat speculative. But one would not be too far off in thinking that the late John R. Connery, S.J., was influential here. Father Connery argued that when quality of life is the central focus, then "the intention is not to free the patient of the burden of using some means, but the burden (or the uselessness) of the life itself. The only way to achieve this goal is by the death of the patient" (*Linacre Quarterly,* February 1988). Therefore, "the intention is the death of the patient"—which Father Connery regarded as "euthanasia by omission," though I am told that he changed his view shortly before his death.

Actually, the situation need not be conceptualized in terms of *life as a burden.* All we need say is that life in a P.V.S. is not a benefit or value to the patient. Therefore, withdrawing nutrition-hydration is withdrawing something from which the patient does not benefit.

This brings us to the central issue in this debate, the notion of benefit. William May *et al.,* see nutrition-hydration for a P.V.S. patient as providing a "great benefit," the preservation of life. So do the Pennsylvania bishops. Father O'Rourke, on the contrary, believes that mere "physiological function bereft of the potential for cognitive-affective function does not benefit the patient" and is, in this sense, useless. Daniel Callahan, the Rev. Dennis Brodeur, John Paris, S.J., the Texas bishops and many others share Father O'Rourke's assessment. So do I.

In deciding what is truly beneficial to a patient, it is useful to distinguish with Lawrence Schneiderman, Nancy S. Jecker and Albert R. Jonsen (*Annals of Internal Medicine,* June 15, 1990) between an effect and a benefit. The authors argue that the goal of medical treatment is "not merely to cause an effect on some portion of the patient's anatomy, physiology or chemistry, but to benefit the patient as a whole." They believe that nutritional support can effectively preserve a host of organ systems of a P.V.S. patient but remain futile. This they conclude because "the ultimate goal of any treatment should be improvement of the patient's prognosis, comfort, well-being or general state of health. A treatment that fails to provide such a benefit—even though it produces a measurable effect—should be considered futile."

This point was made recently by Bishop William Bullock of Des Moines (*Origins*, Jan. 30, 1992). Noting that God gives us life to carry out human activities, Bishop Bullock asserts that "the benefit of care or treatment to prolong the life of a dying person, or of a person for whom these human activities have become very difficult, or even no longer possible, diminishes in proportion to what remains possible for them." Benefit, he states, refers to "possible recovery or a prolongation of at least minimally conscious life." When such a benefit is absent, to omit nutrition-hydration "is not to intend the patient's death, but to permit nature to take its inevitable course."

The determination of what is truly beneficial to us as human persons is a broad human judgment. In all the groups I have polled on this matter, I have found only one person (of thousands) who wished to be maintained indefinitely in a P.V.S., and he did not understand the condition. This should not be taken to suggest that we determine right and wrong by head-counting. That misses the point. The significance of this virtual unanimity is that people do not regard continuance in a P.V.S. through artificial nutrition-hydration a genuine benefit. Effect, yes. Benefit, no.

Let me conclude with a fanciful scenario. Imagine a 300-bed Catholic hospital with all beds supporting P.V.S. patients maintained for months, even years by gastrostomy tubes. Fanciful? Not if the guidelines of the Pennsylvania bishops are followed. Appalling? In my judgment, yes—not least of all because an observer of the scenario would eventually be led to ask: "Is it true that those who operate this facility actually believe in life after death?"

For Reflection and Discussion

1. Compare the positions of this article with those in "Deciding About Death." With which do you agree? Why?

2. Discuss the author's distinction between moral principles and applications to specific questions. Why is this so important to McCormick?

3. What is your own experience of authority in the Church? Do you feel that judgments are imposed? What happens when there is disagreement among the bishops, as in this issue?

4. What is conscience—and how does it fit into this discussion of authority? How is conscience properly formed?

5. What is your reaction to the author's concluding scenario?

Part V:
Appendices

Appendix A: Medical Cases

In light of all the readings and your own reflection and discussion, consider the following cases. Weigh the questions, develop your position, and carefully state your reasons for what ought to be done.

CASE 1: Mr. M was a 58-year-old male who was accurately diagnosed as having inoperable, terminal, metastatic cancer of the lung. Neither radiation nor chemotherapy was appropriate. He was a stoic, alert, cooperative, delightful man. He freely discussed his condition and was aware of his prognosis. He experienced moderate intermittent pain which was controlled by narcotics as required. He was anorexic and ate essentially nothing. Despite pressure from caregivers and family to eat or to be tube fed, he cheerfully refused and was supported in this decision by his primary care physicians.

QUESTIONS: Should euthanasia have been considered in this case? Why or why not? If the patient didn't ask about it, who should? What is the moral value of supervising death by lack of food and water versus hastening the inevitable to reduce burden?

CASE 2: Mrs. Y was a 74-year-old female admitted because of pneumonia. She was demented (though articulate) and insisted on no treatment. In the process of her examination, a lesion was found near her tonsil which proved to be cancer and appeared to be treatable surgically. Since she lacked capacity for informed consent (though she had not been declared legally incompetent), intervention to establish guardianship and to obtain consent for treatment was initiated. Permission to treat the lesion was denied by the courts.

About 18 months later she was readmitted to the same clinical service with advanced inoperable cancer. The state guardian required that she be treated (short of surgery) and in the event of cardiac arrest that she must be resuscitated. Her physicians were intensely frustrated because of the irrationality of the situation. **QUESTIONS:** How would you help Mrs. Y? How would you counsel her physicians? What is the moral value of knowingly prolonging suffering versus enabling the patient to escape? Who decides? Justify your answers.

CASE 3: Mrs. F was a 77-year-old female nursing home resident, strongly supported by her family. She was depressed and anorexic but maintained total mental capacity to make decisions. She requested no treatment and refused food. She developed severe pressure ulcers due to malnutrition and inactivity. She requested not to be hospitalized. The family insisted that she be treated and she finally acquiesced sorrowfully. She was hospitalized, given enteral-nutrition, and treated with surgery and IV antibiotics for her severely infected pressure ulcers. Despite aggressive therapy she did not improve. She became more and more ill and depressed. She experienced significant suffering due both to her illness and to her biotechnological interventions.

QUESTIONS: Should her antibiotics and tube feedings be withdrawn against the family's will? Would this be euthanasia? Why? What are the moral pros and cons of pursuing the various available options in this situation?

CASE 4: AC is a 13-day-old infant girl, born to a 29-year-old mother following a full-term, uncomplicated pregnancy. In the delivery room the nurse noted that the skin on AC's extremities was sloughing. She was transferred to the Newborn Intensive Care Unit (NICU). A skin biopsy done on Day 1 of life was consistent with junctional epidermolysis bullosa, a genetic disease which is usually fatal. (Epidermolysis bullosa is a rare disorder. Approximately 50% of children with the junctional type will die by age 2 years, usually from infection. This is like having a total body burn, so the patient is subject to all the complications of a burn patient, e.g., infection, electrolyte imbalances, etc.) Over the last 13 days her disease has progressed to involve her entire body with the exception of her palms and soles. Her oral mucosa is also involved. In addition, AC's hospital course has been complicated by probable sepsis, hyponatremic seizures, anemia, and inability to feed her orally. Current treatment includes dressing changes every 24 hours, pain medication and sedation (morphine and Fentanyl), antibiotics, blood transfusions as needed, and nutrition via a central line.

AC's family is very involved with her care. Both parents are concerned that AC is suffering, especially during the daily dressing changes. This is their second child. They have a healthy 8-year-old boy at home.

The parents come to you as the attending physician asking you to give their daughter enough pain medication to put her out of her misery.

QUESTIONS: Is euthanasia justified in this situation? Why/why not? What about withdrawal of treatment? Are other options possible? If you were the attending physician, how would you respond to the parents?

CASE 5: AB is a 16-year-old boy with bone cancer of the femur which was diagnosed at age 14. Initially he underwent amputation along with chemotherapy. On routine follow-up, AB was noted to have a nodular lesion in the lung thought to be metastatic disease. Further evaluation with a CT scan showed one additional lesion which was smaller in size. After discussion with AB and his parents, surgery was scheduled for resection of the pulmonary lesions. Prognosis for such patients is uncertain; however, there have been case reports of long-term survival following resection.

At operation six additional lesions were seen. The largest lesion was resected for tissue diagnosis. Following surgery, AB was admitted to the Intensive Care Unit for postoperative care. Over the next 18 hours, AB became progressively more difficult to ventilate, requiring high pressures and rates as well as 100% oxygen. By 18 hours postoperative AB was on maximum ventilator support with continued deterioration of his respiratory status. The attending physician approached AB's parents about discontinuing ventilator support. With the parents' consent to discontinue the ventilator, the attending physician sedated and paralyzed AB, and removed AB from the ventilator.

QUESTIONS: Is the use of the paralyzing agent justified or not? Is this euthanasia or withdrawal of life-support? Are other actions possible? If you were the parents, how would you respond to the physician?

CASE 6: JS was a 20-year-old female with severe mental retardation. She functioned on about the two-year-old level. She also had a very bad seizure disorder requiring multiple medications to keep it under control. She was in the care of one of her sisters. Her parents were deceased. This woman developed progressive kidney failure to the point where hemodialysis was required. Her family chose to begin a course of dialysis therapy, actually over the doctor's recommendations to the contrary. Over the course of several years on dialysis this patient demonstrated progressive violent-type behavior to her caregivers at home. It should be noted that she was a fairly substantial-sized girl at the age of 20. This violence was both verbal and physical at times. In addition, she would refuse to take medications or adhere to diet and fluid prescriptions which were required for optimal therapy of kidney failure. As a result of her noncompliance, she had multiple hospitalizations for seizure-related illness, and fluid overload and electrolyte disturbances. Help from a clinical psychologist and input from a social worker were all without avail. Her sister, who was primary caregiver and held power of attorney over her legal affairs, requested the doctor to withdraw this otherwise healthy patient from dialysis. Withdrawal from dialysis, of course, would mean certain death within five to seven days. **QUESTIONS:** Is withdrawal justified at this time? Would this be intending to kill or allowing to die? How does the physician's earlier recommendation not to use dialysis enter into this decision? If you were the physician, how would you respond to the sister?

CASE 7: RT was a 63-year-old male with multiple medical problems. He had been on hemodialysis for about seven years and for the most part had been enjoying good health. However, he developed progressive problems with liver and heart failure that were not reversible. He had very terrible dialysis treatments related to difficulty removing fluid during hemodialysis. Because adequate fluid could not be safely removed during a hemodialysis treatment, he developed massive swelling of his abdomen and lower extremities. His doctors tried switching him to peritoneal dialysis with the hope that this might help his fluid removal and swelling problems; however, it made no significant difference. He requested that dialysis be discontinued and that he would be made as comfortable as possible while the dying process evolved.

QUESTIONS: Is this decision about "extraordinary means" and therefore justified? Would euthanasia—rather than just making him comfortable—be appropriate here? Who should suggest it? If you were his physician, what would you do in this case?

CASE 8: MS was a 55-year-old female who was a heavy smoker and required hemodialysis therapy. She was discovered to have an abnormal chest X-ray; subsequent evaluations showed a lung cancer. Because of her long-time smoking, she also had emphysema with an underlying problem exchanging oxygen and carbon dioxide because of chronically damaged lungs. The lung cancer was not treatable. She developed progressive pain that was controllable with narcotics. Since the pain pills were self-administered at home on an as-needed basis, she had several episodes of a near respiratory arrest due to the central nervous system depressant effect of the narcotic on her respiratory center, in addition to the baseline problem with oxygen and carbon dioxide exchange resulting from her chronically damaged lungs. She requested continued unlimited supply of narcotic type pain medications, which of course are prescription items, informing her doctor that she would indeed continue to medicate herself with these medications that were provided to her by prescription. She told her doctor she would rather die of an overdose than continue to suffer.

QUESTIONS: If you were the patient, would you be morally justified in deliberately taking an overdose? If you were the physician, would you continue to prescribe the medications? How does this case relate to the one in Timothy Quill's "Death and Dignity" article? Are there other options that ought to be followed?

Appendix B: Glossary

Advance Directives Documents in which individuals can give directions for their future health care if they should become unable to express their views (see living wills and durable power of attorney for health care).

Aid-In-Dying Term used in some public policy propositions to describe euthanasia and/or physician-assisted suicide.

Analgesic Pain reliever.

Cruzan, Nancy, Case 1990 case in which question of withdrawing a feeding tube was debated and decided (the Supreme Court's decision focused only on a state's right to demand clear and convincing evidence concerning the patient's wishes).

Curare One variation produces muscular relaxation, another paralyzes; also a type of poison.

Dementia Insanity.

DNR Do not resuscitate; orders indicating patient's desire not to be revived.

Durable Power of Attorney for Health Care A form of advance directive naming another person as decision-maker when individual is no longer able to make health-care decisions (see proxy and surrogate).

Edema	An accumulation of fluid, causing swelling.
Epidemiology	The science that deals with the incidence, distribution, and control of disease in a population.
Eugenics	A science that deals with the improvement of hereditary qualities by control of reproduction.
Euthanasia	"Easy death"; sometimes a distinction is made between active (causing death) and passive (allowing to die).
Extraordinary Means	Traditional term applied to health care measures that need not be taken because they are futile or excessively burdensome (see "Living and Dying Well" for more on the distinction between extraordinary [heroic] and ordinary means).
Hematocrit	Blood cell density.
Hospice	A form of care in which an interdisciplinary team provides palliative and support services to both the dying patient and the family.
Iatrogenic	Induced by a physician.
Initiative 119	Washington state's proposal to legalize euthanasia and physician-assisted suicide.
Living Will	An advance directive stating the individual's desire concerning health care (for a time when the person can no longer express health-care decisions).

Magisteriolatry   The magisterium is the public teaching office of the Roman Catholic Church (all the bishops together with and under the Pope); magisteriolatry refers to inappropriate deference given to this office (as in idolatry).

Metamyelocyte   An immature white blood cell (mature white blood cells are those cells that ward off infection).

Natural Death Act   Many states now have legislation protecting people's rights to make decisions about dying (e.g., recognizing advance directives).

Neutropenia   Abnormally low number of mature white blood cells (see metamyelocyte).

Nutrition and Hydration   Food and fluids; forms of medically-assisted nutrition and hydration include a nasogastric tube (inserted through the nose into the stomach) and a gastrostomy tube (surgically inserted through the abdominal wall into the stomach).

Palliative Measures   Actions which ease without curing.

Patient Self-Determination Act   Federal legislation requiring health-care institutions to inform patients of their right to make health-care decisions, including advance directives.

Persistent Vegetative State (PVS)   A condition in which the patient has sleep-wake cycles, but demonstrates no awareness of himself or herself or of the environment; a state of deep unconsciousness which is almost always irreversible.

Pluralism	View of reality which holds that there are many different—and valid—understandings; here linked with relativism, implying that one person's view may be as good as another's (vs. some sense of objective reality).
Probabilism	Traditional Roman Catholic view which holds that, concerning a debated moral question, a sound (or probable) opinion may be followed in forming one's conscience.
Proxy	One who takes the place of another (see durable power of attorney for health care).
Quinlan, Karen, Case	1976 case in which question of withdrawing a respirator was debated and decided (she was slowly weaned and survived ten years in a persistent vegetative state).
Relativism	Moral view which holds that all things are relative or arbitrary; "I have my view and you have yours" (vs. some sense of objective reality).
Retractions	Shrinkage or drawing back in • uprasternal: above the breast bone • intercostal: between the ribs.
Substituted Judgment	Judgment made by a proxy.
Surrogate	One who takes the place of another (see durable power of attorney for health care).
Vitalism	View of reality focusing on value of physical life, here implying "Keep the patient alive at all costs."

Appendix C: Sources

Here is a bibliographical list of the articles presented in this book. Appropriate copyright permissions were given by authors and/or journals. Views stated represent those of the authors. Institutional affiliations of the authors are from the time when the article was written.

"Active Euthanasia," *Theological Studies* 53, no. 1 (March 1992) 113-126. John J. Paris, S.J., the Michael P. Walsh Professor of Bioethics at Boston College.

"Active and Passive Euthanasia," *New England Journal of Medicine* 292, no. 2, (January 9, 1975) 78-80. James Rachels, professor of philosophy, University of Miami, Florida.

"Euthanasia," *New England Journal of Medicine* 319, no. 20, (November 17, 1988) 1348-50. Marcia Angell, M.D., Executive Editor of this journal.

"The Physician's Responsibility Toward Hopelessly Ill Patients: A Second Look," *New England Journal of Medicine* 320, no. 13, (March 30, 1989) 844-49. Sidney H. Wanzer, M.D., Emerson Hospital, Concord; Daniel D. Federman, M.D., and S. James Adelstein, M.D., Harvard Medical School, Boston; Christine K. Cassel, M.D., the Pritzker School of Medicine, Chicago; Edwin H. Cassem, M.D., Massachusetts General Hospital, Boston; Ronald E. Cranford, M.D., Hennipin County Medical Center, Minneapolis; Edward W. Hook, M.D., University of Virginia Medical Center, Charlottesville; Bernard Lo, M.D., University of California School of Medicine, San Francisco; Charles G. Moertel, M.D., Mayo Clinic and Medical School, Rochester; Peter Safar, M.D., University of Pittsburgh Medical School, Pittsburgh; Alan Stone, M.D., Harvard Law School, Cambridge;

Jan van Eys, Ph.D., M.D., University of Texas System Cancer Center and School of Medicine, Houston.
"It's Over, Debbie," *The Journal of the American Medical Association* 259, no. 2, (January 8, 1988), 272. Copyright 1988, American Medical Association. Anonymous.
"Death and Dignity: A Case of Individualized Decision Making," *New England Journal of Medicine* 324, no. 10, (March 7, 1991) 691-94. Timothy E. Quill, M.D., The Genesee Hospital, Rochester.
"Medical Science Under Dictatorship," *New England Journal of Medicine* 241, no. 2 (July 14, 1949) 39-47. Leo Alexander, M.D., instructor in psychiatry, Tufts College Medical School; director, Neurobiologic Unit, Boston State Hospital; formerly consultant to the Secretary of War, on duty with the Office of the Chiefs of Counsel for War Crimes, Nuremberg, United States Zone of Germany, 1946-1947.
"Neither for Love nor Money: Why Doctors Must Not Kill," *The Public Interest*, Vol. 94 (Winter, 1989) 25-46. Copyright 1989, National Affairs, Inc. Leon R. Kass, M.D., Addie Clark Harding Professor, The College and Committee on Social Thought, University of Chicago.
"Doctors Must Not Kill," *The Journal of the American Medical Association* 259, no. 14 (April 8, 1988) 2139-40. Copyright 1988, American Medical Association. Willard Gaylin, M.D., The Hastings Center; Leon R. Kass, M.D., the Committee on Social Thought, University of Chicago; Edmund D. Pellegrino, M.D., the Kennedy Institute of Ethics, Georgetown University; Mark Siegler, M.D., the Center for Clinical Medical Ethics, University of Chicago.
"Euthanasia—A Critique," *New England Journal of Medicine*, 322, no. 26 (June 28, 1990) 1881-83. Peter A. Singer, M.D., F.R.C.P.C., University of Toronto; Mark Siegler, M.D., University of Chicago.
Declaration on Euthanasia (USCC Publications Office, Washington, DC, 1980). The Congregation for the Doctrine of the Faith.

"Initative 119: What Is At Stake?" *Commonweal* 118, no. 14 (August 9, 1991) 466-68. Copyright 1991, Commonweal Foundation. Albert R. Jonsen, professor and chairman of the Department of Medical History and Ethics at the University of Washington.

"Euthanasia: Consider the Dutch." *Commonweal* 118, no. 14 (August 9, 1991) 469-72. Copyright 1991 Commonweal Foundation. Carlos F. Gomez, a resident in internal medicine, University of Virginia Health Sciences Center; see his book: *Regulating Death: Euthanasia and the Case of the Netherlands.*

"'Aid-in-Dying': The Social Dimensions," *Commonweal* 118, no. 14 (August 9, 1991) 476-80. Copyright 1991, Commonweal Foundation. Daniel Callahan, director of The Hastings Center.

"Living and Dying Well," *Origins* 21, no. 22 (November 7, 1991) 345-52. The Oregon and Washington Bishops.

"Sources of Concern About the Patient Self-Determination Act," *New England Journal of Medicine* 325, no. 23 (December 5, 1991) 1666-71. Susan M. Wolf, J.D., Philip Boyle, Ph.D., Daniel Callahan, Ph.D., Joseph J. Fins, M.D., Bruce Jennings, M.A., James Lindemann Nelson, Ph.D., all from The Hastings Center; Jeremiah A. Barondess, M.D., New York Academy of Medicine; Dan W. Brock, Ph.D., Brown University; Rebecca Dresser, J.D., Case Western Reserve University; Linda Emanuel, M.D., Ph.D., Harvard Medical School; Sandra Johnson, J.D., St. Louis University; John Lantos, M.D., University of Chicago; DaCosta R. Mason, J.D., American Association of Retired Persons; Mathy Mezey, Ed.D., R.N., New York University; David Orentlicher, M.D., J.D., American Medical Association; Fenella Rouse, J.D., Choice in Dying.

"The Patient Self-Determination Act of 1990," *Clinical Ethics Report* 5, no. 3 (May 5, 1991) 1-10. John J. Paris, S.J., the Michael P. Walsh Professor of Bioethics at Boston College; Kevin J. O'Connell, J.D., an attorney with Hassan & Reardon, Boston.

"Deciding About Death." *St. Anthony Messenger Press* (September, 1989) 23-26. Kenneth R. Overberg, S.J., professor of theology at Xavier University, Cincinnati.

"'Moral Considerations' Ill Considered," *America* 166, no. 9 (March 14, 1992) 210-14. America Press, Inc., 106 West 56th Street, New York, NY 10019, 1992. All rights reserved. Richard A. McCormick, S.J., the John A. O'Brien Professor of Christian Ethics, University of Notre Dame.